It's One Thing After Another!

Other *For Better or For Worse*® Collections

Retrospectives

With Andie Parton

It's One Thing After Another!

For Better or For Worse® 4th Treasury
by Lynn Johnston

**Andrews McMeel
Publishing, LLC**
Kansas City • Sydney • London

Andrews McMeel Publishing, LLC
an Andrews McMeel Universal company
1130 Walnut Street, Kansas City, Missouri 64106

www.andrewsmcmeel.com

14 15 16 17 18 SDB 10 9 8 7 6 5 4 3 2 1

ISBN: 978-1-4494-3717-6

Library of Congress Control Number: 2013943298

www.FBorFW.com

ATTENTION: SCHOOLS AND BUSINESSES

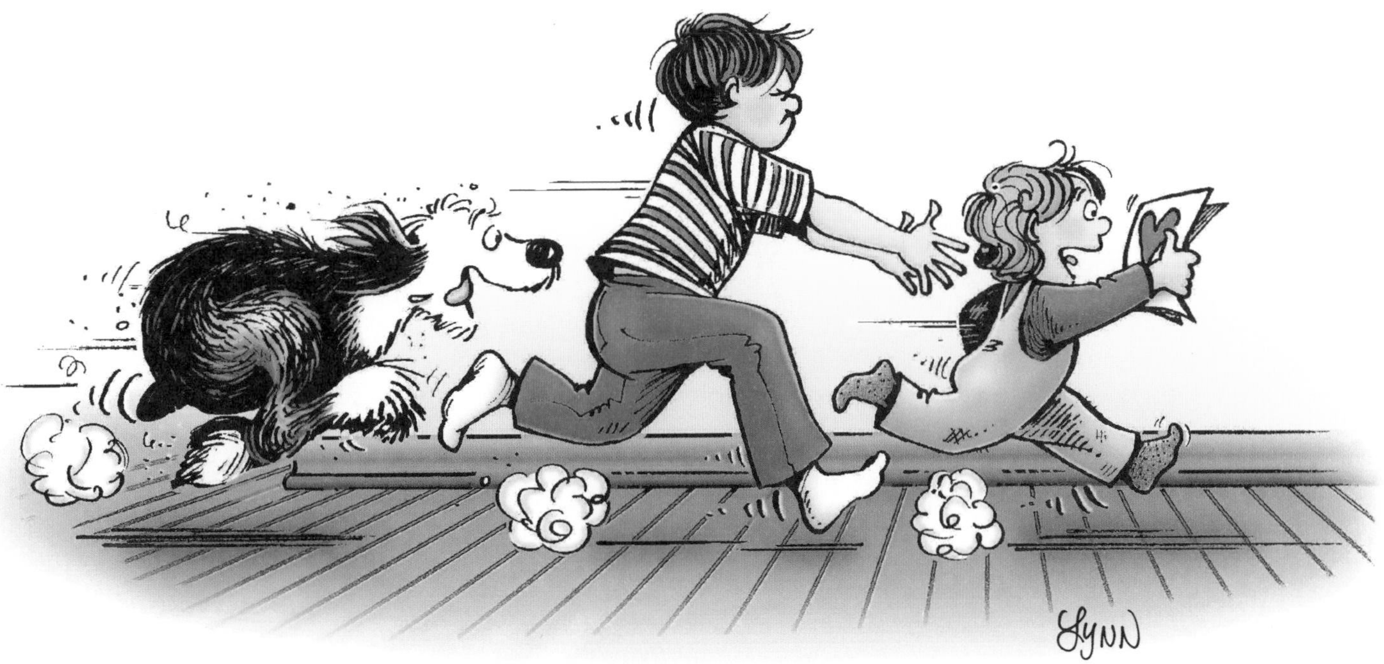
LYNN

Foreword

This fourth treasury is actually the second half of the third treasury: *Making Ends Meet.* Yes, we had to cut the treasuries in half. This was a good thing in that we had this fourth book ready to go well before our deadline, but not so good in that we've had to explain to our readers that we can no longer afford to produce the larger hardcover books. It's a new era. When it comes to publication, the Internet has put a huge question mark over us all! Will the bookshelf become obsolete? Will we look for all of our literature online? Will the printed page disappear forever? Are we that crazy?

As one who is "on the way out," I get no enjoyment from reading transmitted text on an illuminated screen, which can change instantly to anything from GPS to game board. I like books. I like the weight, the texture, the smell, and the shape of them. I like opening a book, turning the pages, positioning a bookmark, seeing how far I've gone, and how much is left to read. I like giving books as gifts. I like owning them. My books are tangible evidence of the journeys I've taken with authors whose stories have captured my imagination; whose talent leaves me breathless and aware. In short, I dread the loss of literature in a form I can feel.

Yes, these next treasuries will be thinner, but they will nonetheless exist! They will be real books (and ebooks most likely). For this I am grateful to my editor, Dorothy O'Brien, her staff, and to my publisher, Andrews and McMeel. For over 30 years, I've had the great good fortune to be syndicated and published by people who believe that things worth doing are worth doing well. I hope you enjoy this fourth collection of cartoons and commentary.

Lynn Johnston

Ours was an "English" household. My mom would often invite someone over for tea, and tea was served with a ritual of cubed sugar and freshly baked cakes. Kids had to be seen and not heard. If we wished to stay in the living room within reach of the desserts, we had to be patient, quiet, and still. This gave us ample time to research the guest's physical attributes and to think of suitable questions to ask later. Sometimes the questions came out before the guest's departure. I made some gaffes, but I don't remember saying anything punishable. What I do remember is my mother telling me something she had once done. One of her mother's tea time guests was a stern, humourless woman who disapproved of children being within hearing distance of an adult conversation. My mom waited and watched in silence as the two women drank and gossiped. Eventually her mother acknowledged her presence and asked if there was anything she'd like to say. Surprised by the opportunity to speak, my mom turned to the haughty lady at the table and said, "You have a very pretty hat. It would look better if it had a smile under it."

When they first came out, the answering machine was a new toy for everyone. Some folks were horrified by the thought of leaving a recorded message, while others became instant hosts of their own daily show. I loved the way folks said, "Hi, I'm not here right now." as if they had gone to that place on "the other side." It was hard to record it right the first time, so I found saying repeatedly that I wasn't there depressing. Kids enjoyed the anonymity and entertained themselves by irritating anyone who had this device, but eventually we all became accustomed to and dependent on the answering machine. Now we're adapting to much more sophisticated toys!

The wildest New Year's Eve party we ever had was in our newly finished rec room in Lynn Lake. Everyone we knew was invited — which meant half the town. Being very rural Manitoba, the pharmacy was also the liquor store, and I went in to order some liqueurs for the occasion. Behind the cash register along the top shelf, pharmacist Bob Clarke had about ten bottles of liqueur on display. When he asked what I wanted to order, I said, "One of each." He knew we were new to town and smiled. Bob then proceeded to order from Winnipeg every kind of liqueur available. Two large, heavy boxes arrived. I was speechless. I had no idea he'd order so many — I was unaware that he was a bit of a prankster. When I looked at him in disbelief, he smiled and said, "Well, you said to order one of each!" To save face and our relationship with the pharmacy, I clenched my teeth and paid for the entire shipment. Ours was suddenly the best stocked rec room in town, and New Year's Eve went on until well into the morning.

This isn't the end of the liqueur story. When we moved to North Bay, along with our boxes of clothing and household goods were the remaining bottles of liqueur. These bottles stayed in our cupboard for years. Aaron left home to seek his fortune, and Katie, now a high school graduate and of legal drinking age, took a bartending course in preparation for summer employment. She wanted to show us some of her skills. She did an inventory of our liquor cabinet and discovered that the contents of every cream- or egg-based liqueur had become like a solid block of cheese inside the bottle. I laughed out loud as I shook the contents, which made a dull, wet thud against the glass. Kate was shocked, "Don'tcha know these things have a shelf life?" It was obvious that we don't drink much, and neither do our friends. We have had many parties since, but none have been as memorable as the New Year's bash with its extensive variety of liqueurs!

5

POW! KA-BLAM!! WHADDYA THINK OF THE NEAT GUN AUNTIE MAVIS SENT ME!?

I DON'T LIKE GUNS, MIKE. AND I FEEL UNCOMFORTABLE AROUND PEOPLE WHO DO.

BUT IT'S PRETEND. SEE?! / I DON'T CARE!

AW, MOM! YOU GOT ABSOLUTELY NO IMAGINATION!

I have always been uncomfortable around guns — even toy guns. Aaron, like most boys, ran around with his friends shooting sticks or fingers or whatever they could find that was shaped like a firearm. When a relative sent him a realistic toy gun, he was thrilled and I was upset. If he had any gun at all, I thought it should be purchased by his parents and given to him along with a stern lecture about weaponry, war, and the seriousness of shooting living things.

MOM'S MAKIN' STUFF FOR THE NEW YEAR'S EVE PARTY, AN' IT LOOKS AWFUL!

CHEESE STUFF, LIVER STUFF, OLIVES MIXED UP WITH FISH ...

HOW COME SHE ALWAYS MAKES THAT STUFF FOR PARTIES? / I DUNNO, MIKE.

BUT AFTER A FEW DRINKS, EVEN HER REGULAR COOKING TASTES GOOD!

CAN WE STAY UP FOR THE PARTY, MOM? PLEASE? WE'LL BE GOOD, HONEST!

NO, MICHAEL. I WANT YOU BOTH IN BED BEFORE ANY- ONE GETS HERE.

AW! NO FAIR! GIMME ONE GOOD REASON WHY I CAN'T STAY UP AN' WATCH YOU GUYS!

BLACKMAIL.

Our log house had an opening next to the top stair, just before you stepped up to the second floor. It was a perfect spy-hole from which the kids could watch what was going on downstairs in the living room. We knew it was there, but we'd forget. Many an evening's get-together was monitored by two silent, pyjama-clad spies, who went undiscovered — unless they snickered or fell asleep at their post!

6

These strips are from a scene in my childhood. The morning after a New Year's Eve party, our house had been left as it was. Bottles of half-finished beer, glasses with the dregs, drying canapés, and stale chips covered the tabletops. Remnants of cigarettes and cigars filled the ashtrays. Alan and I were the first on the scene, and the place was ours!

We drank what was in the bottles and glasses.

HEY, THERE'S A CIGAR HERE! SOMEBODY LEFT A WHOLE CIGAR!

YOU'RE NOT GONNA LIGHT IT?!

JUST ONE END.

AK!! SMELLS LIKE UNCLE DANNY'S PIG BARN! HOW COME ANYBODY WOULD SMOKE THOSE THINGS!?

I DUNNO. MAYBE THEY WANT TO BE NOTICED.

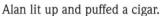
Alan lit up and puffed a cigar.

: SNIFF...SNIFF... — I SMELL SOMETHING BURNING!

WAAAAAAAAAAAAAAAAAAAAAAAAAAAAAAAAAAAAAAAAAAAAAAAAA

JOHN, WAKE UP!

OOH... GROAN! MMMM...

MY HEAD...WON'T STOP RINGING...

IT'S NOT YOUR HEAD, DUMMY, IT'S THE SMOKE DETECTOR!

We had no smoke detectors.

WHAT'S GOING ON!? WHAT'S HAPPENING?!

MICHAEL LIT A CIGAR AN' PUT IT INNA WASTE-BASKET AN' IT CAUGHT FIRE AN' THE ALARM WENT OFF AN' THEN YOU AN' MOM GOT UP!

WELCOME TO 1985.

Our folks didn't suddenly wake up and discover our deeds. Dad went to use the bathroom and found Alan doubled over the biff, and me in the tub smiling stupidly. As I recall, neither of our folks was angry with us for trying out contraband; they were mad at themselves for leaving it there. We all considered it a lesson learned.

This piece of art is from a 1985 calendar (February), which was produced by American Greetings. I began working with American Greetings in 1983 on greeting cards and calendars. Electronic printing systems were taking over from traditional methods, and colourists everywhere were madly experimenting with the new technology. Since my contract gave the artists at American Greetings the freedom to try new ideas, this blotchy, slap-dash style was suggested for *For Better or For Worse*, and I kind of liked it. In fact, it was fun to see what other artists would do with my designs, because it gave everything a different look altogether. This piece was done using brilliant, water-soluble inks. The "wind" in the window was either scratched onto the painting or drawn with a fine white pencil. Leaving the outer edges in black and white was a style that came and went rather quickly, but it was "modern" and quirky at the time.

We have consistently produced every year since the early 80's. Doing a calendar a year doesn't sound like much of a challenge, but producing greeting cards, recall cards, as well as incidental drawings for other projects, made my studio a bit of a prison. I began to work evenings and weekends. I was glad for civic holidays because I could work! I worked on planes, in hotel rooms, and in coffee shops. I was constantly "on." I now had a routine with the strip: writing one day and drawing the next. Everything else was fitted into my life like a puzzle. Looking back, I wonder how I got everything done and still had time to be a mom, a wife, and a friend!

When I was in art school, I was hired to work one summer for Canawest Films, a studio that did commercials and segments of Saturday morning cartoons such as *Abbott and Costello* and *Shazaam*. These were Hanna–Barbera productions, and the Vancouver staff was pressured to churn out as many shows as possible, as fast as possible. We worked a gruelling schedule to keep production going for 24 hours a day. I was in the ink and paint department (something that doesn't really exist any more), and although the job was tiresome and repetitive, I learned more about animation than I could through any course. By the end of the summer, I had decided that I wanted a career as an animator.

I worked as a volunteer apprentice with the director, whenever I wasn't painting cells. Barry Helmer was a great teacher. He gave me characters to design and segments to animate. He showed me how to storyboard and how to

Me (centre) and some of my animation buddies enjoying a lunch break outside the studios.

work with sound tracks, click tracks, and Foley. I loved this challenge. I thought I was on the bottom rung of a ladder I was going to climb and that there was success at the top. Then I got married and everything changed.

Doug and me on our wedding day.

Doug Franks was a television cameraman with the CBC. Television was where several of my high school friends had found work, and through them I was introduced to Doug. Unfortunately, the bottom was falling out of the industry at the time. The 1960s saw many cut backs to public programming in Canada, and it was evident shortly after we were married that Doug would be losing his job. We travelled to Los Angeles with my friend Cecily (to the right of me in the photograph above), an artist who worked next to me at Canawest, and her husband, Larry, who worked for CFUN, a rock-jock radio station in Vancouver. We went as a lark but hoped to find work there … if we were lucky.

Cecily was originally from Los Angeles. Her folks were comic book writers for Disney — her dad had worked as an animator on wonderful shows such as *Fantasia* and *Snow White*. Alpine and Cecil Beard knew all kinds of people in the animation and film industry and were willing to make some connections for us. Cecily and I took our folios and did the rounds. We were both good illustrators, and Jay Ward Studios offered us jobs in their background department starting immediately. We were beyond excited. Jay Ward was famous for *George of the Jungle*, *Rocky and Bullwinkle*, and my personal fave, *Super Chicken*! All I had to do was get a green card, Cecily could move home, and the guys could find something, we were sure! Not so. Radio announcers and television cameramen were everywhere in California. There was no need to hire from out of the country. Both men refused to take "just anything" so their wives could become animators. The four of us drove back to Vancouver. This was heartbreaking, but we followed our men.

Doug and I moved to Ontario after he accepted a position at CHCH TV in Hamilton, and my career took another turn from there. Unable to work in animation, I looked for work in jewellery stores, something in which I had experience. I had just been offered a job when I read an ad in the *Hamilton Spectator*: The Hamilton General Hospital was looking for a graphic artist. I called the number and made an appointment with the head of photography. I then worked all day and into the night making a folio that showed I could do charts, graphs, guts, bones — whatever I thought they'd want to see. This was a good thing. I'd have never been offered the job if all he'd seen was cartoons! This job led to another: medical artist at McMaster University — which, in a series of serendipitous encounters, led to the job I have now. Long story!

Jump ahead to 1985. My comic art career was booming and I was busier than ever. Rod (my second husband) and I had just moved to North Bay, and the proximity of a good airport allowed me to travel more easily and more often. On one of my journeys, I was invited to do a radio show in Toronto, a wonderful show called *This Country in the Morning* hosted by Don Harron, one of my favourite comedians. After the show, he and another guest and I went for coffee at a nearby restaurant, which was a real treat. Sitting at a table nearby was another hero: writer and actor, Gordon Pinsent, to whom I was introduced. Star-struck and stammering, I said, "Mr. Pinsent, I really want to write a play. How do I start?" With a look that said he'd been asked the same question too many times, he replied, "Just do it." I felt silly for asking, but what he said was what I really needed to hear — and I took his advice to heart.

I caught the afternoon flight home that night and couldn't sleep. I decided to write, and I wrote a play called *The Bestest Present*. I sent it by courier to Bill Stevens, owner of Atkinson Film Arts, a small animation studio in Ottawa. He called me right away. He said, "I read your story last night and was really moved by it. Would you like to do an animated television s-pecial?" Excited and in disbelief, I accepted. I couldn't believe this had happened so fast. I was soon on my way to Ottawa to meet Bill and make arrangements to sign the contract. This was the beginning of a huge adventure!

Bill arranged funding through various channels, and we began to work on my first animated film. We chose voices and designed backgrounds, Bill wrote the music, and he sang and was the voice of John. I asked Bill if my children could play the roles of Michael and Elizabeth, and after they did a reading, he agreed. Aaron's friend Scott came on board to add his voice to the opening song, and the recording went off without a hitch. It was so much fun. I travelled to Ottawa regularly for over a year, and our Navajo Aircraft was never more appreciated. Rod was our pilot (and the voice of the postman), so the whole family was involved.

Animation is done by a team of talented artists who are obsessed with what they do, which is a good thing, because it's a hit and miss business with no guarantees. I was honoured to be working with talented illustrators, actors, photographers, sound technicians, and musicians — all focused on a production featuring my work, my characters. They made it all happen; they taught me step by step, all along the way, and we achieved something, which, for me, was amazing.

We all worked for the love of it, and even though it was costly, time consuming, and sometimes maddening, making *The Bestest Present* was one of the happiest times in my life. It won a Gemini award for children's programming. It still runs at Christmas time. I have Bill Stevens to thank for seeing the potential in a short, unsolicited script and Gordon Pinsent for telling me to "Just do it!" This never would have happened if I had taken the job at Jay Ward in Los Angeles … sometimes, disappointment is a blessing in disguise!

Lynn Johnston brings her comic strip family to TV in animated special Mon., 7:30 p.m. on chs. 9 & 13

PHOTO: HAROLD BARKLEY

Lynn's family Christmas

Cartoonist Lynn Johnston's famous family turns tears to Christmas cheers in the first For Better Or For Worse animated special

For better or worse, Lynn Johnston's life imitates art.

On the eve of her television debut, she is juggling the laundry, a burgeoning pile of ironing and "a casserole I'm expected to burn for dinner." She can't answer the ringing phone until she lugs helpless, hopeless Willie, the family mutt, in over the doorstep before he runs away.

In Johnston's real-life family, nestled far from the glare of public acclaim in a small-ish log house outside North Bay, the hectic ups and downs of the fictional Pattersons who cavort across the comic pages of almost 700 newspapers in the cartoon super strip,

For Better Or For Worse, are instantly recognizable.

For Johnston's 60 million readers, Christmas comes early this year with *The Bestest Present*, a half-hour animated film starring John and Elly, Michael and little Lizzie, and Farley the brainless woofer in a touching tale of the true meaning of Christmas joy and goodwill to all.

Like all the family fables concocted by Johnston, this slice of ordinary life has just the right mix of humor, pathos and hearthside drama to make its message both endearing and enduring. Three-year-old Lizzie loses her favorite stuffed bunny; big brother

dreams up a scheme to retrieve it and before Christmas dinner is over, tears are turned to cheers by a lonely widower who is drawn into the family circle and rediscovers the Christmas spirit.

As befits someone who has turned chronicles of everyday catastrophes into a stunningly successful comic strip, Johnston kept much of the work in the family: the television voices of Michael and Lizzie are the voices of her real-life children, Aaron, almost 13, and eight-year-old Kate.

Husband Rod, a dentist like his cartoon alter ego, is the voice of the postman. John-

Lynn's family Christmas

ston herself is the only member of the family circle without a speaking part. But who cares, she says, when she got to direct the production and have her family pay attention to her at last?

Although Johnston insists the strip is not a diary of her day-to-day dilemmas, she admits, "I can't write anything unless I experience it; that's the way I put feeling into the strip."

"The characters in *For Better Or For Worse* behave the way my family behaves and there are similarities between my husband and Elly's on paper: both are lovable,

warm men prone to puns and one-liners. But I create the situations for the strip family. I don't get my two families mixed up.

"The only character I have an identity problem with is Elly — damn it all, she's me. I even cut my hair to break away from her."

But the close identification brings some advantages. "I can be as sarcastic and kidding as I like about someone or something through Elly," Johnston says. "I make fun of myself through her, too — like me, she moans a lot about being 10 pounds overweight even when she's sitting around eating butter tarts."

Johnston's reaction to success hasn't changed since Universal approached her to

do a daily comic strip after the success of her first book, *David, We're Pregnant.* She was expecting Kate and preparing to move to northern Manitoba when Universal asked her for 20 strips right away. She knocked off 20 on her family situation and, much to her amazement, they loved it.

They flew her to Kansas City to sign the deal, but all she felt was shock. "There were all these people with pinstripes and warm handshakes and capped teeth and I felt like a kid from the bush," she recalls. "They left me alone in the boardroom with the contract and it was like an out-of-body experience, watching my right hand sign it."

She rejoices in the fact the family moved to the Manitoba wilderness just as the whirlwind of fame struck, "because it made us inaccessible. I had a brush with celebrity and it's hard to keep your head. People tell you you're wonderful and eventually you start believing it."

Home and family have always come first to the 38-year-old Vancouver-born artist, perhaps because that's where her own gifts were nurtured: Her mother is artistic, two aunts are painters and her father is the family vaudevillian, full of jokes, she says.

Creative at nine on the dot

After the Vancouver School of Art, her career began in an animation studio, then switched to being a medical artist for five years at McMaster University in Hamilton after her first marriage. As soon as son Aaron came along, she quit and freelanced, but separation from her husband forced her to take a full-time job in an ad agency. She was hopeless. "I couldn't be creative at nine on the dot; I used to fall asleep on the job and I was unhappy with Aaron in daycare in a seedy part of town. I quit and freelanced again, going door to door with the baby on my back." She then met her present husband and along came Katy and Universal. Her domestic affairs have caused chuckles in a dozen languages ever since.

In some ways her success doesn't surprise her: "If you've got the gift of humor you can always make a living because people want to laugh, want to be uplifted," she says.

But it doesn't impress her, either. The imminent launching of *The Bestest Present* means she'll have to face a "smozzle" as she calls the party planned for her in Ottawa by the film's producers.

"I'll wear the one elegant dress I own," she says, as only one who lives in jeans can say it. "But I always feel I should be out trick or treating. It's not me."

The understanding mom who appears as Elly is the real Lynn, as is Elly the harried Christmas shopper, the exasperated referee of her children's squabbles and the tender interceder on Lizzie's behalf to the gods that look after little girls' lost bunnies.

Every parent watching will recognize the part of the Patterson household that is also part of theirs and that, for better or worse, keeps it all in the family, as Johnston well knows.

— Helen Bullock

One of the things that plagued families of the 1950s was the need for parents to be right. It was "Do as I say, not as I do," which never made a heck of a lot of sense to me. If Dad swore, swearing was cool. If Mom smoked, smoking was cool too. If what they told us didn't add up, we were quick to object, but the folks were always right — no matter how wrong they were. This was a hard façade to maintain. When I had kids of my own, I discovered that it was much easier to admit a mistake than to try and justify it.

Living in a cold climate means having the kids indoors. I swore that television would not be my babysitter, that my offspring would have wholesome, educational, and creative pastimes. I encouraged them to read, draw, build things out of wood, clay, and paper. I bought board games — we played Scrabble, Monopoly, and Crazy Eights. I let them take apart the vacuum cleaner and roll marbles down the hose. I did everything I could think of to keep them entertained, and they, in turn, participated — as long as I played with them. The plan disintegrated if I decided to leave them and do something else, which is when they begged for television. So, I caved. I gave in. I set them up with food and water and turned on cartoons. I was able to work, clean, do laundry, and get stuff done, while my children bathed in the glow of the tube. I felt guilty, but at the same time … anything that saves a mom's sanity deserves a place in the home.

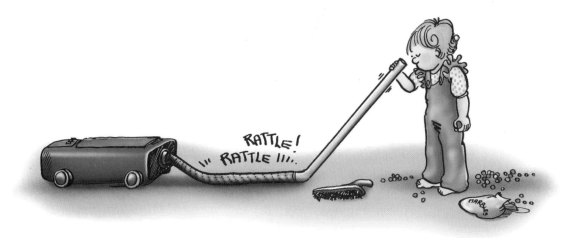

When I was in grade one, I had a friend called Carol Mayes who had survived polio and walked with crutches. (The character Gordon Mayes was named for Carol.) I often went to the washroom with her because she needed help. I also carried her books and her lunch box when she walked home. I was fascinated by her, and when kids began to tease me saying I only liked Carol because I wanted to play with her crutches, I was confused. Did I really like her because of that? It's true, I did like to swing on her crutches and I did find her fascinating because of the scars she had from multiple surgeries. I just thought she was neat. She had been held back several grades because of her illness, and she struggled with spelling and reading. I was a good reader, and our teacher asked me to help her, which I did. The kids who accused me of liking Carol because she had crutches were also jealous of the way I had been singled out to read with her at the back of the room. They eventually had an effect on me. As a small child, I had no way of explaining my friendship. I wanted to be accepted, and I wanted to be liked. I slowly separated myself from Carol, and was relieved when she was sent to another school. Carol was gone. The crutches were gone. I was the same as all the other kids and glad to be so.

I often think of Carol. Her strength of character, the way she thrust herself forward, dragging her feet, the way she smiled through the pain and the curious stares. I recall as if it was yesterday. Now I can say why I liked Carol. Of all the kids in my class, she impressed me as having the most to give — the one who outshone us all.

Looking for a wayward mutt on a night like this is one of the downsides of dog ownership. When our small spaniel, Willy, wandered off, it was usually "Mom" who put on the boots and jacket and went out into the gale to find him. I was convinced he could hear me quite well and was just ignoring me. This was something the kids did too. It infuriated me. At least kids understand a mother's wrath. When a dog comes home to a fuming human, he just pants and wags.

17

JOHN, FARLEY WAS PICKED UP BY SOMEONE IN A BLUE VAN! A MAN IN THE NEXT BLOCK TOLD ME!

BLUE VAN?! WHO IN THE WORLD WOULD WANT TO PICK UP FARLEY?

HERE WE GO, TIM. NO LICENSE, NO COLLAR, NO NOTHING!

EASTGATE ANIMAL POUND

YES, MA'AM... I THINK WE MIGHT HAVE YOUR DOG HERE.

BIG, SHAGGY... ANSWERS TO "FARLEY", DOES HE.

SURE, SURE. YOU CAN COME AND PICK HIM UP.

....BAIL IS POSTED AT 20 BUCKS.

THE CHARGE IS: RUNNING AT LARGE - AND WITHOUT A LICENSE.

YOU'RE LUCKY. THE CHAP WHO CALLED US WANTED TO INCLUDE WILLFUL DAMAGE TO PRIVATE PROPERTY.

WHAT? WHICH ONE OF OUR NEIGHBORS WOULD TURN IN FARLEY?!

CHECK THE ONE WITH THE SNOW SCULPTURE.

EASTGATE ANIMAL POUND

Gary Larson (*The Far Side*) once sent me a Christmas card, which showed a house with a brightly lit window through which you could see a group of wildly partying dogs. In front of the house, on a white lawn, was a snow sculpture of a fat cat. A path of paw prints lead from the door to the snow cat — the side of the cat was yellow! I guess cartoon minds think alike.

I DON'T KNOW WHY I NEVER GOT HIM A LICENSE JOHN. I JUST NEVER THOUGHT ABOUT IT.

YEAH! FARLEY HAD TO GO TO THE POUND 'CAUSE HE WAS CAUGHT WALKING DOWN THE STREET WITHOUT A LICENSE!

MOM?

YES, ELIZABETH?

YOU GOT A LICENSE FOR ME?!!

MOM...DO WE HAFTA KEEP FARLEY TIED UP IN THE YARD?

YES. HE'S BEEN JUST TOO HARD TO HANDLE LATELY.

BUT, MOM... HE'S AT THE END OF HIS ROPE!

SO AM I.

OK... COME ON IN.

UGH! YOUR FEET ARE FULL OF SNOW, YOU SHED EVERYWHERE, YOU'RE ALWAYS GETTING INTO TROUBLE!

SOMETIMES I WONDER WHY WE GOT YOU IN THE FIRST—

SLURP!

- DON'T KISS ME WHILE I'M LECTURING YOU!

Sheep dogs have big, wide feet, and their toes are webbed to some extent. This means that a snowy walk will result in wads of frozen snow plugging the dog's foot pads. I'd have to spread his toes and pull each chunk of snow out of the crevices — and with it, remove hair and dirt as well. It's a messy process, and the only rewarding thing about it is the look of relief on the dog's face when it's done!

19

This was done for our family Christmas card in 1982.

HEY, THIS IS A NEAT MAGNIFYIN' GLASS YOU GOT FROM SANTA, LIZZIE!

NEAT! I CAN SEE ALL THE LITTLE KNOBS ON YOUR TONGUE! WOW! THERE'S MILLIONS OF 'EM!

GO SHOW MOM!

MICHAEL! DID YOU PUT HER UP TO THIS?!!

I'M GLAD MICHAEL'S TAKEN AN INTEREST IN MUSIC, GEORGIA.

TA-TA-TA WAAAH... TATTICA TAT-TAT....

YES. IT DOES A LOT TO DEVELOP ONE'S PERSONALITY!

YOU TOOK AN INTEREST IN THE ACCORDIAN WHEN YOU WERE A KID, DIDN'T YOU, ELLY?

YEAH.

...MOTHER SAID IT WOULD DEVELOP MY BUST.

When I was a kid, a travelling salesman came to the door selling piano accordions. I'm not kidding. With every purchase, they threw in a year's worth of lessons. My mother, wanting me to play something (that wouldn't swallow half the living room and take ten years to pay off), actually considered buying one. Here was a piano-like instrument that was almost portable! I liked polkas and accordion music in general, but the cool factor was lacking. I declined. A real piano would have been great, but this was not the same! In desperation, she promised me that playing the accordion would increase my bust size. For a budding teen, this argument had merit, but the piano accordion still wasn't my thing.

Years later, when I was living in southern Ontario, I met some musicians from Newfoundland. Caught up in my love for east coast music, I bought myself a button accordion. This I learned to play not too badly, and after a while, it showed. I was indeed building up bulges where none had been — on my arms. I actually had pipes! I knew then that the old arm-pumping exercise to the cry of "We must, we must, we must improve our bust!" was hogwash. The only sure way to enhance the un-enhanceable is through surgery! I still play my accordion, but only for sympathetic friends, and I don't really care about the bust line. I do have a word of advice, however: Ladies, it's a fine instrument, but never play an accordion in the nude!

Being 'exposed' in his sister's cartoon strip causes no problems for local music teacher

By DAN BLACK
Staff Writer

He teaches instrumental music at Brockville's Thousand Islands Secondary School and "For Better or For Worse", Alan Ridgway is somewhat of an international celebrity.

A seemingly intense man with an eye for excellence and an ear for music appreciation, Ridgway, 35, has — thanks to his artistic sister — something in common with Charlie Brown, Herman and even Dagwood Bumstead.

He is the personality behind Uncle Phil — a cool and lovable cartoon character in Lynn Johnston's popular comic strip "For Better or For Worse".

"I find it quite amusing," said Ridgway, with a bright smile forming in his heavy brown beard. "Sometimes I have to swallow my pride, but the pleasure I get from Lynn's strip certainly outweighs any embarrassment."

The strip, which appears daily in hundreds of newspapers (including The Recorder and Times), is syndicated under Kansas City-based Universal Press.

Today, Johnston, who along with her younger brother was raised in the Vancouver area, earns "a comfortable living" and occasionally hobnobs around the world from her North Bay home with cartoon geniuses Jim "Garfield" Davis and Jim "Herman" Unger.

"Her's is somewhat of a Cinderella story," notes Ridgway. "She went from a layout artist to an international celebrity. The whole family takes a lot of pride in her."

All of the characters in the strip are take-offs of people in Johnston's life. Their first names are the middle names of family members and friends.

And while Phil is cool and entertaining, Ridgway regards himself as "subtly funny."

"She has the uncanny ability to turn everyday events into something very humorous and touching," he added.

Ridgway's favorite strip is the one where Phil, a jazz musician, asks his nephew, Michael, (who is Johnston's son Aaron in real life) about his trumpet practising.

Says Phil: "Come on, Mike, how are you going to get anywhere with this thing if you don't practice?!"

Responds young Michael: "I do practice, Uncle Phil. I practice all the time!"

"Okay... show me something you've practiced," insists Phil — arms folded tightly beneath a jutting chin.

The final frame of the strip shows Michael balancing his trumpet on the end of his left index finger and Phil hiding the frustration in his face behind the palm of his hand.

"I can certainly relate to that strip," says Ridgway, who teaches music to grades nine through 12 students both at TISS and Brockville Collegiate Institute. "It shows the frustration of being a music teacher and it shows the novelty or the quick-thinking of youth."

Beyond the comic page and apart from his sister, Ridgway is better known for his musical talent.

He is a published musician who after receiving his musician union card at age 14 went on from one challenge to another, including seven years with the Stratford Festival Theatre Orchestra.

"I enjoyed Stratford immensely," he says, "but I also felt I wasn't being utilized to my full potential. After a while, I felt like a cog in a wheel and so I decided it was time to move on and look for another challenge."

Local high school music teacher Alan Ridgway is the man behind the Uncle Phil character in the cartoon in Lynn Johnston's popular strip "For Better or For Worse." (Staff photo by Dan Black)

Today, Ridgway lives near Kemptville and in the summer is an avid canoeist on the Rideau River. He also has time to compose his own music — music which may someday be used for instruction purposes at TISS and BCI and music which may eventually wind up as the score for a "For Better or For Worse" television cartoon.

And while his sister's work may reach new audiences through the television screen, Ridgway maintains TV was never an influence in the Ridgway home.

"We were the last people on the block to have a television set," he said. "A great deal of our entertainment in the home was self-generating. She took

to art and I took to music. Mom and dad didn't force us in any direction. They just encouraged us."

While Ridgway has gone from being a professional musician to a high school music teacher and novice canoeist, cool-headed Phil has failed to make any transformation. But Ridgway believes it may only be a matter of time before Phil the musician becomes Phil the teacher and Phil the canoeist.

"Phil doesn't have a lot to do with the outdoors — yet," he added.

Ridgway and his sister visit each other about every three months and during these get-togethers they talk about the

strip, but don't go out of their way to generate ideas.

Says Ridgway: "The ideas generate themselves. The information and the gags she uses in the strip come from interpersonal relationships she observes in the people around her. Her humor is subtle, but very down-to-earth and meaningful."

Still, Ridgway says he's glad Phil doesn't make it into the strip every day.

"It tends to be an expose," he adds. "Our foibles are there for the public to see and read about. I really don't mind — and besides Lynn said if she ever ran out of ideas, she'd just have another child."

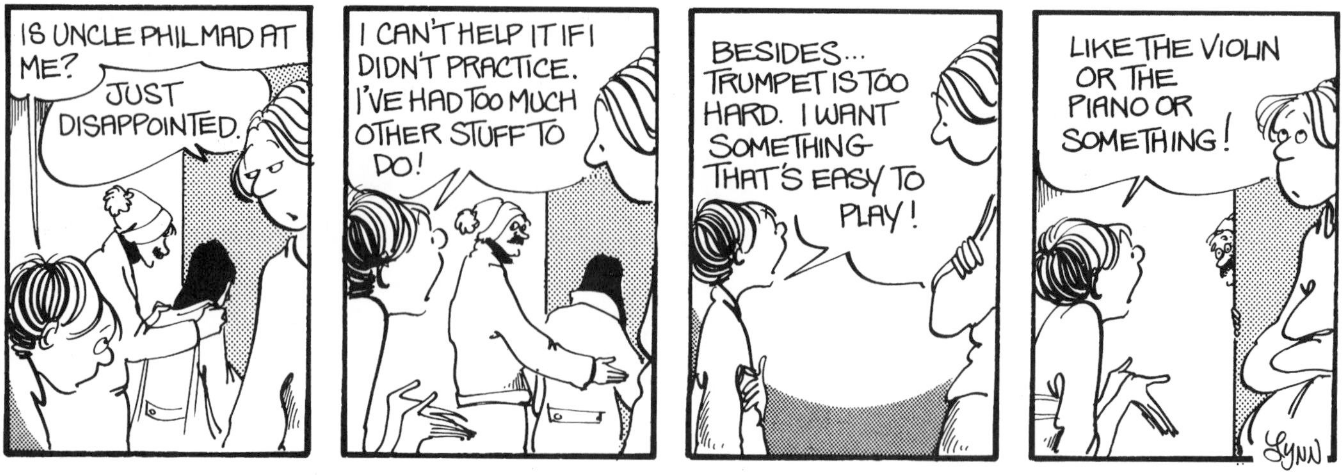
IS UNCLE PHIL MAD AT ME?
JUST DISAPPOINTED.
I CAN'T HELP IT IF I DIDN'T PRACTICE. I'VE HAD TOO MUCH OTHER STUFF TO DO!
BESIDES... TRUMPET IS TOO HARD. I WANT SOMETHING THAT'S EASY TO PLAY!
LIKE THE VIOLIN OR THE PIANO OR SOMETHING!
LYNN

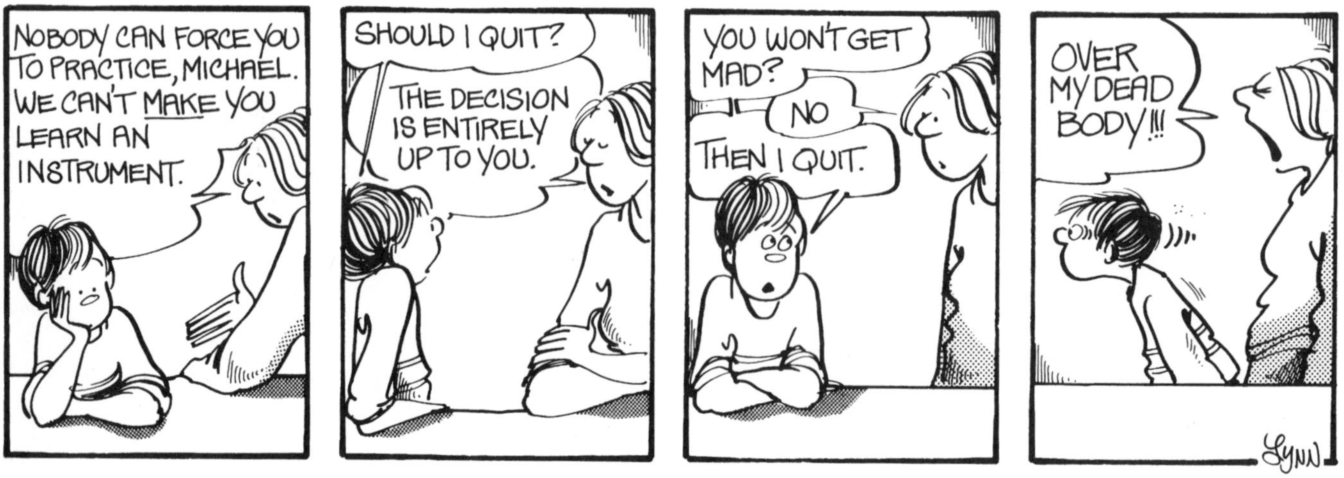
NOBODY CAN FORCE YOU TO PRACTICE, MICHAEL. WE CAN'T MAKE YOU LEARN AN INSTRUMENT.
SHOULD I QUIT?
THE DECISION IS ENTIRELY UP TO YOU.
YOU WON'T GET MAD?
NO
THEN I QUIT.
OVER MY DEAD BODY!!!
LYNN

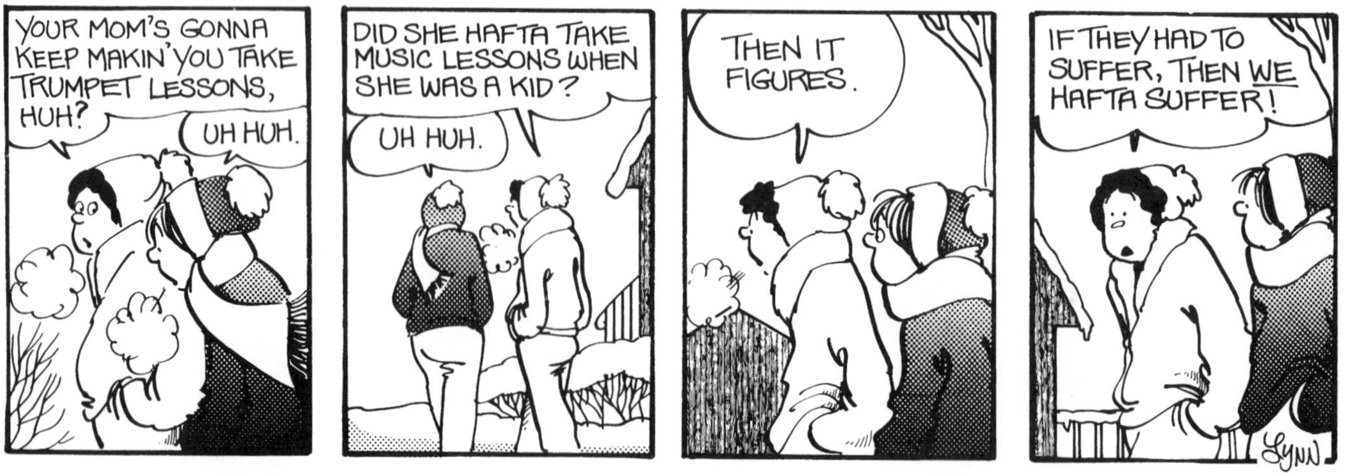
YOUR MOM'S GONNA KEEP MAKIN' YOU TAKE TRUMPET LESSONS, HUH?
UH HUH.
DID SHE HAFTA TAKE MUSIC LESSONS WHEN SHE WAS A KID?
UH HUH.
THEN IT FIGURES.
IF THEY HAD TO SUFFER, THEN WE HAFTA SUFFER!
LYNN

I took my kids to fast food joints. I knew the value of cheap, fast, and fried, and it had everything to do with convenience. Tiled floors and washable seating, disposable plates, cups, and cutlery offered respite from kitchen duties and the possibility of communicating with another adult (with kids the same age). It also meant my offspring would eat everything on their plates. It might not be with sustenance, but their stomachs would be full. I ushered my charges, unapologetically, into plastic indoor playgrounds. I ordered the specials, the biggies, and meals — which came with toys. I too ate with gusto, knowing that what I was doing was addictive, that I was introducing my children to substances I wanted them to avoid. Still, the positive outweighed the negative: an hour of freedom vs. a hassle at home. I plead guilty to falling for an easy solution to lunch.

I can't remember the last time I went to a fast food joint, but I know the time will come when I will fall off the wagon again. I look forward to sitting at one of those colourful plastic tables with burgers, onion rings, and a rot-gut pop while my granddaughter romps in the plastic kid-proof play area, her stomach full of fries. I'll count the useless calories in the grub that I'm eating and try not to feel guilty for enjoying every bite!

When I drew this strip, I weighed 130 lbs. I was in the best physical shape I'd ever been and I still felt chubby. Like most women, I was down on myself for not being shaped like the girls on the covers of magazines! No matter how hard I exercised or how much weight I lost, I'd never be able to achieve that model shape. The "ideal" was never going to be me.

I have been going through old photographs lately looking for things to put in this book and I came across a rare photo of yours-truly in a bathing suit. The first thing I said to myself was, "Wow! I didn't look so bad after all!" Strange how your perception of self can change over the years.

And, no … you can't see the photo!

My mom used to put my hair into what she called "bunches." She would pull my hair so tight, my eyes watered and the elastics made my head ache. When I had a daughter, I decided I wouldn't force anything like this on her, but I did want to learn how to do French braids. Kate wouldn't let me practice. No matter how I approached the subject, she was uninterested, until I offered to PAY her to let me braid her hair. Eventually this didn't work, and I gave up. I figured that I'd never see my girl with her thick, dark tresses in a hairstyle I loved. Until one day, she appeared with a perfect set of French braids, neatly tied together with a white bow. She had done them herself!

I did these strips after agreeing to look after a friend's two-year-old. Both my kids were in school, and my home was no longer baby-proof. I had forgotten how to feed, carry, talk to, and otherwise live with a toddler and was right out of my element. To add to this, my charge was the spawn of "New Age" parents who felt that discipline curbed a child's natural curiosity. In other words, the kid was a terror. His mother arrived before I called and begged for mercy. Thankfully, she never asked again!

LOOK, LIZZIE! RICHARD IS HERE FOR A VISIT!

WOULD YOU WATCH HIM WHILE I START SUPPER?

UH HUH.

YOU WATCH HIM, NOW. ARE YOU SURE YOU CAN WATCH HIM?

UH HUH.

ARE YOU WATCHING HIM, ELIZABETH?

UH HUH.

MOM, BABY RICHARD'S PLAYING IN THE KITCHEN CUPBOARDS!

I KNOW. HE'S FINE, HONEY.

HE'S TAKEN ALL THE CANS OFF THE SHELVES.

I KNOW. HE'S FINE.

HE'S STACKING THEM UP IN PILES.

HE'S FINE.

AN' HE'S TAKEN ALL THE LABELS OFF 'EM.

HE'S **WHAT?!**

Katie loved to play on the lazy Susan where I kept all my canned goods. As long as I could hear the rumble of the sturdily built shelves turning, I knew she was safe and not getting into trouble — so I thought. As she rode around one day, she amused herself by removing all the labels from the cans. We had mystery meals for months afterwards!

WHY IS RICHARD CRYING?

MAYBE HE'S TIRED, LIZZIE.

MAYBE HE MISSES HIS MOMMY. MAYBE HE'S GOT AN UPSET TUMMY. MAYBE IT'S A TOOTH COMING IN....

WAAAHHH

YEEOWWLLL!

...MAYBE HE'S OUT TO GET ME!!

As a new mother, with no one close by to advise me, there were times that I truly believed my son was "out to get me!" When you do everything possible to stop a baby from crying and they still go on and on and on, it's easy for a novice to think a baby does things like this on purpose. I came very close to shaking him one night and called my social worker the next day for help. I can see why some parents just can't cope — especially if they're on their own.

YOU PUTTING HIM IN MY BED?

SHHH...

RICHARD'S SLEEPING... WE DON'T WANT TO WAKE...

SLAM!

HIYA, MA-WHAT'S TO EAT?!

WAAAAAAHHHH..

I THINK...YES, I THINK I AM CAPABLE OF GREAT PHYSICAL VIOLENCE.

YOWLLL!!

I DIDN'T MEAN TO WAKE HIM! HOW WAS I TO KNOW THERE WAS A BABY SLEEPING HERE?

HIYA, RICKY! WANNA COME TO MICHAEL?

OH, HE'S SO CUTE! AREN'T BABIES CUTE, MOM?!

UH HUH.

IT'S A NATURAL CAMOUFLAGE TO ENSURE THEIR SURVIVAL.

I DON'T KNOW WHERE ANNIE IS, SO I GUESS YOU'LL BE HAVING DINNER WITH US, KIDDO.

OH, WOW! I'LL GET THE HIGH CHAIR FROM THE CRAWL SPACE!

I'LL FIND THE BIBS AN' THE PLASTIC PLATES AN' THE BABY SPOONS!

SO. HOW DO YOU LIKE YOUR STEAK?

YA-GAH!!

SQUISH MUSH SMUSH SPLT

WELL, IT'S BEEN A LONG TIME SINCE WE HAD A BABY AT OUR TABLE!

YEAH! ISN'T HE NEAT?

SPLUSH MUSH

IT'S NOT VERY OFTEN WE HAVE A DINNER GUEST WHO MAKES US LOOK GOOD!

OH, ELLY—I'M SORRY TO HAVE BEEN SO LONG!

SINCE YOU HAD THE BABY I, UH.... DID SOME SHOPPING. YOU KNOW HOW IT IS!!

AREN'T YOU A LITTLE ANGRY, EL? SHE LEFT HIM AN AWFULLY LONG TIME.

OH. I GUESS NOT.

I KNOW HOW IT IS!

This was obviously done before cell phones. Nowadays there's almost no excuse for not explaining late kid retrieval!

31

We got Farley as a puppy in the fall. The first snow was so much fun. Like any baby, he was thrilled to play in it and would bounce into a snowdrift — right up to his ears. The ravine behind our house was quite steep, and in winter, we had no choice but to slide down if we wanted to walk along the creek at the bottom. Farley watched my husband and me slide down the hill on our toboggan, and with a little coaxing, he stepped forward, sat down, and slid all the way down, too. It was so funny, we laughed till we cried. All that winter, he would slide down the hill. We photographed him and made our friends watch. Summer came, and the following winter, we thought Farley would carry on sliding. He didn't. He had no - interest at all in getting his seat wet and clogged with snow. I can't say that I blame him. We, at least, had protection! I guess it goes to show you that even dogs grow up and become sensible.

32

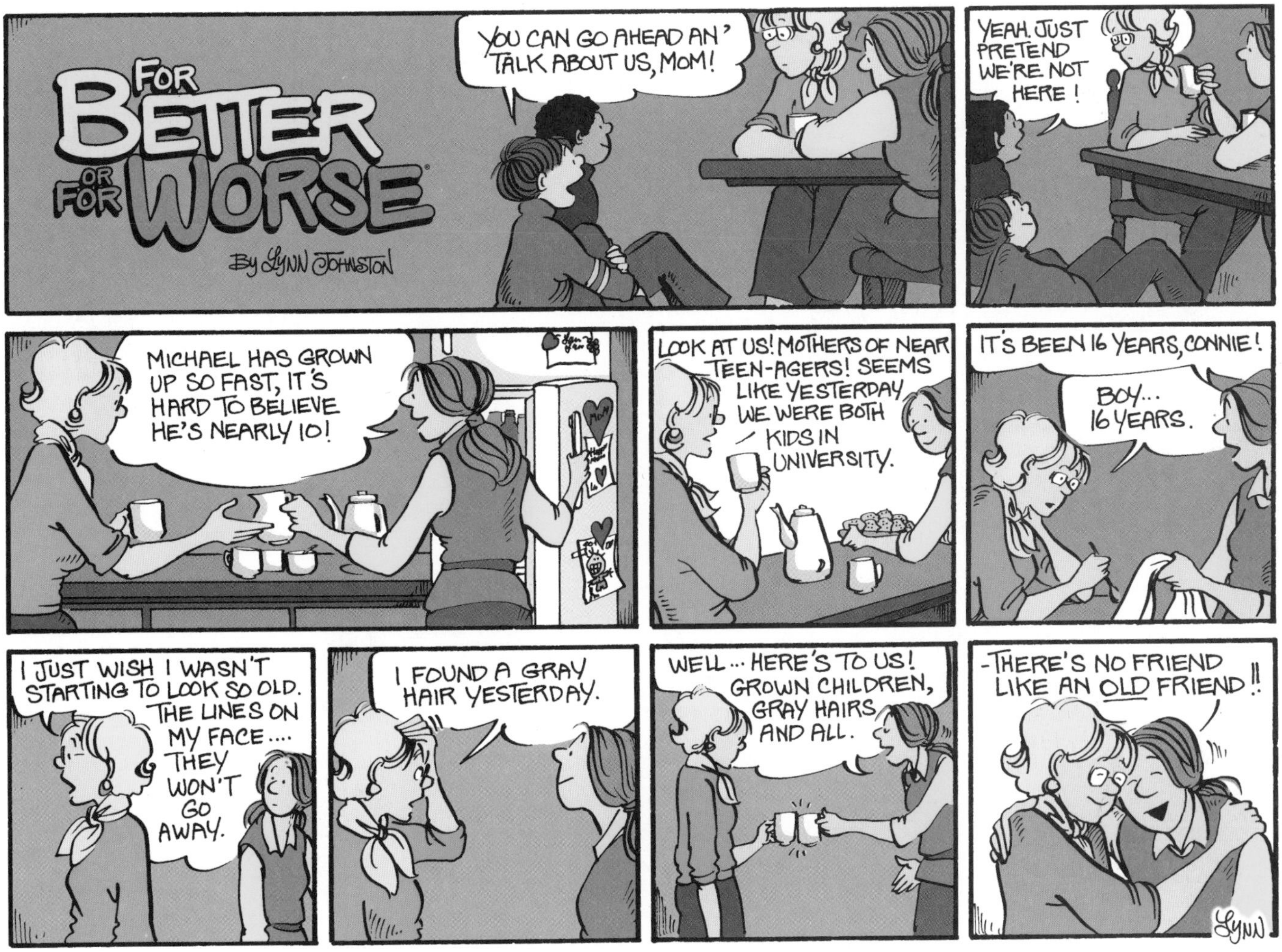
FOR BETTER OR FOR WORSE
BY LYNN JOHNSTON
YOU CAN GO AHEAD AN' TALK ABOUT US, MOM!
YEAH. JUST PRETEND WE'RE NOT HERE!
MICHAEL HAS GROWN UP SO FAST, IT'S HARD TO BELIEVE HE'S NEARLY 10!
LOOK AT US! MOTHERS OF NEAR TEEN-AGERS! SEEMS LIKE YESTERDAY WE WERE BOTH KIDS IN UNIVERSITY.
IT'S BEEN 16 YEARS, CONNIE!
BOY... 16 YEARS.
I JUST WISH I WASN'T STARTING TO LOOK SO OLD. THE LINES ON MY FACE.... THEY WON'T GO AWAY.
I FOUND A GRAY HAIR YESTERDAY.
WELL... HERE'S TO US! GROWN CHILDREN, GRAY HAIRS AND ALL.
-THERE'S NO FRIEND LIKE AN OLD FRIEND!!
LYNN

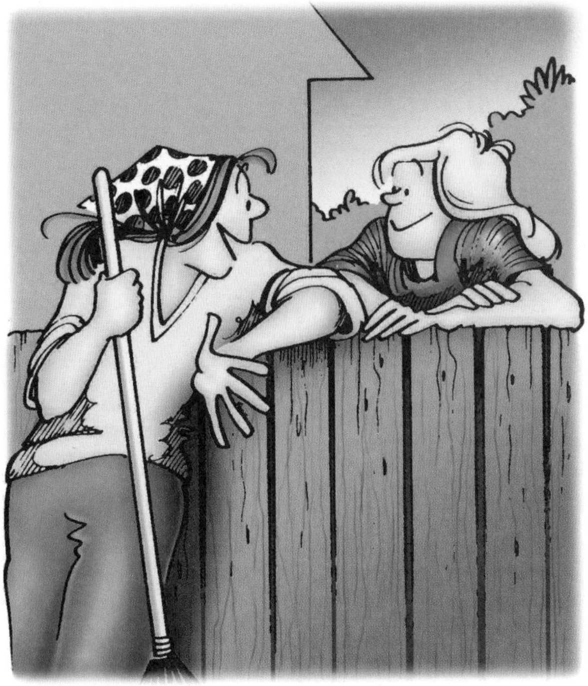

KNOW WHAT I'D LIKE TO GET ELLY FOR VALENTINE'S DAY, JEAN?

ONE OF THOSE GREAT BIG, FANCY, HEART-SHAPED BOXES OF CHOCOLATES!

IMAGINE ME BUYING HER SOMETHING AS SILLY AND SENTIMENTAL AS THAT!

... COULD YOU PICK ONE UP ON YOUR LUNCH HOUR?

MICHAEL, YOUR SCHOOL PARTY IS COMING UP. YOU'D BETTER GET ALL YOUR VALENTINES DONE!

I GOT TWO PACKAGES OF CARDS, THE NAMES OF ALL THE KIDS IN YOUR CLASS, AND A SPECIAL CARD FOR YOUR TEACHER.

THERE! ALL YOU HAVE TO DO IS SIT DOWN AND WRITE OUT EVERYBODY'S NAME.

SIGH..... EVERY YEAR I GOTTA GO TO ALL THIS TROUBLE!

HEY, THERE'S DEANNA, MIKE! FIRE ONE AT THE BACK OF HER HEAD! GO ON, DO IT, DO IT, DO IT!!

AWW-YOU'RE NOT GONNA DO IT, 'CAUSE YOU LIKE HER, DON'TCHA, MIKE! MICHAEL LOVES—

I DO NOT!!

THE DARNED THING'S STUCK TO THE FUZZ ON MY MITT.

HAVE A TOUGH DAY, HONEY?

MY BEST ASSISTANT IS QUITTING, MY HYGIENIST IS SICK, I TRIED IN A BRIDGE THAT DIDN'T FIT, THEY SHUT THE WATER OFF AND MY FOOT IS KILLING ME!!

LEAVE DADDY ALONE, LIZ. HE'S IN A BAD MOOD.

WHEN CAN I TALK TO HIM?

WAIT 'TIL HIS EYES STOP BUGGING OUT.

DON'T WIGGLE THE CUTTER. WE WANT THE EDGES NICE AND SHARP!

THERE! NOW, WE CAN PUT THE SPRINKLES ON AND GET THEM INTO THE OVEN!

THESE ONES HAVE COOLED A LITTLE BIT, MOM. CAN I HAVE ONE NOW?

DADDY?... WOULD YOU LIKE A WARM HEART?

My brother once hurt his leg in a soccer game and had to wear a cast. As his leg healed, the cast became unbearably itchy. Mom discovered a couple of her best knitting needles missing and found them in Alan's room. He had been using them to shove down the cast to relieve the itching. In fact, he had made so many holes with them all over the cast, he had to have it taken off and replaced. Some story lines bring back all kinds of memories!

Here I used Letrafilm, the now archaic method of adding black and white texture to cartoons destined for the newspaper. This is a wood grain pattern, and after it came out in the paper, I realized just how badly it reproduced! Sometimes this way of adding depth to a strip looked fine on the original art, but when reduced to the printed format, it became blotchy, muddy, and rough. I was constantly learning about what worked and what didn't!

NOW, YOU SAY YOU DROPPED A LARGE WEIGHT ON THIS FOOT?

YES...IT WAS A...HEH...WELL, IT WAS A TURKEY. 25 LBS. ...FROZEN.

AH. YES. I SEE. THAT WOULD BE AN ACCIDENT ONE WOULD WISH TO FORGET!

FORGET IT?! WE'RE STILL EATING IT!!

I received many letters expressing thanks for showing a Jewish doctor in this strip. I also received a few letters of complaint! I drew the yarmulke — because I have Jewish relatives, my ex-husband and I were married in a civil service by a Rabbi (a great friend of the family), and I have always enjoyed Jewish humour. It was interesting to see how a small symbol of one man's faith could elicit such a strong response.

FREE AT LAST! I CAN SCRATCH, I CAN SLEEP! I CAN HAVE A BATH!!

WHY ARE YOU SMILING?! YOU'VE NEVER HAD TO PUT UP WITH WHAT I'VE JUST BEEN THROUGH!

ELLY, I'VE JUST SPENT 6 WEEKS WITH A CAST ON MY FOOT. YOU DON'T KNOW WHAT DISCOMFORT'S LIKE!!

TRY BEING PREGNANT FOR 9 MONTHS.

CONGRATULATIONS ON GETTING YOUR CAST OFF, JOHN!

WE KNEW YOU'D BE UNCOMFORTABLE WEARING A SHOE JUST YET, SO THE GIRLS AND I BOUGHT YOU SOME SLIPPERS TO WEAR AROUND THE OFFICE.

GEE. THANKS.

Our small wartime house on Fifth Street had a wood and coal furnace. Warm air was forced through grates in the floor, and these grates were used for everything from drying socks to warming up Plasticine. Plasticine was (and still is) a superb modelling material with which we played endlessly. Heating the house was costly, so our home was often quite cold. We would play on the floor near one of the floor grates, and the smell of warming Plasticine is something I can still recall. I also remember scraping the melted stuff off the floors and the grates when we'd forgotten to remove it.

In our elementary school, we had those large water-filled metal heaters, shaped like a row of packaged hot dogs. Having used the heating system at home for melting stuff, I was intrigued by the possibilities presented by these heaters! At one end, there was an L-shaped valve, which had a small indentation on the top. This tiny valve was very hot, and interestingly, a wax crayon fit into the indentation perfectly. Within a few days, the classroom heaters had a rainbow of melted wax on one end, and an APB was put out for the guilty party. Due to my already colourful reputation, I was detained posthaste and sent to the principal's office. Another memory I have is of scraping melted crayon off the heaters at school, a punishment to fit the crime!

Another gift from the horse's mouth. Any time I got my husband into a clothing store, it was a special occasion. He hated to think about his attire. As long as he was comfortable, he didn't much care about his image! He'd buy a year's worth of clothing in one shot. The salesman would make sure that ties went with shirts, socks matched trousers, and that everything fit accordingly. Dressing him for a special occasion was much easier when there was a plan of attack. Still there were lapses, and this exact exchange took place before a dinner we had to attend.

This is a sketch done for Sharper Cards. It was rejected as a recall postcard, but I like it anyway!

Here's a story for you: The province of Manitoba had just decreed that people trained as dental nurses would be licensed to do check-ups, cleanings, small fillings, and extractions on children. Rod's dental practice had expanded to include three First Nations villages, and he needed someone to offset the load. I was on my way to Winnipeg with Aaron (who had a doctor's appointment) when an interesting application came in. Debbie had very good references and was willing to move up to Lynn Lake. Rod asked me to interview her in Winnipeg, so Debbie and I arranged to meet in the hospital cafeteria while Aaron had his appointment. I sat at a table with a coffee and waited for Debbie to arrive. Right on time, a stunningly beautiful girl with a long blonde hair, deep blue eyes, and a voluptuous figure came into the room, wearing a black low-cut cocktail dress. She put out her hand and introduced herself. I got her a coffee, and the interview began. Debbie was wonderful. I immediately liked her and knew she would work well with our team. I asked her if she could move up north as soon as possible. "You mean I've got the job?" she asked in amazement. "Absolutely," I said, "you are exactly the kind of person we're looking for." I watched Debbie as she adjusted herself in her seat. She was blushing. "There's just one thing I want to know," I continued, "why on earth did you wear a cocktail dress to this interview?" "Well," she smiled, "when I told my friends I was being interviewed by the dentist's wife, they told me I'd never be hired. So I decided to blow off the interview by dressing up!" I laughed. We both did. Debbie was not only beautiful, she had a wicked sense of humour. She worked for us for four years and was one of the best staff members we ever had.

One of the things interviewers will often ask a cartoonist is, "Of all the punch lines you've written, which is your favourite?" and the cartoonist will typically say, "Well. I haven't written it yet." Or something like that. This is my favourite punch line!

41

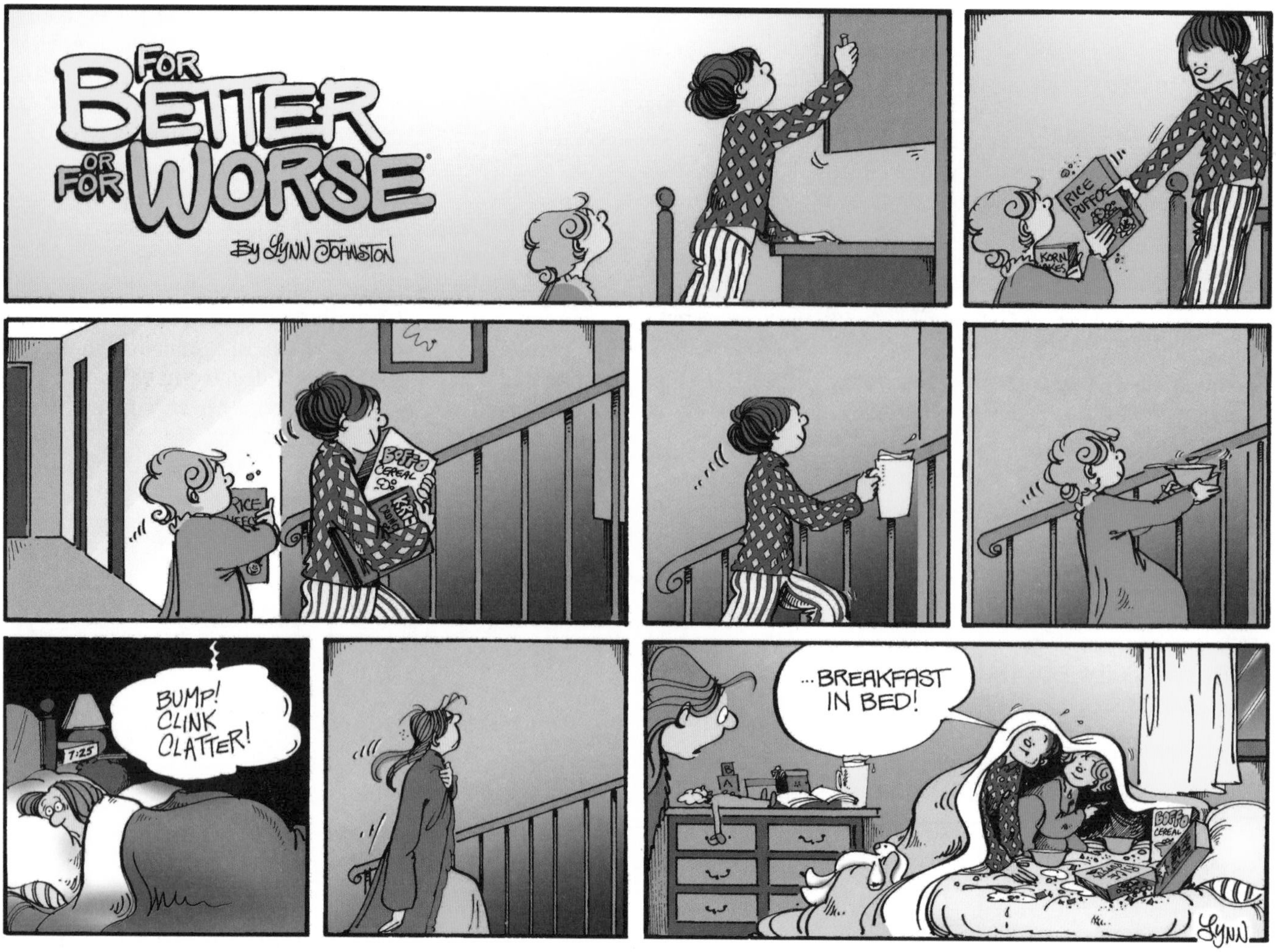
FOR BETTER OR FOR WORSE
By Lynn Johnston
RICE PUFFOS
BOFFO CEREAL
7:25
BUMP! CLINK CLATTER!
...BREAKFAST IN BED!
BOFFO CEREAL
LYNN

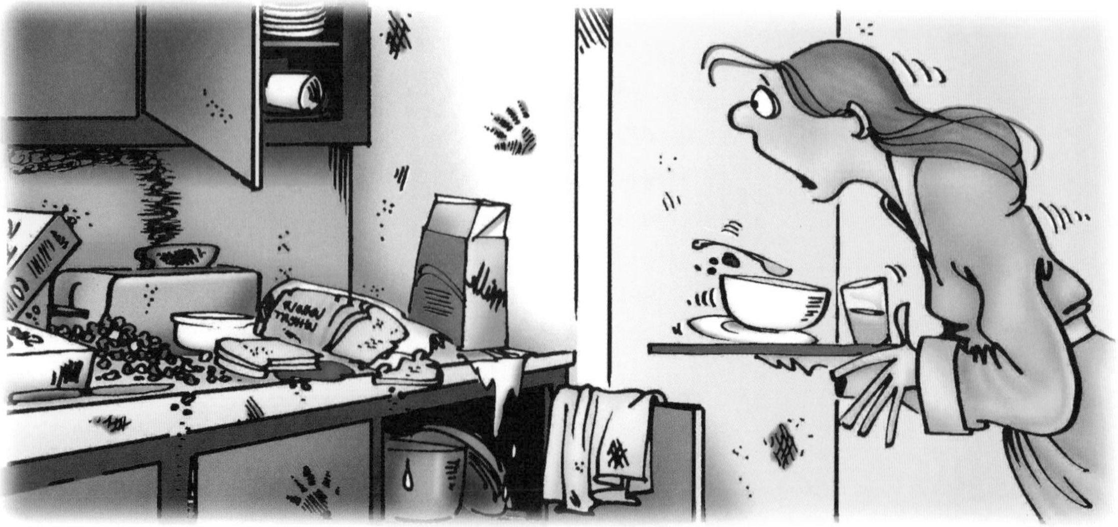

I'M WORKING LATE TONIGHT, MIKE. COULD YOU GET SOMEONE ELSE TO DRIVE YOU TO HOCKEY?

AWW, YOU'VE BEEN WORKING EVERY DAY LATELY. I THOUGHT THIS JOB WAS S'POSED TO BE PART TIME!

I KNOW, MIKE. IT'S JUST THAT RIGHT NOW THEY REALLY NEED ME!

SO DO I !!

GUILTY! WHY DO THEY ALWAYS MAKE ME FEEL GUILTY?

I LIKE MY JOB. I NEED MY JOB.

I'M JUST ONE MORE WOMAN DOING SOMETHING FOR ME FOR A CHANGE!

... I'M JUST ONE MORE GUILTY WOMAN.

ELLY, I'M GLAD YOU'RE HERE. I WAS SUPPOSED TO GO TO WINNIPEG NEXT WEEK, BUT I CAN'T MAKE IT.

... COULD YOU ATTEND THIS WORKSHOP IN MY PLACE?

ME?!!!

SUE, I'D HAVE TO GET SITTERS, ORGANIZE MY HOUSE, I COULDN'T POSSIBLY ...

HERE ARE THE TICKETS, THE HOTEL IS TAKEN CARE OF ....

43

ME? TAKE OFF TO WINNIPEG JUST LIKE THAT? SUE, THEY'D THINK I WAS CRAZY!!!

...SPACIOUS HOTEL ROOM, A BATHROOM ALL TO YOURSELF, DINING OUT, NEW PEOPLE TO MEET, INTERESTING CONVERSATION... TIME ... ALONE ...

ELLY, ARE YOU REALLY GOING TO TURN THIS DOWN?

...I'D HAVE TO BE CRAZY!!!

I DON'T BELIEVE IT. THEY WANT ME TO GO ON A BUSINESS TRIP! ME!

BUT, WHAT WILL JOHN SAY? WHAT ABOUT HIM? WHAT ABOUT THE KIDS??

...I'D FEEL SO GUILTY ABOUT LEAVING THEM. I'D FEEL SO GUILTY... AND SO SELFISH...

FOR AN HOUR OR SO - AT LEAST!

A BUSINESS TRIP TO WINNIPEG? SOUNDS LIKE A NICE OPPORTUNITY TO ME, EL!

REALLY?! YOU WOULDN'T MIND?

WE CAN SURVIVE ON MY COOKING FOR A FEW DAYS, CAN'T WE, KIDS!

IT DEPENDS...HAVE THEY DISCOVERED AN ANTIDOTE?

At the time these strips were done, I was travelling a great deal. I went on book tours, I did speaking engagements, and I attended various fairs and comic art related events. Sometimes, we went as a family, but more often, I went alone.

One of my many "chalk-talks."

HOW COME YOU GOTTA GO AWAY, MOM?

IT'S BUSINESS, HONEY.

...BESIDES, IT'LL BE NICE TO GET AWAY FROM THINGS!

...YOU'RE ONE OF THE THINGS...

I'M GOING TO MISS YOU, EL.

IT'S ONLY FOR A COUPLE OF DAYS.

I JUST WORRY ABOUT YOU TRAVELING ALONE, THAT'S ALL.

JOHN, I'M A CAPABLE WOMAN! I CAN LOOK AFTER MYSELF. I CAN MANAGE PERFECTLY WELL ON MY OWN!

.... MAYBE THAT'S WHAT I'M AFRAID OF.

My frequent absences were a great thing for my business, but they were not such a good thing for my family.

Most moms didn't have the opportunity I had to travel, so to make this a more believable story, I had Elly go on a "once only" short trip to attend a workshop for the library — even though she was just a volunteer. (Yes, her contribution to the library made her eligible for this perk, despite the complaints I had from librarians!)

If nothing else, travelling gave me an opportunity to get out of the house — a house in which I often felt like a prisoner.

I have met many interesting folks on my travels. When I'm travelling alone on a plane, I wonder if I can guess what the person next to me does. If my seatmate and I are both keen to engage in conversation, I discover I am always wrong; I can never guess by looking at another passenger what they are like and what they do for a living. This intrigues me.

My brother-in-law, Ralph, was a textile designer. One of the things he would do was to feel the fabric you were wearing and announce what it was made of. He also played the organ and wrote music for the United Church. We called him "a man of the cloth."

47

Because they are, in essence, public speakers, I find ministers and priests to be engaging conversationalists — and unless I brooch the subject, they rarely talk about religion.

One of the things I had to teach myself was to have small bills ready for tips and to know how much to give for which service.

Hard to believe that the invention of the wheeled suitcase took so long!

I was taught to sew at a very early age. As soon as I could manage a needle and thread, I was darning socks and patching trousers. One of the first "grown-up" gifts I received was a sewing box of my own — into which my mother had put all of the things I would need, including a thimble, which was just my size. I kept the sewing case until it fell apart, and up until a few years ago, I still had the tiny scissors my grandmother used for cutting thread. Sewing has always been something I've enjoyed — as long as I didn't have to follow a pattern or make something fit!

AAH... A HOTEL ROOM FOR TWO WHOLE NIGHTS!

NO COOKING, NO CLEANING, NO KIDS... JUST ME!

I HAVEN'T BEEN BY MYSELF FOR AGES AND AGES AND AGES!

HELLO, STRANGER.

I do love checking into a clean, attractive hotel room — knowing that I don't have to wash the porcelain receptacles or change the sheets. When I was a busy mom, this was a luxury I craved!

KNOCK KNOCK

ROOM SERVICE!

UH?

OH, MY GOSH - I FORGOT TO SET MY ALARM!!

COULD YOU BRING THE TRAY BACK LATER, PLEASE? I'M NOT DRESSED! I LOOK AWFUL!

THAT'S OK, LADY. I'M USED TO IT....

I'M MARRIED.

PUPPETS with a PURPOSE

PUPPETS AS TEACHERS
THEATRE WORKSHOP
INTRODUCTION
PUPPET M
BOOK

o READING
o WRITING SKILLS
o UNDERSTANDING SELF
o M   APPLICA
    ENCY
    TH

SALON

Welcome

REGISTRATION

NAME TAGS

HEH, HEH ... HELLO THERE, MRS... UH... PATTERSON!

NEARSIGHTED, MY FOOT!!

This story line was based on the trip I made annually to Winnipeg to attend "Contact." This event was a venue for performers willing to travel to the north to showcase their talent and to meet the community representatives who would hire them. I was the rep for Lynn Lake. It was my pleasure to hire performers and arrange the various stops on their tours in our area. I have remained friends with a number of wonderful people who were billeted with us when they came to town.

A friend of mine was working as a volunteer in a school, helping kids who had trouble reading. It was her observation that the kids thought to be slow to learn were often the fastest to make good decisions and show good judgement. I thought this was a nifty "So there!" to the "smart" kids who teased them!

When I was ignored in a restaurant by a waitress more interested in a table full of gents, I retaliated by doing a strip about it. Once a waitress myself, I knew that, even if you're busy, it's still possible to be courteous!

HOLY COW! IS IT EVER RAINING!!

THE SNOW'S ALMOST GONE, AN' THERE'S MUD PUDDLES EVERYWHERE!!

OH GOOD. ...IT MUST BE SPRING.

HOTDOGS? AGAIN?!— BUT, WE HAD 'EM LAST NIGHT— AN' FOR LUNCH TOO!

OK. WHY DON'T WE JUST PACK UP AND GO OUT FOR SUPPER.

WHAT ARE YOU GOING TO ORDER, MICHAEL?

I DUNNO.

GUESS I'LL HAVE A HOT DOG.

WHAT IF MOM NEVER COMES BACK?—EVER!

AWW—SHE'S COMING BACK, ELIZABETH—I KNOW SHE'S COMING BACK!

SHE LEFT SOME OF HER MOST VALUABLE STUFF HERE!

US!

I TALKED TO MY KIDS ON THE PHONE LAST NIGHT - THEY SURE MISS ME!

ELLY, YOU'VE ONLY BEEN AWAY TWO DAYS! DON'T GO FEELING GUILTY ALREADY!

CLAIRE - I'D FEEL GUILTY NO MATTER HOW LONG I WAS AWAY!

SO - NEXT TIME TAKE TWO WEEKS!

MY KIDS WOULD HAVE LOVED THAT LAST WORKSHOP! WE'D HAVE HAD TO DRAG THEM AWAY!

MINE TOO. THEY WOULD HAVE GONE CRAZY! - ABSOLUTELY WILD!!

THEY WOULD HAVE BEEN SO EXCITED ABOUT THE MUSIC, THEY WOULDN'T HAVE BEEN ABLE TO SIT STILL!

YEAH! .... IT'S A GOOD THING THEY'RE NOT HERE.

THAT WAS OUR LAST LECTURE, CLAIRE. IT'S OUR LAST NIGHT HERE - OUR LAST NIGHT OF FREEDOM.

SHOULD WE CELEBRATE?

DEFINITELY!

TO US! TO WOMEN! TO FRIENDSHIP!!

HAPPENS EVERY TIME YOU LET 'EM OUT OF THE KITCHEN, FRANK.

I went to a bar with one of the women from the workshop, to celebrate our new friendship and to mourn the end of a wonderful event. We were in our 30s, and guys at another table made suggestive comments and lewd gestures the whole time we were there. I remember thinking, "I make smart-ass comments for a living, but I can't think of one clever put-down to fling at these Neanderthals." It was frustrating!!!

NOW... LET'S SEE... I'VE BOUGHT STUFF FOR THE KIDS, SOME CLOTHES FOR JOHN....

I VISITED HIS FOLKS, HIS SISTER AND TWO OF MY RELATIVES....

IF I RUSH, I CAN GET IN SOME MORE SHOPPING BEFORE I LEAVE FOR THE PLANE!

12:24

THESE BUSINESS TRIPS SURE ARE EXHAUSTING!

SALE

NOW. HOW AM I GOING TO GET ALL THIS STUFF INTO MY SUITCASE?

UGH! GRUNT... MMPH!!

AAAH!!

CLICK!

'SCUSE ME, MA'AM-YOU'VE LEFT A SKIRT, SOME SHOES AND TWO BLOUSES IN THE CLOSET!

MOM'S COMING HOME! MOM'S COMING HOME!!

SETTLE DOWN! GET YOUR JACKETS ON! STOP JUMPING AROUND!

CUT IT OUT! LEAVE THE DOG! GET YOUR SHOES! HURRY UP!!

MOM'S COMING HOME! MOM'S COMING HOME!!

THERE SHE IS! MOM'S HOME! SHE'S HERE!

KNOW WHAT, MOM? KNOW WHAT?

WHAT, HONEY?

EVEN IF YOU BROUGHT ME SOMETHING ... I'M NOT GONNA ASK IF YOU BROUGHT ME SOMETHING!

IT WAS A WONDERFUL TRIP, JOHN! THE COURSE WAS SUPER, I LEARNED A LOT, I MET SOME FANTASTIC PEOPLE ...

I LOVED BEING ON MY OWN, IT DID ME A WORLD OF GOOD!

I'LL HAVE TO GO AWAY MORE OFTEN!!

GUESS WHAT, MOM! WE GOT SOMETHING TO SHOW YOU!

NO, LIZZIE! SHHHH...

WE DID IT ALL BY OURSELVES - AN' YOU'RE GONNA LOVE IT!!

NO! YOU'RE GONNA SPOIL...

WE CLEANED UP THE HOUSE ALL BY OUR- AAAAAAAH!!

YOU DUMMY, ELIZABETH! I WANTED HER TO BE SURPRISED!

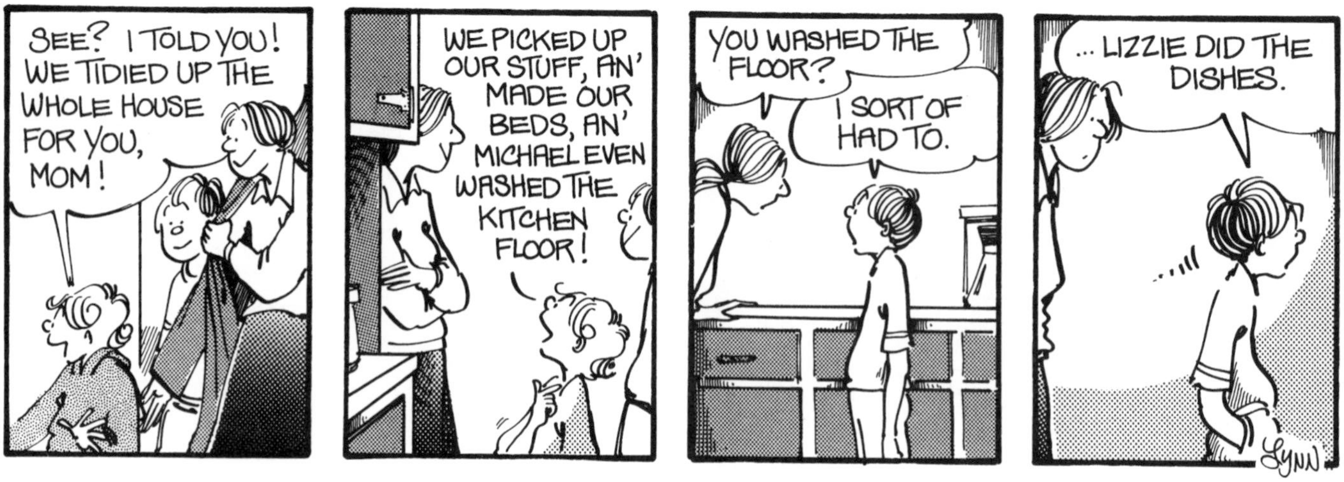
SEE? I TOLD YOU! WE TIDIED UP THE WHOLE HOUSE FOR YOU, MOM!
WE PICKED UP OUR STUFF, AN' MADE OUR BEDS, AN' MICHAEL EVEN WASHED THE KITCHEN FLOOR!
YOU WASHED THE FLOOR?
I SORT OF HAD TO.
...LIZZIE DID THE DISHES.
Lynn

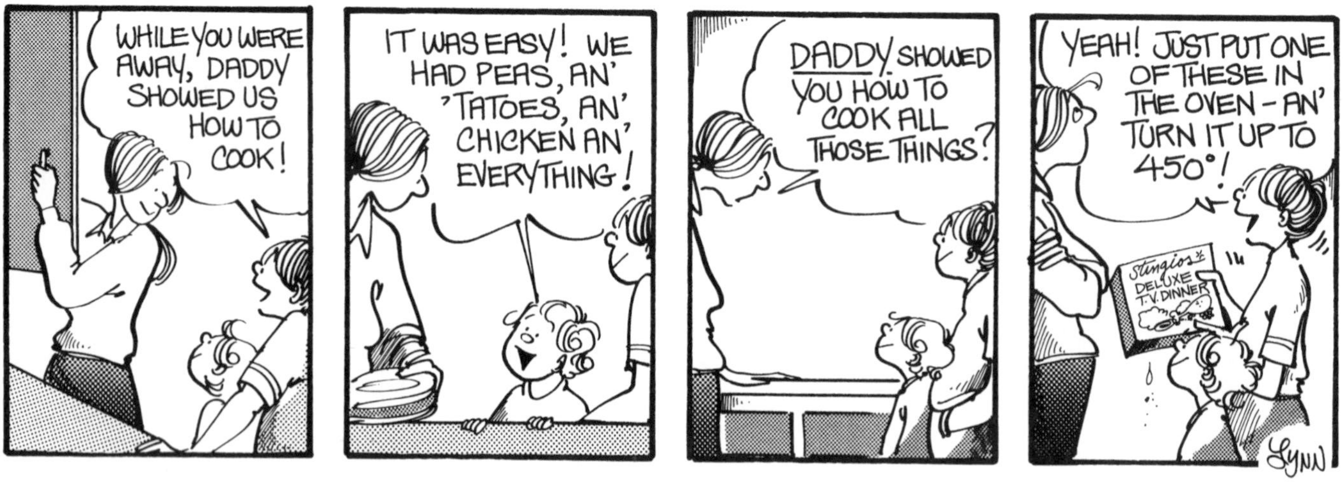
WHILE YOU WERE AWAY, DADDY SHOWED US HOW TO COOK!
IT WAS EASY! WE HAD PEAS, AN' 'TATOES, AN' CHICKEN AN' EVERYTHING!
DADDY SHOWED YOU HOW TO COOK ALL THOSE THINGS?
YEAH! JUST PUT ONE OF THESE IN THE OVEN - AN' TURN IT UP TO 450°!
DELUXE T.V. DINNER
Lynn

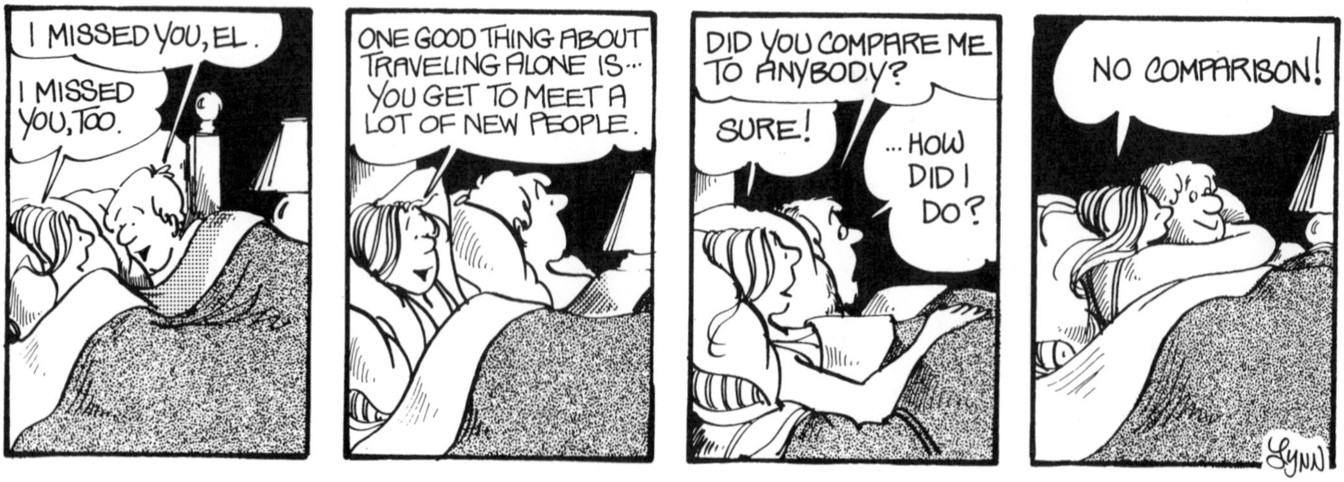
I MISSED YOU, EL.
I MISSED YOU, TOO.
ONE GOOD THING ABOUT TRAVELING ALONE IS... YOU GET TO MEET A LOT OF NEW PEOPLE.
DID YOU COMPARE ME TO ANYBODY?
SURE!
...HOW DID I DO?
NO COMPARISON!
Lynn

The real story behind this strip was quite different from what you see here. It began with a dream. I was on a dock on Bowen Island, waiting for the ferry to arrive. It came in with a rush of water and a hiss from the engines, and when it pulled in, the hull hit the wooden pilings and the waves pushed it up and down against them, making an awful, rhythmic scraping sound. This became so loud, it woke me up. There I was in bed, with my arm around my husband, and he was snoring … with the same rhythmic, grating sound!

Mrs. Baird was a background character who was meant to be put aside once Farley came into the family (her hobby was breeding Old English sheepdogs). To tie in with this, I also did a few strips about her being a friendly neighbour. I guess her short appearance struck a chord with some readers who asked to see her more often. In this Sunday page, I have her working in her greenhouse and talking to Michael — in a way that enabled me to say more about her personality and her past.

If Mrs. Baird was based on anyone at all, it would have been the ladies who lived across the street from us when I was growing up in North Vancouver. They were sisters, the "Miss Stewarts." They taught kindergarten and piano and were endlessly patient with me. I made a habit of going to their home uninvited and was rarely told that they had no time. When I needed an extra hug or another grown-up opinion, I headed for the Miss Stewarts' house and twisted the ringer on the front door to be let in.

Not long ago, I was in North Vancouver and I went for a nostalgic walk down Fifth Street. Their old wood frame house is still there, though mine is now a condo complex. A notice was on their fence to say the house and the one next door would soon be condos as well. I'm glad I got to see it one more time. There have been many unforgettable folks in my life, and these two ladies are certainly among them!

I got my first real burn from my curling iron. I was in a hurry; it flew out of my hand, and stupidly, I tried to catch it. I had to wear a bandage on my hand for two weeks. The pain and the inconvenience made me aware of how dangerous these things can be, so when my kids were around, I was extra careful with it. I made sure they knew it could be dangerous, that it was not a toy and should never be played with. I was certain that my lecture was well heeded until the day I noticed my curling iron had been put away "differently." When I examined it, I saw nylon and some other substance melted to the barrel. I never found out what my kids had been doing with it or what they had destroyed, which reminds me: Now that they are adults, they tell me stories of "what really happened" when I wasn't looking — I'll have to ask about the curling iron!!

POKE POKE

LIZZIE, IF YOU WANT SOMETHING TO GROW, YOU HAVE TO PLANT A SEED OR A BULB FIRST.

THERE. NOW YOU HAVE YOUR VERY OWN DAFFODIL. WE'LL JUST WATER IT AND WAIT FOR IT TO GROW!

NOTHING'S HAPPENING!

DADDY.... YOU CAN TELL IF A ANIMAL IS A GIRL ANIMAL OR A BOY ANIMAL, CAN'T YOU?

UH HUH.

... SO, HOW CAN YOU TELL IF A WORM IS A BOY WORM OR A GIRL WORM?

WELL?

... HE SAYS THE BOYS HAVE DEEPER VOICES.

A question like this would have made my parents get out the encyclopaedia and look up the answer. My mother especially enjoyed teaching us stuff about plants and animals and would easily pick up a snake or a spider to show us it was something to admire. She was responsible, I'm sure, for my brother's degree in biology and my years working as a medical artist!

MOM, CAN CHRIS AN' BABY RICHARD COME IN TO PLAY?

ALL RIGHT—BUT DON'T GET ANY MUD AND SAND ON THE FLOOR.

WE WON'T!

LOOK AT YOUR HANDS!

GO INTO THAT BATHROOM RIGHT NOW, ALL THREE OF YOU!

DO YOU WANT US TO WASH THEM?

The towels in our family bathroom were often filthy. Alan and I would "wash" our hands but were always in too much of a hurry to use soap!

NO COOKIES?

LIZZIE, I HAVEN'T HAD TIME TO BAKE COOKIES!

HERE. YOU CAN EACH HAVE ONE OF THESE.

WANNA COOKIE? ....THEY'RE HOME-BOUGHT.

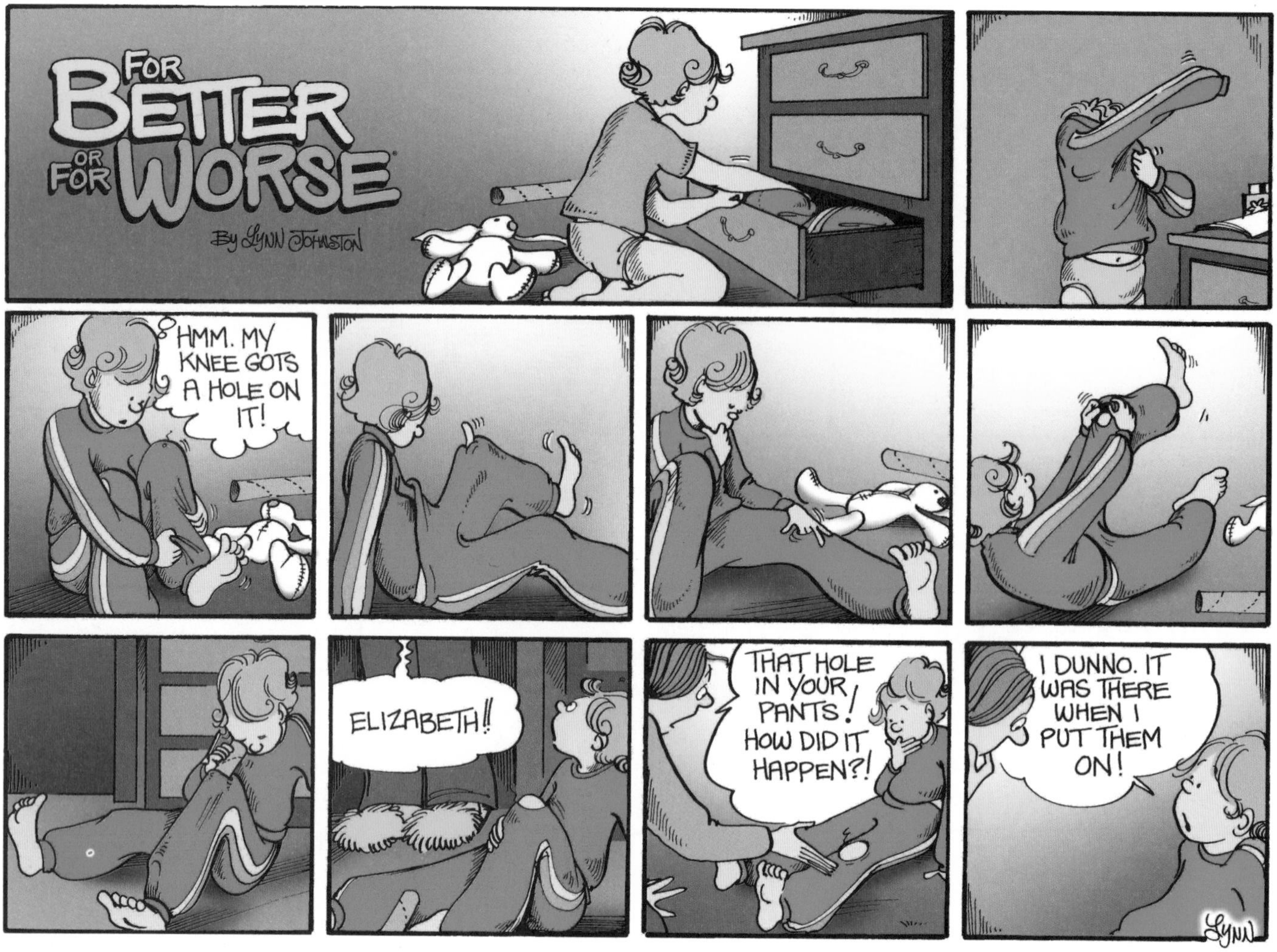
FOR BETTER OR FOR WORSE
BY LYNN JOHNSTON
HMM. MY KNEE GOTS A HOLE ON IT!
ELIZABETH!!
THAT HOLE IN YOUR PANTS! HOW DID IT HAPPEN?!
I DUNNO. IT WAS THERE WHEN I PUT THEM ON!
LYNN

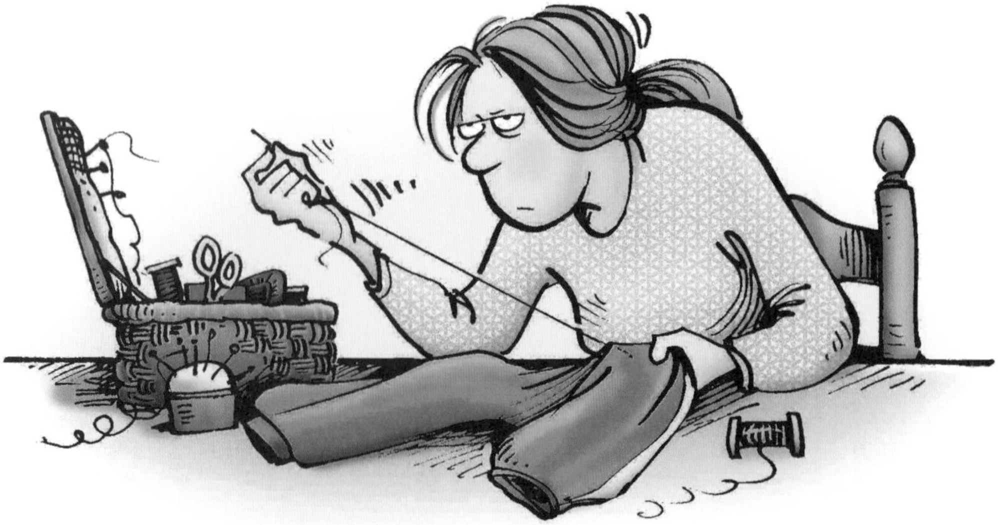

CAN'T MIKE AN' LAWRENCE COME IN, MOM?

NO. I TOLD THEM YOU ALREADY HAD TWO FRIENDS IN, AND THAT'S ENOUGH.

THEY CAN'T COME IN?

NO.

OH. ...THAT'S TOO BAD.

NA-NA NA-NAAAA NAH!

MAAAH! LIZZIE'S MAKIN' FACES AT US THROUGH THE WINDOW!

MICHAEL, YOU'RE TOO OLD TO LET A 4-YEAR-OLD GET THE BEST OF YOU!

I'M NOT LETTIN' HER GET THE BEST OF ME!

—THIS IS THE WORST OF ME!!

WHAT'S THE MATTER, EL?

THE KIDS BOTH HAD FRIENDS OVER TODAY, AND I SPENT ALL MY TIME WIPING NOSES AND BEING REFEREE!

THEY WERE UNDER-FOOT ALL DAY DRIVING ME CRAZY. WHY DO I DO THIS TO MYSELF?!!

BECAUSE...IN A FEW YEARS THEY'LL DRIVE YOU CRAZY WONDERING WHERE THEY ARE!

This was true. My house and my yard were always full of kids, and though it sometimes became a chore, I always knew where my children were!

HEY, MOM! CAN I HAVE MY ALLOWANCE?!

SHHH! THIS IS A LIBRARY. HOW MANY TIMES HAVE I TOLD YOU NOT TO BARGE IN TO THE PLACE WHERE I WORK?!

DOES EVERYTHING I SAY JUST GO IN ONE EAR AND OUT THE OTHER?!!

WAIT... COULD YOU SAY THAT AGAIN?

The library where Elly volunteered was based on the library in Dundas, Ontario, where I went with Aaron to borrow toys and books and to take in the free events put on for kids. There were readings, films, children's shows, and an annual yard sale — the profits from which went to buy the toys we all borrowed and appreciated so much. That library was a resource and a refuge, and even though these images were sparse in detail, I felt I was "there" when I drew them!

AWW GEE, $2.50

MIKE, IF YOU NEED EXTRA MONEY, YOU HAVE TO EARN IT.

SIGH... SO WHAT CAN I DO THAT WON'T TAKE A WHOLE LOT OF TIME, AN' WON'T BE TOO HARD, AN' GET PAID FOR DOIN' IT?

YOUNG MAN, YOU AND I ARE GOING TO HAVE TO HAVE A LONG TALK!

SOUNDS OK. HOW MUCH WILL YOU PAY ME?

DADDY, MOM SAYS YOU MIGHT HAVE A JOB I COULD DO TO EARN SOME MONEY.

SURE! YOU COULD SWEEP OUT THE GARAGE AND VACUUM THE CAR!

WHERE'S THE EXTENSION CORD? WHICH BROOM DO I USE? I CAN'T FIND THE ATTACHMENTS TO THE VACUUM CLEANER!

HOW MUCH WILL I GET FOR DOING ALL THIS WORK?

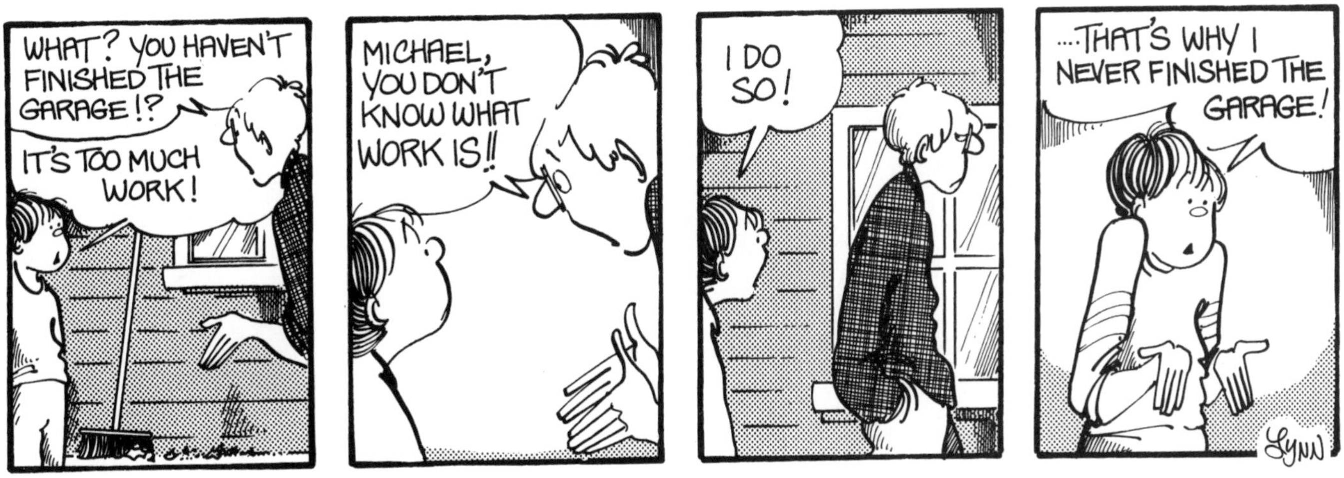
WHAT? YOU HAVEN'T FINISHED THE GARAGE!?
IT'S TOO MUCH WORK!
MICHAEL, YOU DON'T KNOW WHAT WORK IS!!
I DO SO!
....THAT'S WHY I NEVER FINISHED THE GARAGE!
LYNN

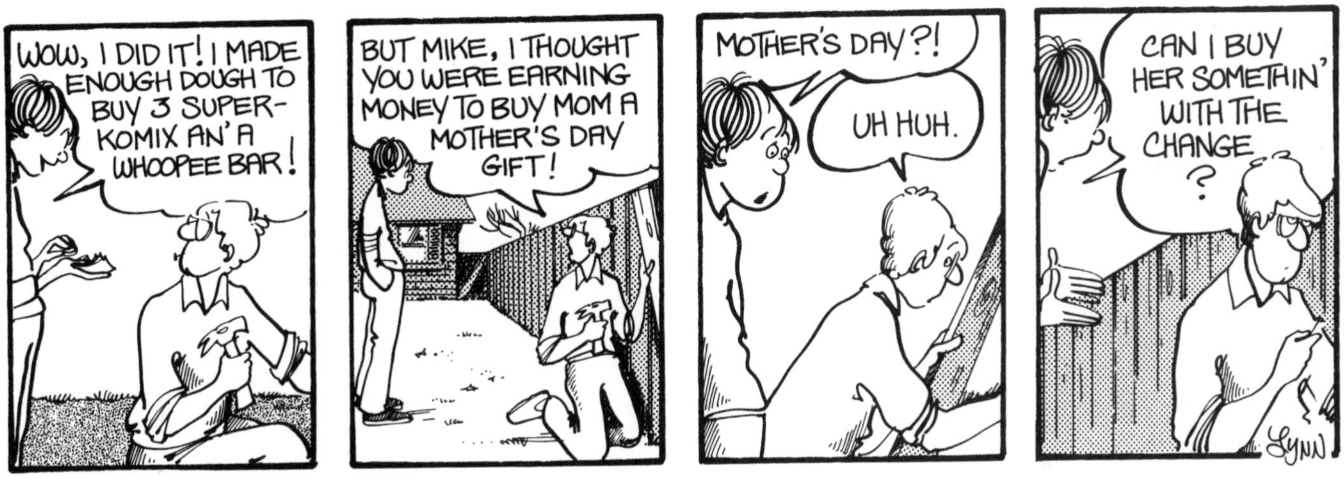
WOW, I DID IT! I MADE ENOUGH DOUGH TO BUY 3 SUPER-KOMIX AN' A WHOOPEE BAR!
BUT MIKE, I THOUGHT YOU WERE EARNING MONEY TO BUY MOM A MOTHER'S DAY GIFT!
MOTHER'S DAY?!
UH HUH.
CAN I BUY HER SOMETHIN' WITH THE CHANGE?
LYNN

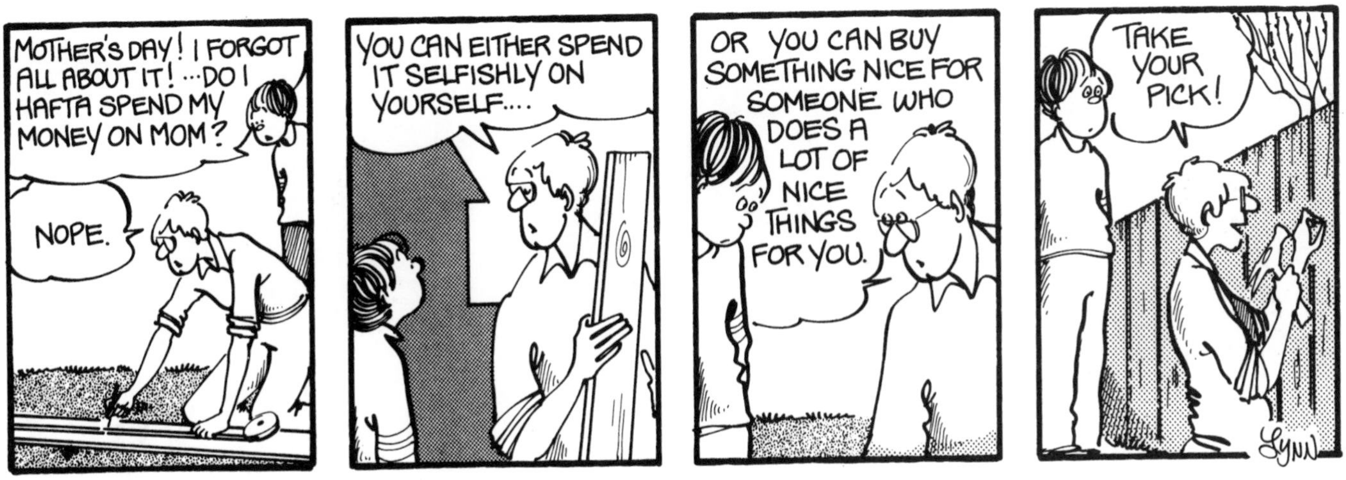
MOTHER'S DAY! I FORGOT ALL ABOUT IT! ...DO I HAFTA SPEND MY MONEY ON MOM?
NOPE.
YOU CAN EITHER SPEND IT SELFISHLY ON YOURSELF....
OR YOU CAN BUY SOMETHING NICE FOR SOMEONE WHO DOES A LOT OF NICE THINGS FOR YOU.
TAKE YOUR PICK!
LYNN

When I was in high school, I went out with a guy whose dad was a florist. I would often wait for Ken at the family flower shop, taking the opportunity to look into the big refrigerated room where the flowers were stored. I'd sneak into the back room where vases were kept and arrangements were designed. It was exciting. I loved the ambience, the colours, and the smell, and when Ken gave me a corsage, I kept it for as long as I could. Flowers are still my favourite gift — to give and to get!

I'M GLAD I DECIDED TO GET ROSES! MOM WILL REALLY LIKE –

GASP! OH, NO! IT'S BRAD LUGGSWORTH!!

...I'M CARRYIN' A BOUQUET OF DUMB FLOWERS – AN' I HAFTA RUN INTO THE MEANEST GUY IN SCHOOL!

WHATCHA GOT IN THE BAG, NERD-HEAD? PANSIES?

There had to be a bad guy in the picture, so Brad Luggsworth was introduced. His last name just popped into my head. It suited him. Brad was out to get Michael Patterson and anyone he hung out with. I don't know why he set Michael in his sights, but that's the way it was. Brad was a large kid, a slow learner with a chip on his shoulder who threw his weight around. *FBorFW* had become a "story strip." New characters provided great material, but they added to a growing "cast" as well.

HAH! SO, PATTERSON HANGS OUT IN FLOWER SHOPS, EH?

DON'T, BRAD – THEY'RE FOR MY MOM, AN' –

LEMME SEE IN THERE, WIMPO!

GIMME THAT! – UH?

BRAD? BRAD LUGGSWORTH?

THE CARNATIONS YOU WERE TO PICK UP ARE READY!

JOHN? ...THESE ROSES! THEY'RE FROM MICHAEL!

SHHHH! THEY'RE FOR MOTHER'S DAY. YOU'RE NOT SUPPOSED TO FIND THEM UNTIL TOMORROW!

ROSES. ...HE BROUGHT ME ROSES.

MICHAEL ...YOU MAKE BEING A MOM... JUST FINE!

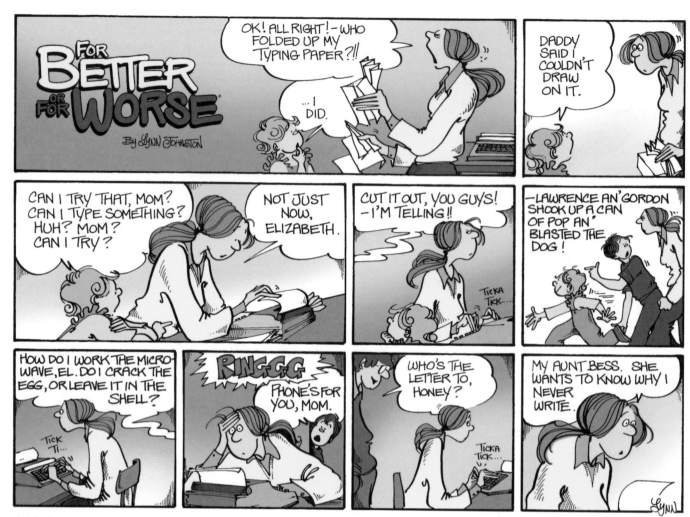

Aside from getting out the message that chaos always happened when I needed to think, I did owe a letter to my aunt Bessie. This was a way to tell her I was thinking about her and get some work out at the same time. Unfortunately, Bessie never read the paper the day this was released, but I did write the letter I owed her!

Tic! Ticka Tap! Tik Tappity

---well, that's all the news I can think of,
I'll leave some space - Elizabeth wishes to
add a few lines.
Love Elly

p ppk g g 3 3 3 zzzz8! !&O O OS S SMi i i i j j i j j
f f f f f f f f f f b b b??2 2222777!!& ooo ou u u
L L L d d dc c c caaaaaE E E E E E E FE E E E...

My brother and I fought over trivia; my kids fought over stupid things, too. Whether it's caused by boredom or the need to establish territory, fighting between siblings seems to be unavoidable. My mother would say, "You two are LOOKING for an excuse to fight!" And we were.

I always liked to make a figure of speech into a punch line. This one worked so well, I used it as the title to a collection book.

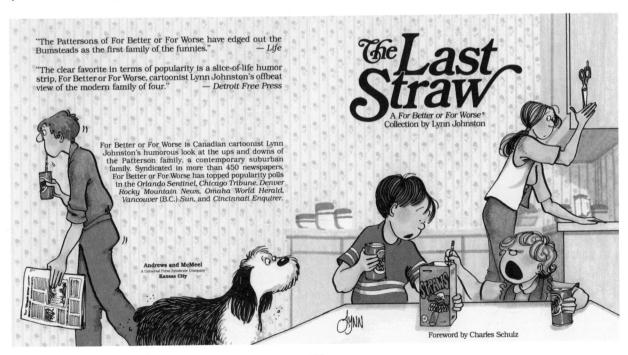

For the new release of this strip, the dialogue was changed to read, "Hey, guys, what's short and round ..." I knew I would still get negative mail but perhaps fewer complaints than when it was first printed. People don't want to see derogatory remarks of any kind, even if it's exactly what two little boys would say. I could have deleted the strip, but I rather liked the gag!

HEY, LOOK AT THAT! THE CAKE RAFFLE IS TODAY!

HOME ECONOMICS
CAKE RAFFLE
TODAY
25¢ PER TICKET
OR
5 FOR A DOLLAR

AREN'T YOU GONNA GET SOME TICKETS?

NAH. I WENT AN' FORGOT MY MONEY.

CAKE RAFFLE

...WELL, I GUESS I COULD GIVE YOU ONE OF MINE — ON ONE CONDITION...

—YOU GOTTA GIVE IT BACK IF IT WINS!

QUIET, EVERYONE... WE'RE GOING TO DRAW THE WINNING NUMBER FOR THIS WEEK'S CAKE RAFFLE.

I CAN'T WAIT— IT'S CHOCOLATE FUDGE THIS TIME!

READY? THIS WEEK'S LUCKY NUMBER IS... 661!!

GASP!

CONGRATULATIONS, BRAD LUGGSWORTH!

I DON'T BELIEVE IT! I JUST DON'T BELIEVE IT!

WHAT'S THAT, MIKE?

EVERY WEEK WE HAVE A CAKE RAFFLE AT SCHOOL—AN' THIS WEEK BRAD LUGGSWORTH WON!

HE'S STUPID AN' HE'S MEAN — EVERYBODY HATES HIM — WHY HIM? WHY DID IT HAFTA BE HIM?!

BECAUSE, MIKE... SOMETIMES A LOSER REALLY NEEDS TO WIN.

Behind closed doors, I had a dopey, mommy-to-doggie vocabulary, which I shared with Farley alone. I even had a song I sang to him, and later, I made up a song for Willy, our small black spaniel. While openly criticizing other pooch-parents for talking baby talk to their canine family members, I was doing the very same thing. My dogs appreciated it. This was a language we shared in the privacy of my home. This Sunday page allowed readers into our secret world. I believed that the sheer stupidity of what Elly was saying would be taken as "made-up cartoon dialogue," but not so. I received several letters from readers telling me they used the exact same words of endearment!

This cartoon was done specifically as a message to my son. Word for word, grimace for groan, I expressed my outrage in the most visible and lasting way possible. When the strip appeared in the *Toronto Star*, I showed it to him hoping that he would be shocked into changing his evil ways. I said that millions of people had read it and now knew about the way he treated his laundry — and ME! Aaron read the dialogue thoroughly and said, "I get the gag, Ma, but what's your point?"

JOHN... COULD YOU HELP ME GET THIS BATHING SUIT ON?

MMMM MMHH

WHEW! THANKS.

IT WAS NOTHING...

SORT OF LIKE PUTTING SHEETS ON A WATER BED!

Waterbeds were all the rage in the '80s, so we bought one. It was a miserable thing. The heater was defective, so the mattress was often clammy and cold. Putting the sheets on took practice. We had to pull up the edge of the mattress, then work a band of elastic under this blubbery, rolling water-filled sack while skinning our knuckles on the frame. It occurred to me that it was kind of like dressing something warm, large, and flabby!

(GROAN) I LOOK AWFUL! I CAN'T GO OUT ONTO A BEACH LIKE THIS!

WHY NOT, FOR HEAVEN'S SAKE? YOU'RE OVER 35, YOU'VE HAD TWO KIDS... YOU'RE ENTITLED TO SPORT A FEW EXTRA ROLLS!

ACCEPT THE FACT THAT YOU'RE A LITTLE CHUNKY AND...

— SO MUCH FOR HONESTY IN MARRIAGE.

SO, HE SAYS TO ME, "ACCEPT THE FACT THAT YOU'RE A LITTLE CHUNKY!"

I'M TELLING YOU, ANNIE, I WAS SO MAD !!!

IF ONLY I COULD LOSE 10 LBS. I'D....

...WHY DO THE SKINNY ONES COME TO ME FOR SYMPATHY?!

76

This punch line was ahead of its time; today, it might be a viable reality show!

I got away with this drawing, perhaps because there was no Internet to give me an instant blast for inconsistency: The car isn't backing into the garage. It somehow hit the frame while backing OUT!

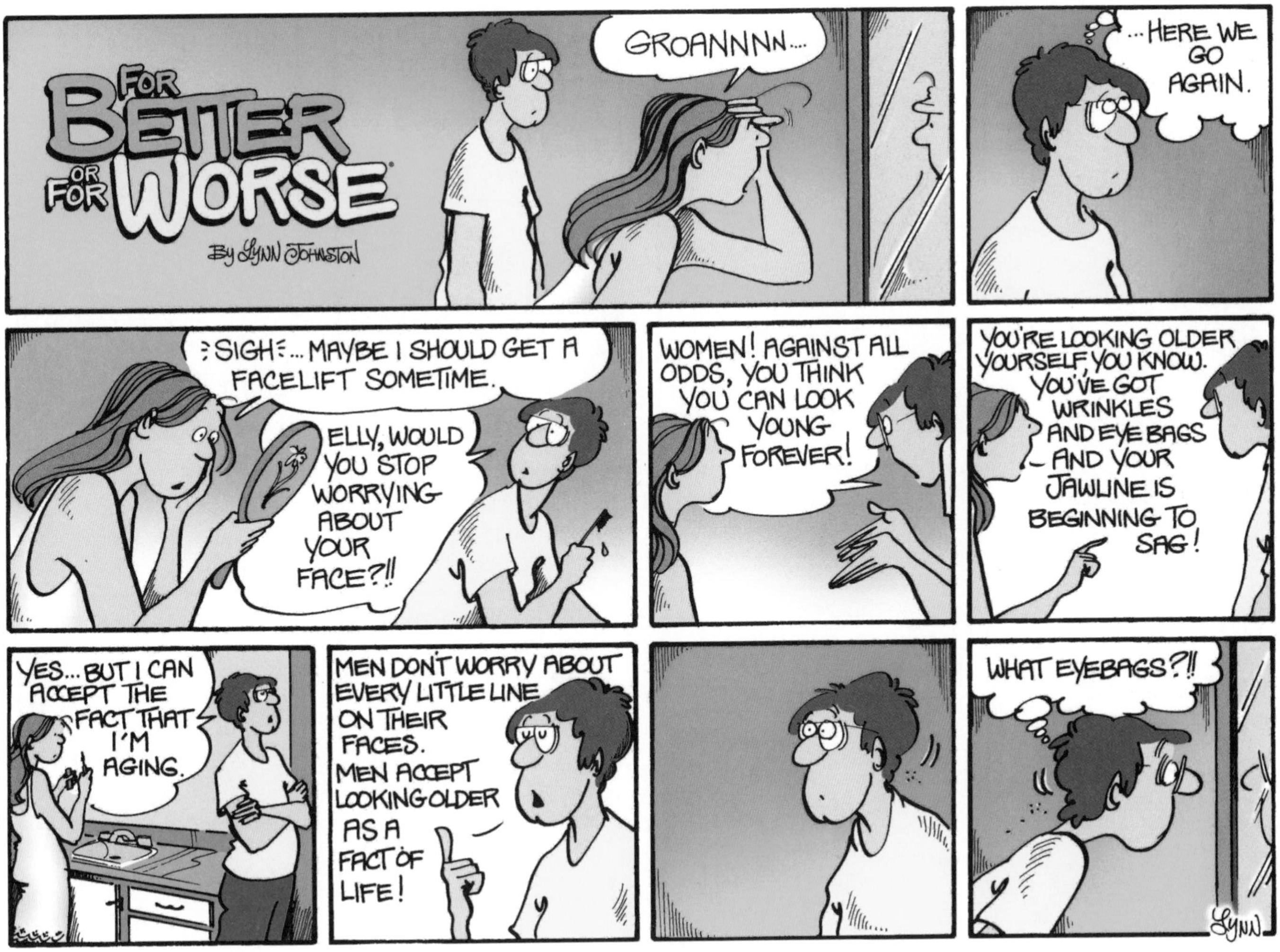
For Better or For Worse
By Lynn Johnston
GROANNNN....
...HERE WE GO AGAIN.
SIGH... MAYBE I SHOULD GET A FACELIFT SOMETIME.
ELLY, WOULD YOU STOP WORRYING ABOUT YOUR FACE?!!
WOMEN! AGAINST ALL ODDS, YOU THINK YOU CAN LOOK YOUNG FOREVER!
YOU'RE LOOKING OLDER YOURSELF, YOU KNOW. YOU'VE GOT WRINKLES AND EYE BAGS - AND YOUR JAWLINE IS BEGINNING TO SAG!
YES... BUT I CAN ACCEPT THE FACT THAT I'M AGING.
MEN DON'T WORRY ABOUT EVERY LITTLE LINE ON THEIR FACES. MEN ACCEPT LOOKING OLDER AS A FACT OF LIFE!
WHAT EYEBAGS?!!
LYNN

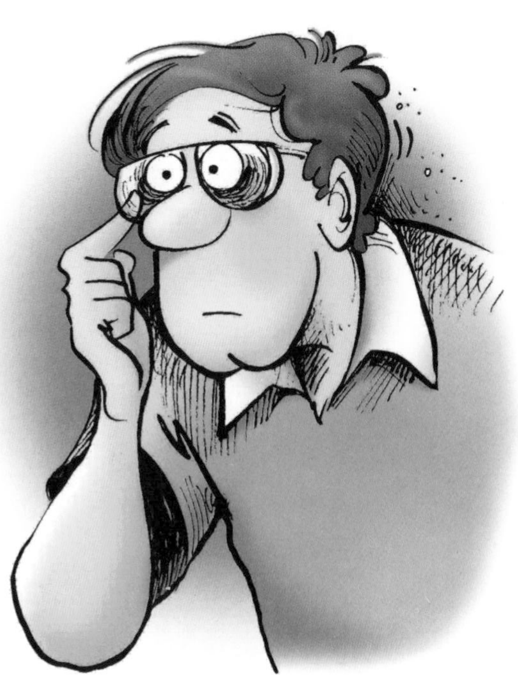

UNH! UGH! GASP!...THIS TREE MUST WEIGH 100 LBS.!!

"UNTIE SACKING, BURY ROOT BALL COMPLETELY, WATER WELL..."

WHAT DO YOU THINK HONEY? LOOK OK?

YEAH.

BUT I WANTED IT OVER THERE!

Having moved to a more southerly clime, we were able to grow real plants! I went crazy finding ornamental trees and flowering perennials to fill our garden. I dug and I trimmed. The job was bigger than I had imagined, so I hired a lady to help me. She would arrive with her young children in tow; I'd feed and water them while she did the same for the garden. Eventually, we had a beautiful place to live, surrounded by pine forests and open fields.

YOU KNOW THOSE FLOWERS YOU JUST PLANTED BY THE GARAGE, MOM?

UH HUH!

WHAT ARE THEY CALLED?

THEY'RE BEGONIAS, HONEY. WHY DO YOU WANT TO KNOW?

MICHAEL'S STANDING ON 'EM.

Begonias do very well here, and the blossoms can grow to an amazing size. Aaron and Katie liked to break them off and bring them in, along with the ants that infested them!

WHEW! GARDENING'S GOOD EXERCISE! I FEEL THINNER ALREADY!

LOOK AT ME, JOHN - DO I LOOK THINNER?

WELL?

WHAT CAN I SAY THAT WON'T GET ME INTO TROUBLE?

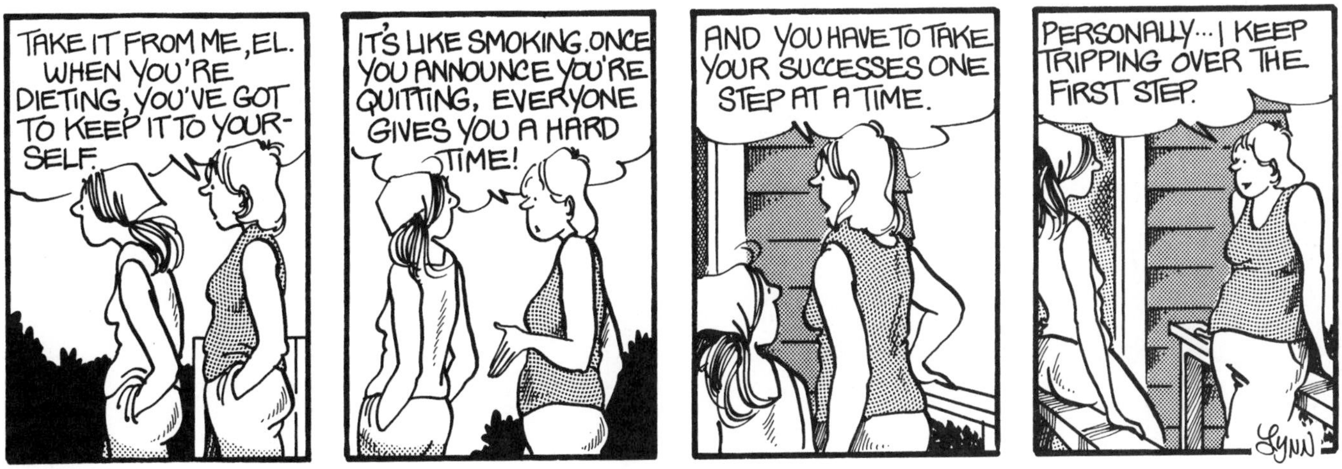
TAKE IT FROM ME, EL. WHEN YOU'RE DIETING, YOU'VE GOT TO KEEP IT TO YOURSELF.
IT'S LIKE SMOKING. ONCE YOU ANNOUNCE YOU'RE QUITTING, EVERYONE GIVES YOU A HARD TIME!
AND YOU HAVE TO TAKE YOUR SUCCESSES ONE STEP AT A TIME.
PERSONALLY... I KEEP TRIPPING OVER THE FIRST STEP.
LYNN

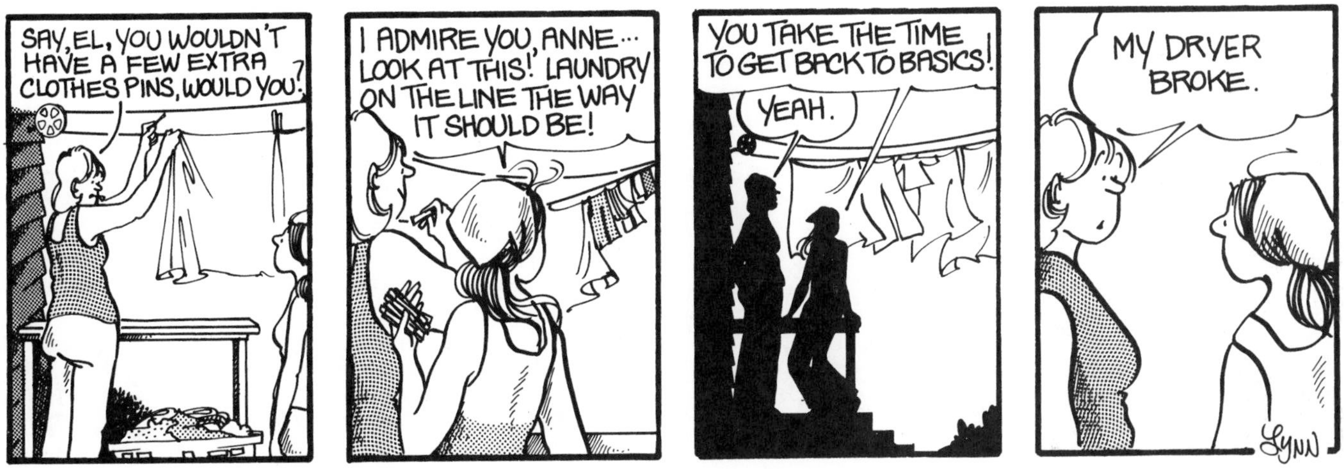
SAY, EL, YOU WOULDN'T HAVE A FEW EXTRA CLOTHES PINS, WOULD YOU?
I ADMIRE YOU, ANNE... LOOK AT THIS! LAUNDRY ON THE LINE THE WAY IT SHOULD BE!
YOU TAKE THE TIME TO GET BACK TO BASICS!
YEAH.
MY DRYER BROKE.
LYNN

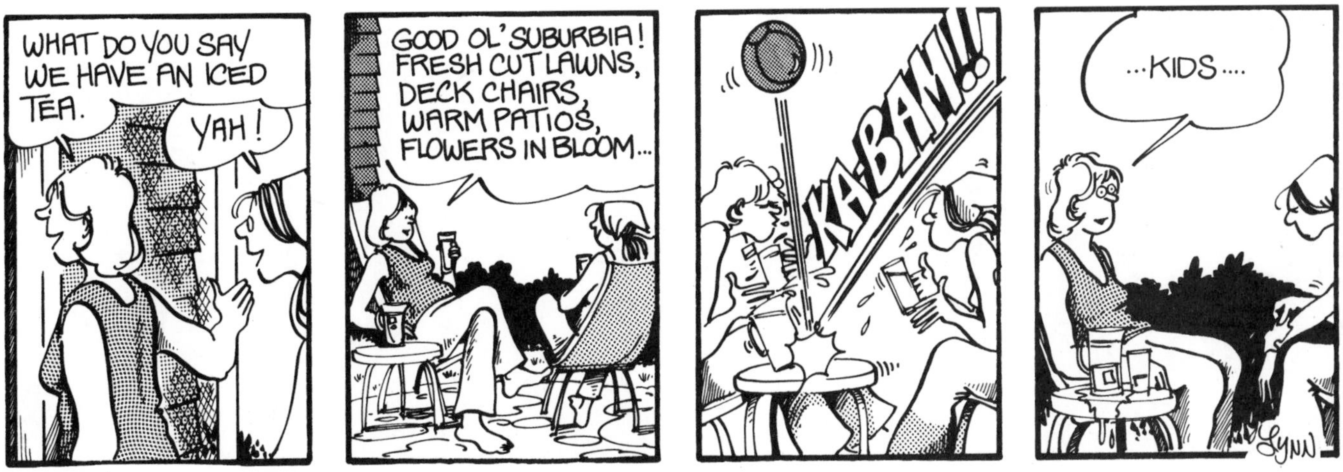
WHAT DO YOU SAY WE HAVE AN ICED TEA.
YAH!
GOOD OL' SUBURBIA! FRESH CUT LAWNS, DECK CHAIRS, WARM PATIOS, FLOWERS IN BLOOM...
KA-BAM!!
...KIDS....
LYNN

MOM, RICHARD KEEPS EATIN' THE SAND IN THE SANDBOX!

WELL, TELL HIM NOT TO.

HE SAYS IT'S PUDDING. TELL HIM IT'S SAND!

I DID, BUT—

OH, ALL RIGHT!!

YOU'VE GOT TO ADMIT, ANNIE, HE'S CHEAP TO FEED!

I remember being so into mud pies that I really expected to taste fresh baking when I bit into them. I can even recall the taste of dirt and the feeling of sand between my teeth. Why, then, can't I remember my own cell phone number?

I THOUGHT THAT YOUR FIRST KID WAS THE HARDEST TO RAISE— BUT THIS ONE DRIVES ME CRAZY!

HE'S THE MOST STUBBORN, HARDHEADED, TEMPERA-MENTAL PERSON I'VE EVER KNOWN.

GA-GA?

LOOKS CAN BE DECEIVING.

BUNGA!

NO BUNGA.

BUNGONGONG!!

NO. BAD. NOT LIKE!

WAN BUNGA! MAMA, GIM-BUNGA—NOW!!

WE HAVE OUR OWN LANGUAGE, RICHARD AND I.

... SOUNDED MORE LIKE A CONVERSATION BETWEEN CHEETAH AND JANE

STEVE'S DOWNTOWN, ELLY, AND I'VE GOT THE CAR. COULD I LEAVE THE BOYS WITH YOU?..

WELL... I... UH....

THANKS, EL... I'LL ONLY BE AN HOUR OR SO.

I DON'T MIND TAKING THEM FOR AN HOUR.... IT'S THE "OR SO" THAT BOTHERS ME!

MICHAEL, HONEY... CHRIS AND LIZZIE ARE PLAYING NICELY DOWNSTAIRS...

WOULD YOU WATCH BABY RICHARD AND SEE THAT HE STAYS OUT OF TROUBLE?

BUT MOM, I'M DOIN' STUFF... AN' HE'S A REAL NUISANCE !!

BESIDES THAT.... HE'S NOT HOUSE-BROKEN.

HERE IT IS— I FOUND IT IN THE CRAWL SPACE!

BOY, GOOD THING YOU KEPT ALL OUR BABY JUNK. IT COMES IN HANDY!

COME ON, RICHARD, LET'S—

NO WAVNA!

MOM FORGOT TO TELL YOU— HE'LL ONLY GO ON HIS OWN POTTY.

JOHN, WOULD YOU GO NEXT DOOR AND GET RICHARD'S POTTY? I'M BABY-SITTING AND IT'S THE ONLY ONE HE'LL USE!

PLEASE HURRY!

JOHN? WHAT'S TAKING SO LONG?

ANNIE LOCKED HER *!@✗ DOORS !!

In real life, this didn't happen; the story grew around the idea of Elly babysitting, and I kept saying to myself, "what if?" It's the sort of thing you do when you're lying in bed and wondering where your teenaged kids are. You come up with all kinds of "what ifs"! When you look after little ones, the troubles encountered are often bathroom related, so this was my imagination running wild!

ELLY, NO KID HAS TO HAVE HIS OWN POTTY! TELL HIM HE CAN —

BUT HE'S CRYING! CAN'T WE GET IN THROUGH A WINDOW?

BREAK INTO A HOUSE FOR A POTTY? ARE YOU CRAZY?!!

... SHE'S CRAZY!

OK, OK — THIS WINDOW SEEMS TO BE LOOSE. — THERE!

SHE KEEPS HIS POTTY IN THE LOWER HALL BATHROOM.

THIS IS RIDICULOUS. I HOPE NOBODY FINDS OUT I BROKE INTO A HOUSE FOR A ...

RING-ALINGA LINGA AL RING ALING

84

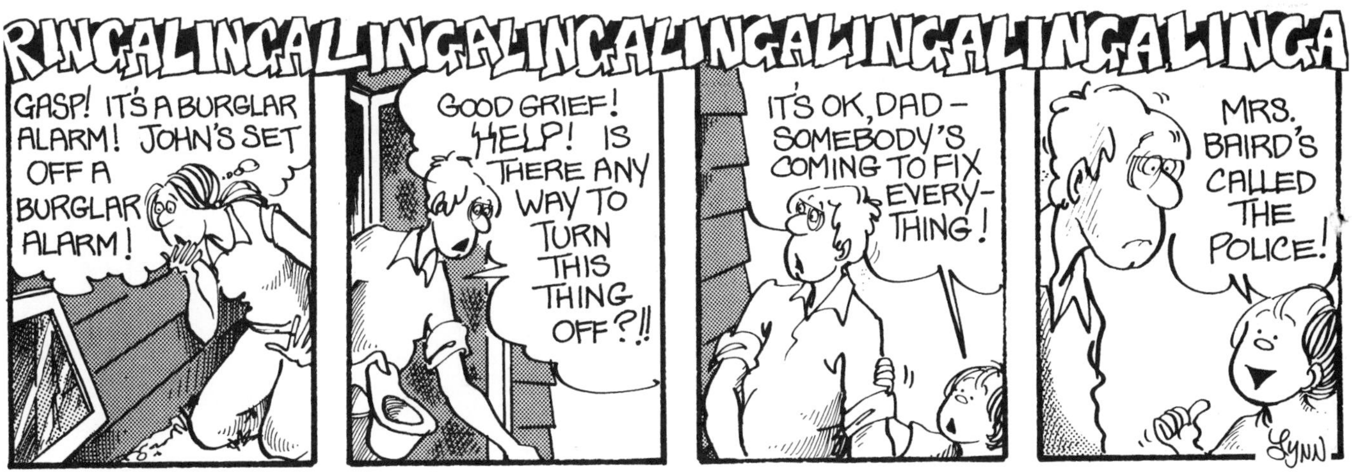
RINGALINGALINGALINGALINGALINGALINGALINGA
GASP! IT'S A BURGLAR ALARM! JOHN'S SET OFF A BURGLAR ALARM!
GOOD GRIEF! HELP! IS THERE ANY WAY TO TURN THIS THING OFF?!!
IT'S OK, DAD - SOMEBODY'S COMING TO FIX EVERYTHING!
MRS. BAIRD'S CALLED THE POLICE!
LYNN

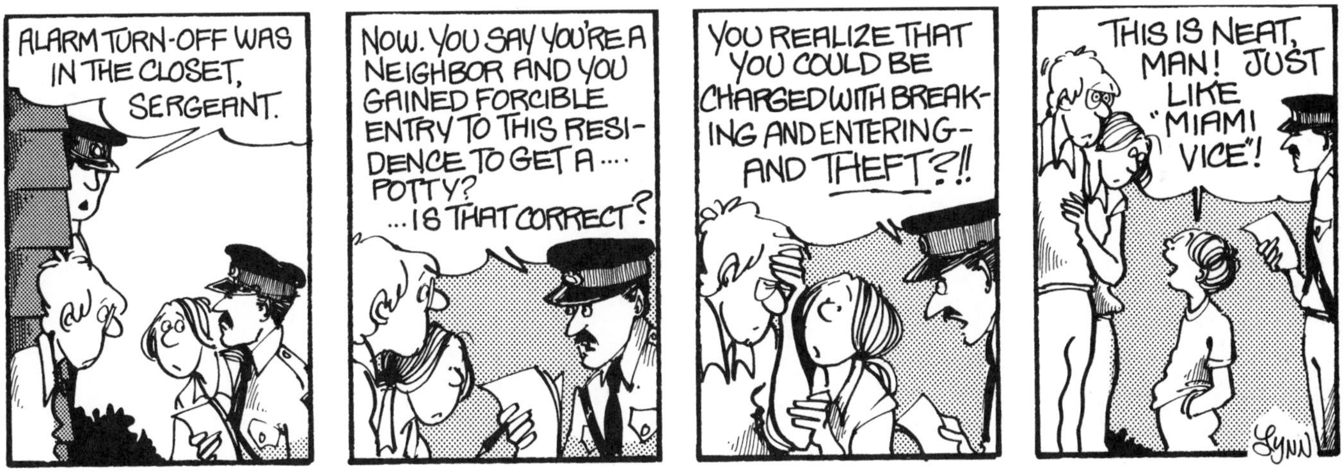
ALARM TURN-OFF WAS IN THE CLOSET, SERGEANT.
NOW. YOU SAY YOU'RE A NEIGHBOR AND YOU GAINED FORCIBLE ENTRY TO THIS RESIDENCE TO GET A.... POTTY? ...IS THAT CORRECT?
YOU REALIZE THAT YOU COULD BE CHARGED WITH BREAKING AND ENTERING - AND THEFT?!!
THIS IS NEAT, MAN! JUST LIKE "MIAMI VICE"!
LYNN

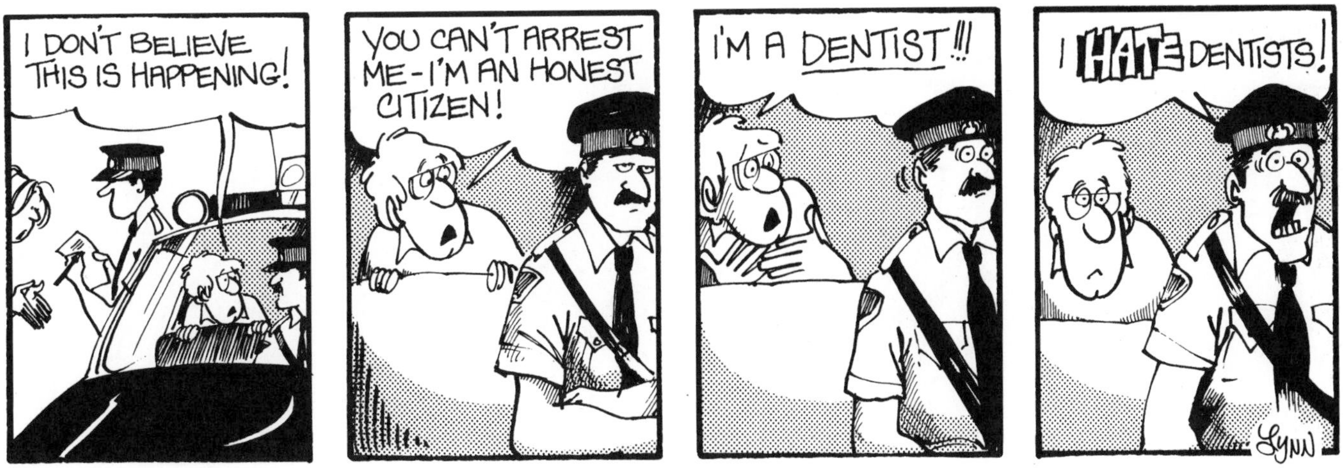
I DON'T BELIEVE THIS IS HAPPENING!
YOU CAN'T ARREST ME - I'M AN HONEST CITIZEN!
I'M A DENTIST!!!
I HATE DENTISTS!
LYNN

This idea came from a situation in which a friend's house was broken into, and she was upset that the police had seen her unwashed dishes and her unmade bed. I remember thinking: Like wearing good underwear in case of an emergency, you should keep your house tidy in case it's robbed!

I'VE NEVER BEEN SO EMBARRASSED IN MY LIFE!

THE ENTIRE NEIGHBORHOOD WATCHED ME GET ARRESTED, FOR HEAVEN'S SAKE!

OH WELL... I GUESS SOME DAY WE'LL LOOK BACK AND LAUGH AT...

I SAID **SOME DAY**!

Lynn

DADDY'S IN A BAD MOOD - SO I WANT YOU BOTH TO GET INTO YOUR P.J.s AND INTO BED. NOW!

AWW!

LET'S GO, LIZZIE!

BUT I DON'T WANNA GO TO BED!

THE TROUBLE WITH YOU IS YOU DON'T LISTEN. SHE SAID GET INTO BED....

SHE NEVER SAID WE HAD TO SLEEP!

Lynn

My philosophy was, "I don't care if you sleep or not, just go to bed and be quiet." A light on was okay, books and toys were okay. It seemed to me that an hour was all it took for the offspring to weary and crash!

NEED A HUG, DADDY?

Lynn

87

My mother had a day of the week for laundry. Rain or shine, she washed on Wednesday, and there was an order to the way she hung the clothes on the line. Sheets, towels, and good clothing was hung first — so it could be seen and appreciated by the neighbours. Underwear and things not meant for public scrutiny were hung closer to the house. These things were easily reached by standing on the rungs of our porch railing, and often fell prey to my brother — whose pranks with Mom's unmentionables were legendary.

After our neighbour's big dog, Teddy, died, their daughter, Tootie (our babysitter), bought a small fuzzy pup, which she called "Noby" — short for "Nobody." Noby was a sweet, easygoing little pooch who put up with just about anything the local kids would do to her. One day, Alan decided to dress her up in Mom's underwear. Noby dutifully stood still while bra and panties were administered. Al expected a wild struggle for freedom, but Noby stood still. Frustrated by the lack of action, Al lifted Noby up and placed her inside a sheet, which had been doubled so it could hang on the lower line. Noby went crazy. She squirmed and howled, and we worried that she'd tear the sheet open. Tootie soon came to her rescue. She pulled Noby out of the sheet, cuffed my brother on the side of his head, threw the bra and panties on the lawn, and went home.

I picked up the underwear and put it back on the line. The sheet was left to dry. Later, when Mom pulled in the laundry, I watched as she folded it. When she got to the underwear, she frowned, wondered why it looked unwashed, but kept on folding. Then she reached for the sheet. There in the middle was a mess of dirt and dog hair. Mom looked at me and said, "Where's your brother?" Alan, of course, was gone. I was close at hand and received the brunt of her wrath. After a thorough tongue-lashing, I was sent to my room — Al had to wait. Nothing was said when he came home, and I was furious. I thought I had taken the blame for everything! Later that evening it was clear that justice prevailed. When Al pulled the blankets back on his bed, there was the dirty sheet. Grossed out and grumbling, he slept on it for a week!

FOR BETTER OR FOR WORSE
BY LYNN JOHNSTON
ENEMY DESTROYER STILL IN SIGHT-AND OUR WEAPONS ARE PARALYZED!
WE CAN'T STAY SUBMERGED ANY LONGER, CAPTAIN-WE'RE RUNNING OUT OF AIR!
GASP!
U-BOAT ON THE HORIZON, SIR... ENEMY AIRCRAFT ARE-
MICHAEL! ARE YOU STILL IN THAT BATH?!!
GET OUT RIGHT NOW... IT'S PAST YOUR BEDTIME!
LOOK AT YOU- YOU'RE ONE BIG WRINKLE!
YOU WERE IN THERE NEARLY 2 HOURS! HOW CAN YOU STAY IN THE BATH FOR SO LONG?
TWO HOURS IS NOTHING!
I WAS IN A TUB FOR NINE MONTHS ONCE!
LYNN

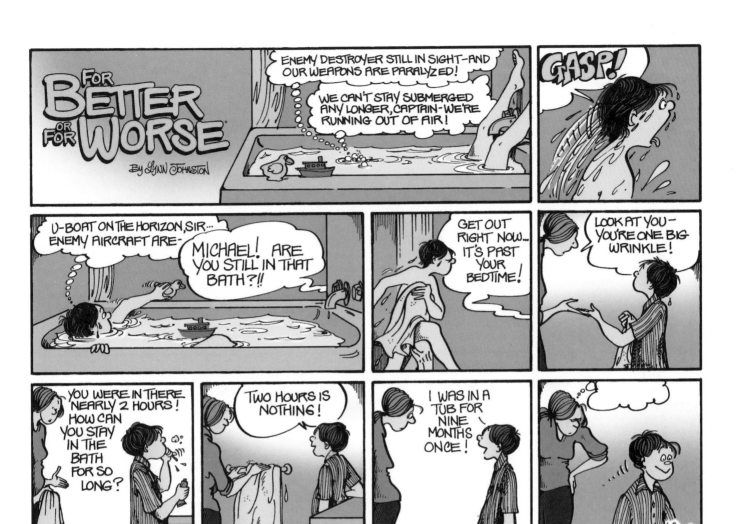

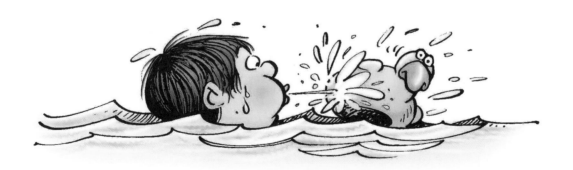

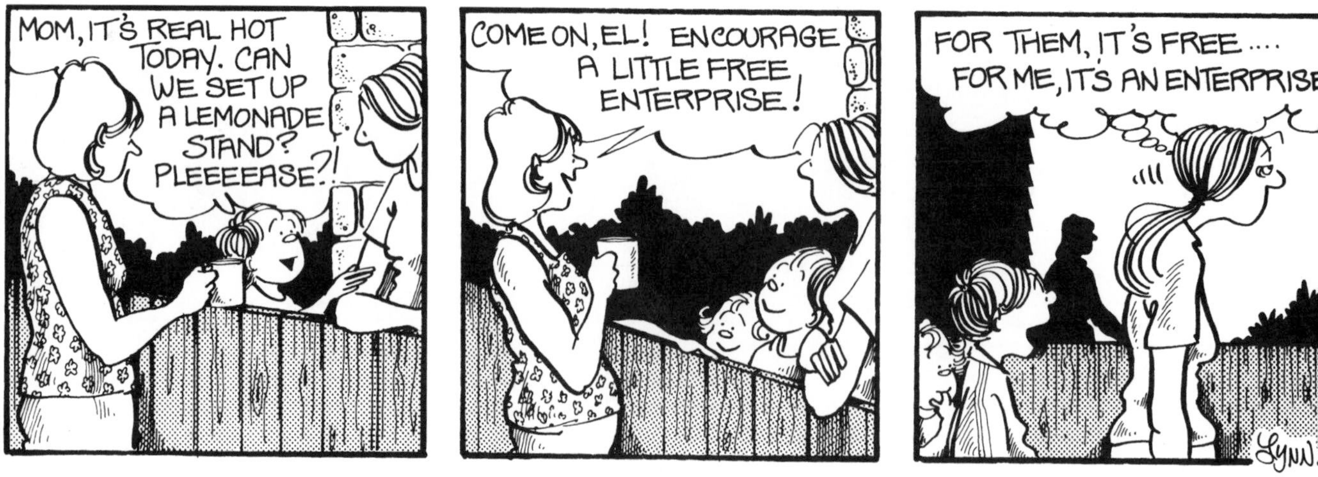
MOM, IT'S REAL HOT TODAY. CAN WE SET UP A LEMONADE STAND? PLEEEEASE?!
COME ON, EL! ENCOURAGE A LITTLE FREE ENTERPRISE!
FOR THEM, IT'S FREE.... FOR ME, IT'S AN ENTERPRISE.
LYNN

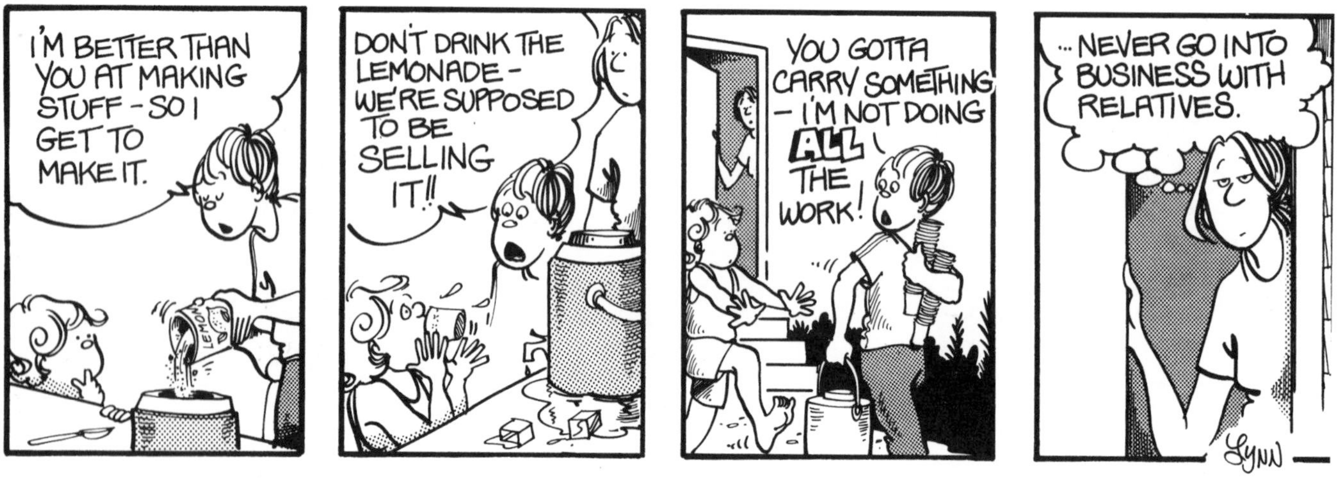
I'M BETTER THAN YOU AT MAKING STUFF - SO I GET TO MAKE IT.
DON'T DRINK THE LEMONADE - WE'RE SUPPOSED TO BE SELLING IT!!
YOU GOTTA CARRY SOMETHING - I'M NOT DOING ALL THE WORK!
...NEVER GO INTO BUSINESS WITH RELATIVES.
LYNN

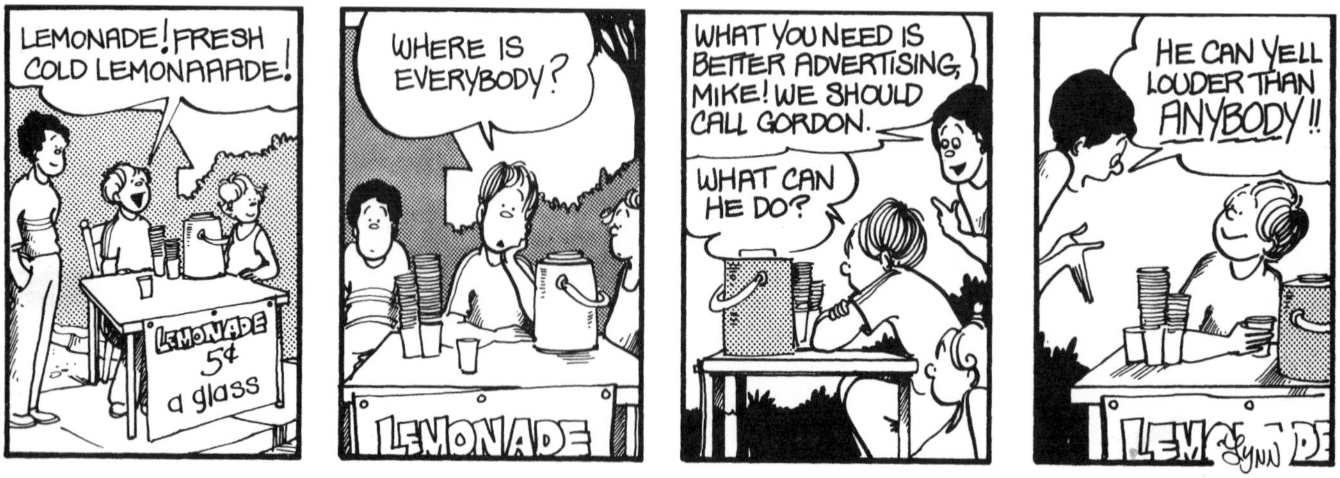
LEMONADE! FRESH COLD LEMONAAADE!
LEMONADE 5¢ a glass
WHERE IS EVERYBODY?
LEMONADE
WHAT YOU NEED IS BETTER ADVERTISING, MIKE! WE SHOULD CALL GORDON.
WHAT CAN HE DO?
HE CAN YELL LOUDER THAN ANYBODY!!
LYNN

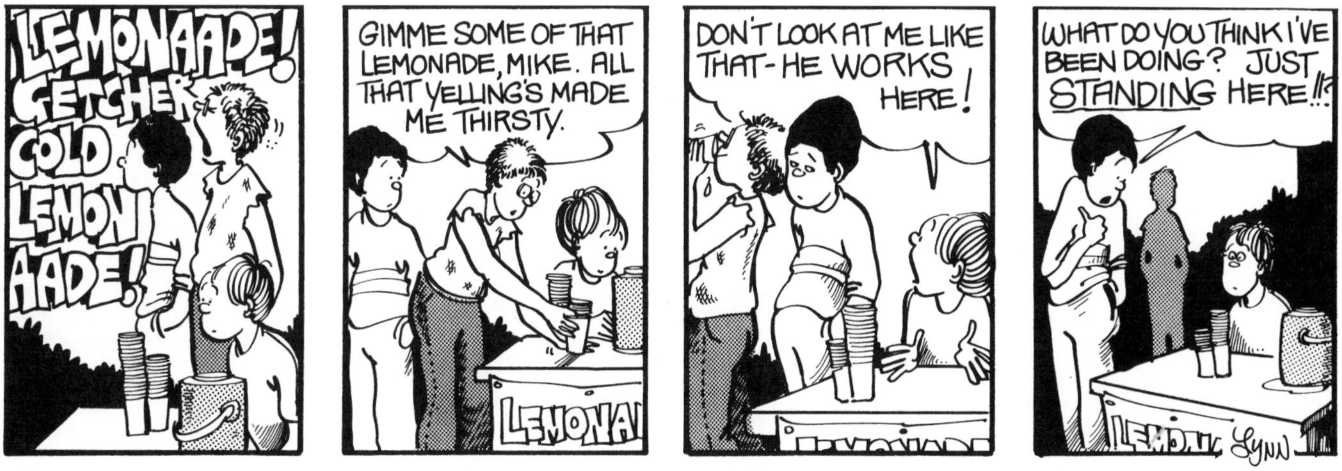
LEMONAADE! GETCHER COLD LEMON AADE!
GIMME SOME OF THAT LEMONADE, MIKE. ALL THAT YELLING'S MADE ME THIRSTY.
DON'T LOOK AT ME LIKE THAT- HE WORKS HERE!
WHAT DO YOU THINK I'VE BEEN DOING? JUST STANDING HERE!!?
Lynn

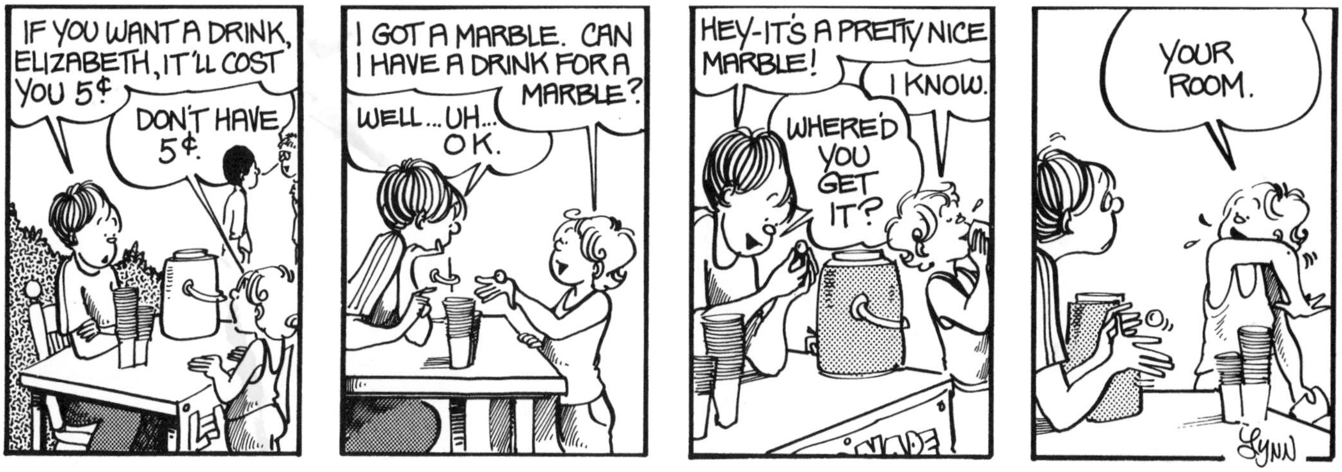
IF YOU WANT A DRINK, ELIZABETH, IT'LL COST YOU 5¢
DON'T HAVE 5¢.
I GOT A MARBLE. CAN I HAVE A DRINK FOR A MARBLE?
WELL...UH... OK.
HEY-IT'S A PRETTY NICE MARBLE!
I KNOW.
WHERE'D YOU GET IT?
YOUR ROOM.
Lynn

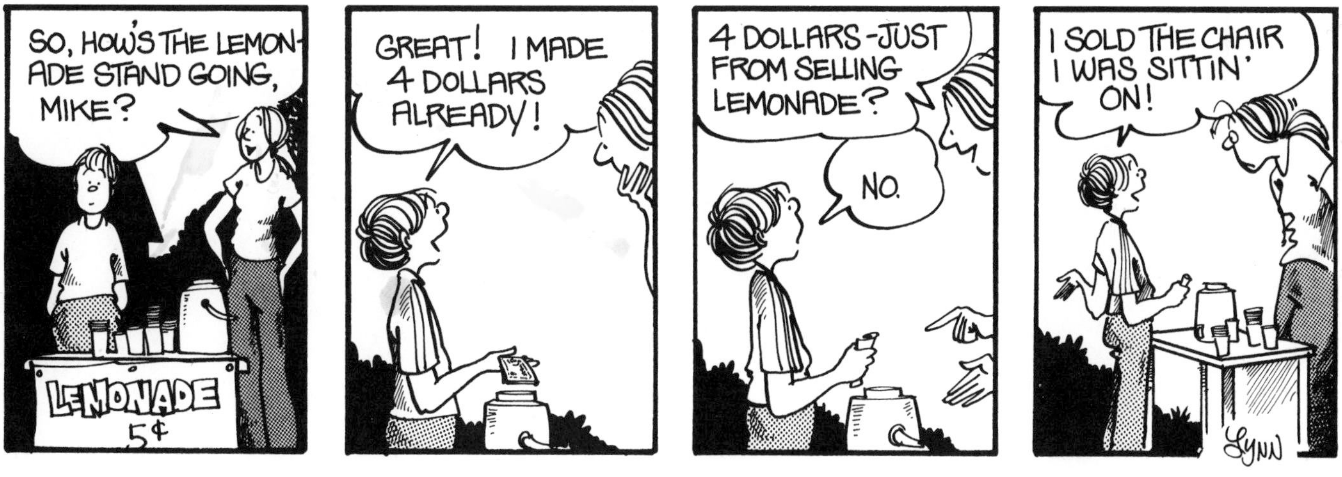
SO, HOW'S THE LEMONADE STAND GOING, MIKE?
LEMONADE 5¢
GREAT! I MADE 4 DOLLARS ALREADY!
4 DOLLARS -JUST FROM SELLING LEMONADE?
NO.
I SOLD THE CHAIR I WAS SITTIN' ON!
Lynn

I was on the periphery of hippiedom during the '60s. Never too far out or too far in, just one of the middle masses who liked the concept of "make love, not war" — but I also wanted to make a living. I had the long hair, the tattered sweaters, the jeans, and the vocabulary, and with this, I fit in. I often hung out with people who did drugs. I talked like they did so they'd think I'd "et" (the in-word for having taken drugs), and accept me as just another "head." I liked being an outcast without the risks! Art school connected me with some very smart, creative, and outrageous people — most of whom remained under cover; people didn't identify themselves the way they do now. The youth of today are more openly different. They advertise their eccentricities. They know how to be cool!

If I were 16 right now, I would dye my hair blue, wear mostly black, have a small tat, and turn my tunes up loud! I'd have a few piercings. I'd do subversive cartoons and improv comedy while secretly planning a career in music and medicine. I'd hang out with the Goths, go to churches, mosques, and synagogues looking for truth and enlightenment. And I'd be a vegan — just 'cause it would bug my mother. I'd backpack in Europe, play my guitar on street corners, write poetry, and ponder the meaning of life. I'd be into the Internet: animating, chatting, and exploring it all. If I were 16 right now, I'd be hanging out with the girls in this cartoon — I like to think they are simply a much younger me.

I think I've told you that Ruth, my mother-in-law, was a weaver. She must have had three looms going at once and extras for friends who wanted to learn. Thrifty and thoughtful, she kept every scrap of fabric and every piece of yarn. The cut ends from her warps and weavings, called thrums (there's a name for everything!), were kept for stuffing and felting and for birds' nests — which I thought was neat. In early spring, Ruth would go for long walks in the woods and leave handfuls of thrums along the way for the birds to find. An avid birder, she would then retrace her steps and watch for nests, which had been made with her threads. Determined to see me do the same, she gave me a basket of thrums to distribute. We were well into nesting season, and when I still hadn't thrown the thrums, she began to grumble. Annoyed and lazy, I tossed the threads onto our lawn and forgot about them until the lawn needed mowing. I started the mower and was happily going along when suddenly the thing seized with a loud, metallic THWANGGGGG. Smoke came out from under the cowling with a burning rubber smell. I unplugged the mower and turned it over. Strangling the blade was a broad band of colourful, smouldering thrums.

WHAT'S MOM DOING?

SHE'S TRYING TO WRITE AN ARTICLE FOR THE PAPER.

DON'T TALK TO HER.

YOU'LL RUIN HER TRAIN OF BLANK.

HERE, MOM — WE MADE YOU AN INSTANT COFFEE!

GAKKK!

DO YOU LIKE IT?

DID WE MAKE IT OK?

WAS TWO TABLESPOONS FULL ENOUGH?

IT'S FINALLY FINISHED! WANT TO READ MY ARTICLE, JOHN?

"...RIDING HIGH ON THE WINGS OF THEIR IMAGINATIONS, CHILDREN MORE AND MORE ARE TURNING TO BOOKS FOR THEIR ENTERTAINMENT."

THAT'S NICE, EL.

THANKS. WHERE ARE THE KIDS?

WATCHING TV.

94

HOW CAN YOU TWO SIT INSIDE AND WATCH TV ON A DAY LIKE THIS?!!

FIND SOMETHING ELSE TO DO—AND DO IT OUTSIDE!

HERE IT IS, NEW BARFO DOG FOOD—WITH A TASTE DOGS CAN'T RESIST!

YES, SIR! THE RICH FLAVOR OF LEFTOVERS! JUST LOOK AT OL' FIDO DIG IN!

HEY! WHAT ARE YOU GUYS DOING?!!

CHANGING CHANNELS!

WE DON'T WANNA BE THE AUDIENCE ANY MORE, MIKE—WE WANNA BE ON TV FOR A CHANGE.

BUT, YOU WERE ON ALREADY!

NOT FOR VERY LONG!

WELL, IT WAS MY IDEA TO MAKE A TV, SO I'M THE STAR AN' YOU HAFTA DO EVERYTHING I SAY.

...IT'S LONELY AT THE TOP....

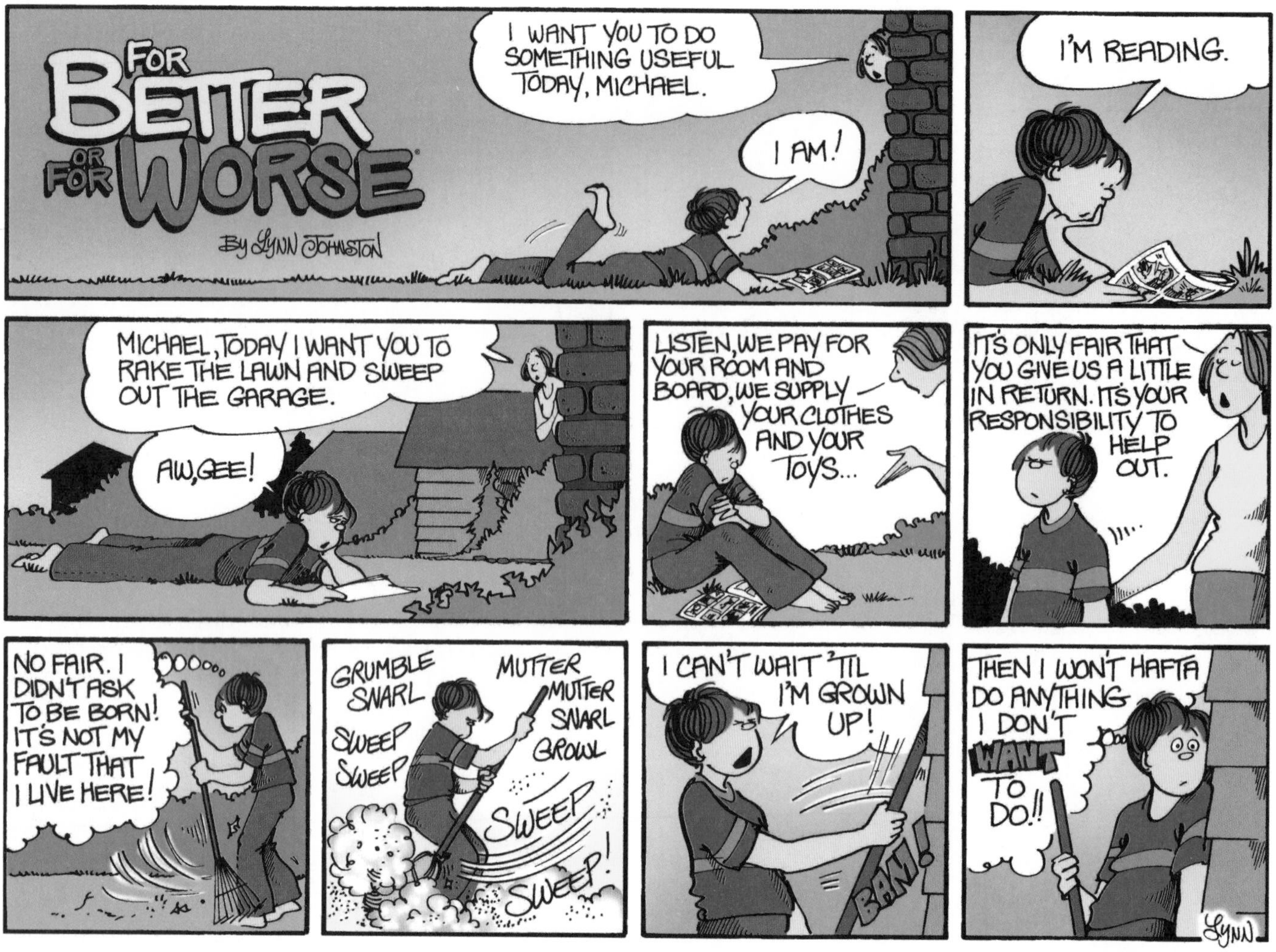
FOR BETTER OR FOR WORSE
BY LYNN JOHNSTON
I WANT YOU TO DO SOMETHING USEFUL TODAY, MICHAEL.
I AM!
I'M READING.
MICHAEL, TODAY I WANT YOU TO RAKE THE LAWN AND SWEEP OUT THE GARAGE.
AW, GEE!
LISTEN, WE PAY FOR YOUR ROOM AND BOARD, WE SUPPLY YOUR CLOTHES AND YOUR TOYS...
IT'S ONLY FAIR THAT YOU GIVE US A LITTLE IN RETURN. IT'S YOUR RESPONSIBILITY TO HELP OUT.
NO FAIR. I DIDN'T ASK TO BE BORN! IT'S NOT MY FAULT THAT I LIVE HERE!
GRUMBLE SNARL
MUTTER MUTTER SNARL GROWL
SWEEP SWEEP
SWEEP
SWEEP!
I CAN'T WAIT 'TIL I'M GROWN UP!
BAM!
THEN I WON'T HAFTA DO ANYTHING I DON'T WANT TO DO!!
LYNN

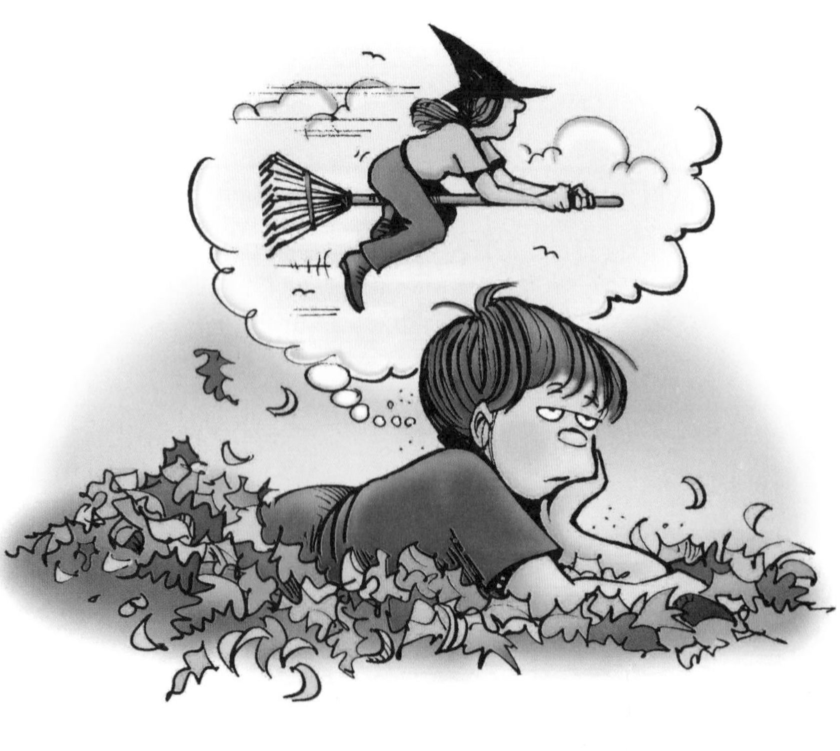

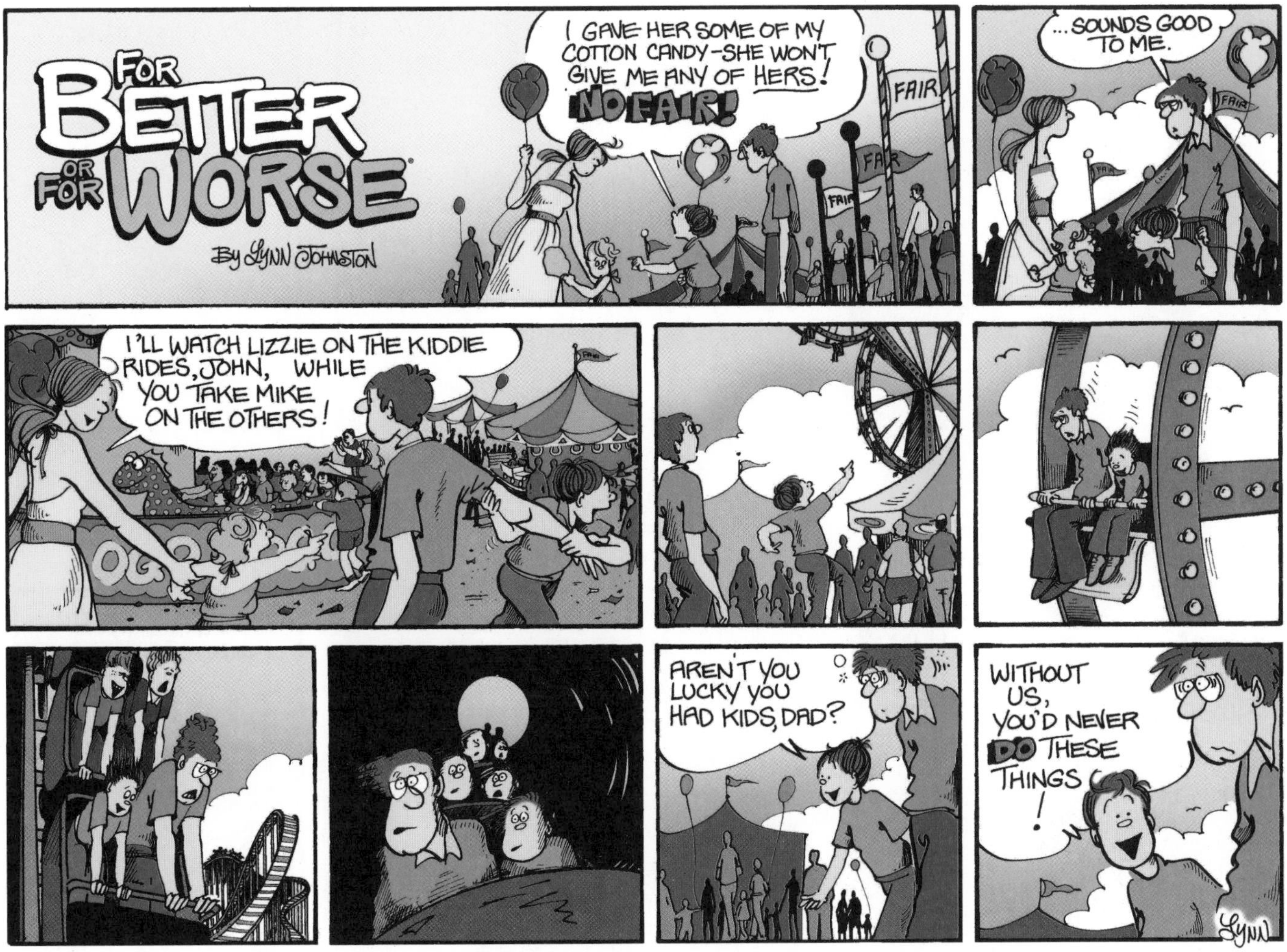
FOR BETTER OR FOR WORSE
BY LYNN JOHNSTON
I GAVE HER SOME OF MY COTTON CANDY-SHE WON'T GIVE ME ANY OF HERS! NO FAIR!
FAIR
...SOUNDS GOOD TO ME.
I'LL WATCH LIZZIE ON THE KIDDIE RIDES, JOHN, WHILE YOU TAKE MIKE ON THE OTHERS!
AREN'T YOU LUCKY YOU HAD KIDS, DAD?
WITHOUT US, YOU'D NEVER DO THESE THINGS!
LYNN

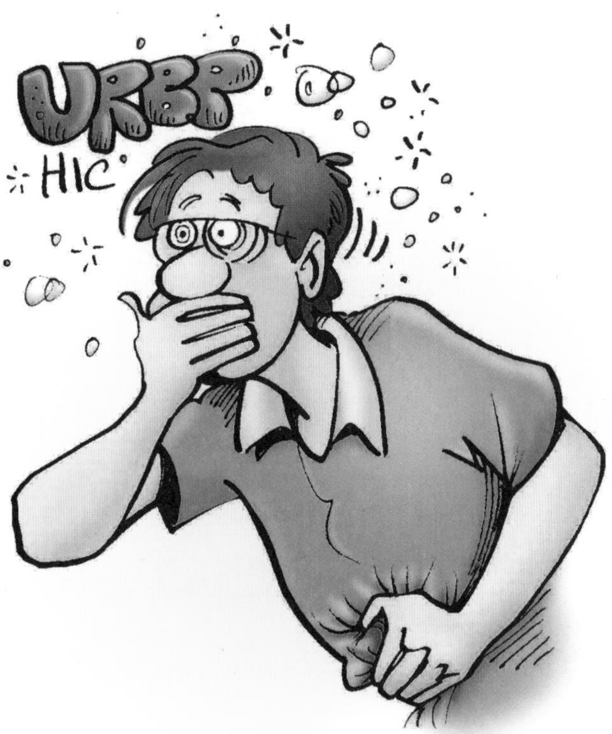
URBP
HIC

In the Canadian north, you learn to live with flies. Legends, stories, and songs have been written about them, and no amount of spray will protect you when the season is nigh. I used to complain about the mosquitoes on the west coast, but the black flies, deer flies, and mosquitoes in northern Ontario make wimps out of them. On the GOOD side, the country here is beautiful!

Our new location came with great big trees. This posed a new set of conditions, which included rooftop sweeping, eves trough cleaning, climbing threats, and lost projectiles. As soon as we set up our badminton net, the shuttlecocks went up and didn't come down again. We either hoped for a wind or bought new ones and eventually turned to volleyball.

Doug and Ina Harrison lived on Trout Lake — about a mile down the road from us, close to my in-laws. Ruth and Ina were great friends. The Harrisons' dock was a favourite place for these ladies to sit and have tea, and our kids were welcome, too. Katie and Aaron spent hours on the Harrisons' dock, swimming and fishing, and enjoying the company of Doug and Ina, who became "adopted grandparents." This strip was to thank them for their kind generosity. I gave them the original.

Aaron and his buddy in front of our old cabin showing off
the fish they caught on Berge Lake (Ruth admiring the catch
through the window).

I'd occasionally buy the *National Enquirer* if I recognized the celebrity on the cover — and cared! I did, however, buy the *News of the World* regularly. Who could resist headlines like the ones I had fun with in this strip?! The stories were so wonderfully preposterous, I secretly wished I was one of their writers. A few years before this fine rag went belly up, I read a headline that was very similar to "Octogenarian gives birth to triplets" (panel three), and I hoped it had come from this strip!

WHAT'RE YOU DOING, ELIZABETH?

DADDY SAID IF I DUG LONG ENOUGH, I COULD DIG DOWN TO CHINA!

CHINA! BUT THAT'S RIGHT THROUGH THE CENTER OF THE EARTH!!

I GOT ALL DAY.

MICHAEL! PHIL'S HERE FOR YOUR TRUMPET LESSON!

HAVE YOU SEEN YOUR BROTHER, ELIZABETH?

UH-HUH.

WELL... WHERE IS HE?

HE TOLD ME NOT TO SAY.

HOW 'BOUT IF I POINT!

LAST LESSON OF THE SEASON, MIKE! LET'S GET GOING...

NOW, DID YOU PRACTICE THE DUET?

NOPE.

YOUR SCALES?

NO.

HOW ABOUT YOUR TONGUE EXERCISES?

AND I GAVE UP A CAREER AS AN ELECTRICIAN FOR THIS?!!

PFFTT

102

THIS BARBECUE IS A WONDERFUL IDEA, ELLY!

I BROUGHT A BIG PLATE FULL OF RAW VEGGIES!

DID YOU BRING A DIP?

I DUNNO... GEORGIA POINTED AT ME, AND THEY BOTH STARTED LAUGHING.

Johnny Hart (*Wizard of Id* and *BC*) was a wonderful cartoonist and a great friend. One of my favourite cartoons shows BC hitchhiking. Rock after rock rolls by, but the riders won't pick him up. Then the "camera" pulls back to show a sign slightly ahead of where BC is standing. It says, "CAUTION. DIP IN THE ROAD."

WHO EXACTLY IS COMING TO THIS BARBECUE, EL?

OH, A FEW FRIENDS AND NEIGHBORS— THAT'S ALL.

ANY SPECIAL OCCASION?

WE'RE PAYING BACK EVERYONE WHO'S INVITED US TO DINNER OVER THE LAST 6 MONTHS!

YOU DID A SUPERB JOB ON THE STEAKS, PHIL.

THANKS, CONNIE.

IT'S A NICE PARTY, EL. ...UM... WHO IS THE REDHEAD TALKING TO PHIL?

OH, JUST AN OLD CHUM—A MUTUAL FRIEND OF OURS.

YEAH. I BET HE'S STILL CRAZY ABOUT HER!!

103

JOHN, I DIDN'T KNOW THAT CONNIE WOULD BE HERE WITHOUT TED!

HOW WAS I TO KNOW THEY'D JUST BROKEN UP AGAIN?

ANYWAY... PHIL AND GEORGIA ARE TOO WELL ESTABLISHED TO LET ANYONE COME BETWEEN THEM.

Here's another example of "what if?"

REMEMBER THAT TIME IN MONTREAL? IT WAS INCREDIBLE! WE—

OH, UH-CONNIE, I'D LIKE YOU TO MEET GEORGIA.... GEORGIA, THIS IS, UH, CONNIE!

NICE TO MEET YOU —I'VE HEARD SO LITTLE ABOUT YOU!

WHAT'S WITH PHIL?

HE INTRODUCED CONNIE TO GEORGIA.

SO THE OLD GIRLFRIEND AND THE NEW ONE ARE FACING OFF, ARE THEY?

WHAT'S HAPPENING, PHIL? ARE THEY FIGHTING OVER YOU?!

IT'S WORSE THAN THAT —THEY'RE COMPARING NOTES!

THE SECRET TO STAYIN' UP LATE AT A GROWN-UP PARTY IS NOT TO LET 'EM KNOW YOU'RE AROUND!

YOU GOT A BOTTLE OF CHERRIES—I'M TELLING! MAAAAAH!

WHAT'S THAT? ARE THE KIDS STILL UP?

THE SECRET TO STAYIN' UP AT A GROWN-UP PARTY IS TO GAG YOUR KID SISTER!

NOW, YOU ASK LAWRENCE IF HE WANTS TO SLEEP ON THE BED OR ON THE AIR MATTRESS.

I WANT THE BED! IT'S MY BED!

I KNOW, BUT HE'S A GUEST, AND WE'RE BEING POLITE.

I DON'T WANNA BE POLITE—I WANNA BE COMFORTABLE!

...I'LL BE POLITE.

IS THE PARTY OVER YET?

NOPE, THERE'S SOME PEOPLE LEFT.

MY MOM'S STILL TALKING TO YOUR UNCLE PHIL'S GIRLFRIEND.

YES, PHIL AND I HAD A CASUAL FLING. I'M SURE HE HARDLY REMEMBERS.

MY OLD FLA-A-AME...

EXCUSE ME, CONNIE, COULD I TALK WITH YOU? SURE.

LOOK, I'M SORRY ABOUT YOU AND TED...

YEAH - WE HAVE AN ON-AND-OFF RELATIONSHIP.

EVERY TIME I GET ON THE SUBJECT OF MARRIAGE... HE TAKES OFF!

Lynn

I KNOW WHAT YOU'RE GOING TO SAY, ELLY - AND I HAVE NO INTENTION OF MESSING UP THINGS BETWEEN PHIL AND GEORGIA

HEAVEN KNOWS, I'VE GOT ENOUGH ON MY PLATE!

...WANT A PICKLE?

Lynn

TED SAYS HE FEELS CONFINED, EL. HE WANTS TO DATE SOMEONE ELSE FOR A CHANGE.

I DON'T THINK I COULD STAND IT IF I SAW HIM OUT WITH ANOTHER WOMAN!

THAT'S GOING TO HAPPEN, CONNIE. WHAT DOES HE EXPECT YOU TO DO ...MOVE?

I PUT MY HOUSE UP FOR SALE THIS MORNING.

Lynn

YOU'RE MOVING?!! I'VE BEEN OFFERED A JOB IN THUNDER BAY.

IT'S A GOOD ONE, EL, I'LL BE A LAB SUPERVISOR!

AFTER ALL THESE YEARS, IT'S A STEP IN THE RIGHT DIRECTION!

A STEP?! THUNDER BAY IS 1,200 MILES AWAY!!

I chose Thunder Bay as Connie's new destination because it's a nice place to live and a long way from southern Ontario, where Elly lived. I had also received an honorary degree from Thunder Bay's Laurentian University a short while before writing this story, and the city was still strong in my mind. I became a doctor of letters. WOW! After receiving the award, I called my mother to tell her, and she replied, "A doctor of letters? That's ridiculous! You haven't written to me for MONTHS!"

THE SUN – Monday June 3, 1985

For better or worse, she's got a doctorate

Now there are two doctors in the house. Canadian cartoonist Lynn Johnston, whose strip For Better of For Worse appears in The Sun, was awarded an honorary doctorate of letters degree Saturday at convocation ceremonies at Lakehead University, in Thunder Bay. Johnston's husband is a dentist, as is the husband of her comic-strip heroine Elly.

JOHNSTON... *receives Lakehead doctorate*

107

SELLING YOUR HOUSE?!! BUT CONNIE, WE'VE BEEN NEIGHBORS FOR YEARS! WE'VE BEEN CLOSEST FRIENDS!

AND WHAT ABOUT YOUR FOLKS? WHAT ABOUT LAWRENCE? WHAT ABOUT HIS SCHOOL? HIS FRIENDS?...

WHAT ABOUT **ME**?!!!

This sentiment reflects the feeling I had when my women friends moved away from Lynn Lake. In this small town, good friends kept me sane. When my friend Nancy Lawn left for Edmonton, I told her I was happy for her, and I really was! I congratulated her husband on his promotion and transfer, and I earnestly wished them well. As they drove away, I waved and smiled until their car disappeared, and then I cried. I cried for all the good times we could have had. I cried for me.

YOU'RE RIGHT. MOVING IS GOING TO BE EARTH-SHATTERING FOR BOTH OF US FOR A WHILE.

BUT WE'LL HANDLE IT. LAWRENCE IS STRONG. HE'LL SURVIVE O.K.

HOW DOES HE FEEL ABOUT LEAVING?

I DON'T KNOW.

.... I HAVEN'T TOLD HIM YET.

YOU WEREN'T JEALOUS OF CONNIE, WERE YOU, GEO?

OF COURSE NOT.

I MEAN, IT DIDN'T BOTHER YOU THAT I SPENT SOME TIME WITH HER THIS EVENING, DID IT?

NOT AT ALL.

YOU WEREN'T WORRIED ABOUT ME GOING OUT WITH...

HONEY, I TRUST YOU!

LOOK, GEORGIA—IF IT BOTHERS YOU, LET'S **TALK** ABOUT IT!!

PHIL, I DON'T OWN YOU... IF YOU WANT TO TALK TO SOMEONE, THAT'S YOUR RIGHT!

BESIDES, CONNIE MEANT A LOT TO YOU— YOU *HAD* TO SPEND SOME TIME WITH HER.

YOU'RE SO UNDER-STANDING, GEORGIA. YOU'RE SO WONDERFULLY UNDERSTANDING!

THIS TIME.

O.K., ANIMALS, IF YOU'RE NOT DOWN FOR BREAK-FAST IN 10 MINUTES, YOU'LL HAVE TO WAIT 'TILL LUNCH!

YOU'RE AWFULLY SERIOUS, WHAT'S GOING ON?

MOM! LAWRENCE IS *MOVING*!

IT'S TRUE! I FOUND OUT 'CAUSE THE REAL-ESTATE AGENT LEFT A MESSAGE ON OUR ANSWERING MACHINE.

HE (SNIFF) WASN'T GONNA TELL ME!

SOMETIMES ONE'S ARMS JUST DON'T SEEM BIG ENOUGH.

WHAT IS IT, MIKE— SOMETHING WRONG?

THERE'S A "FOR SALE" SIGN ON LAWRENCE'S LAWN. WHY DO THEY HAFTA MOVE, DADDY? WHY?!!

NOTHING STAYS THE SAME IN LIFE, MIKE. WE HAVE TO ACCEPT CHANGES.

I CAN ACCEPT CHANGES.

LAWRENCE COULD MOVE IN WITH US!!

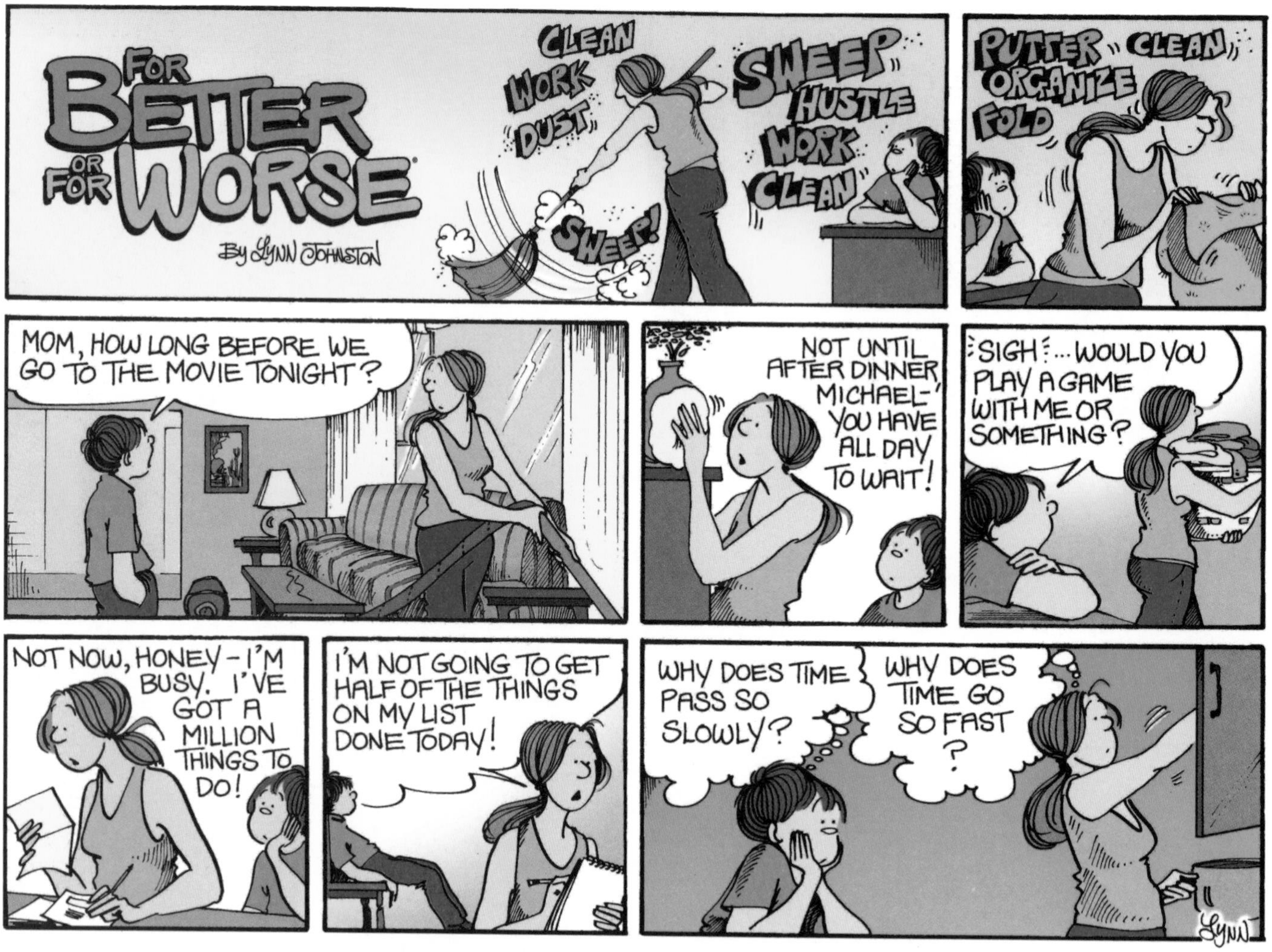
FOR BETTER OR FOR WORSE
BY LYNN JOHNSTON
CLEAN
WORK
DUST
SWEEP!
SWEEP
HUSTLE
WORK
CLEAN
PUTTER
CLEAN
ORGANIZE
FOLD
MOM, HOW LONG BEFORE WE GO TO THE MOVIE TONIGHT?
NOT UNTIL AFTER DINNER, MICHAEL - YOU HAVE ALL DAY TO WAIT!
SIGH... WOULD YOU PLAY A GAME WITH ME OR SOMETHING?
NOT NOW, HONEY - I'M BUSY. I'VE GOT A MILLION THINGS TO DO!
I'M NOT GOING TO GET HALF OF THE THINGS ON MY LIST DONE TODAY!
WHY DOES TIME PASS SO SLOWLY?
WHY DOES TIME GO SO FAST?
LYNN

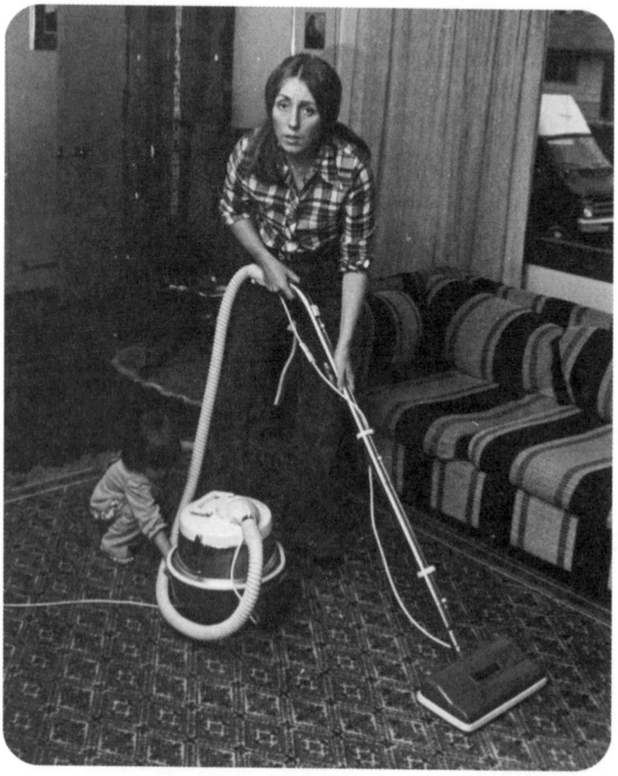

I did this Sunday page after I was squeezed in half by a sadistically designed lawn chair. I brought the chair into my studio and drew the exact position it was in when it maimed me. I felt relieved and vindicated even before the art was published. This job came with unlimited and curative benefits. I was jubilant when I took the chair to the dump.

DON'T BRING ANY DIRT IN HERE! PICK UP THOSE SHOES!

PUT AWAY THOSE COMICS, DON'T SIT THERE — GO OUTSIDE!

THE REAL ESTATE LADY WILL BE HERE WITH PEOPLE ANY MINUTE, AND I WANT THIS HOUSE TO BE PERFECT!

WE HAVEN'T MOVED OUT YET... AND ALREADY IT'S NOT MY HOUSE.

Lynn

WHO'S THAT? SOME PEOPLE TO LOOK AT THE HOUSE.

THERE IS A FULL BATHROOM AND TWO BEDROOMS UPSTAIRS.

THE KITCHEN IS SPACIOUS, WITH LARGE CUPBOARDS THAT ARE....

ISN'T THAT WHERE YOU FOUND THE MICE LAST SUMMER?!

Lynn

HERE'S A PICTURE OF THE TOWNHOUSE WE'RE GONNA HAVE IN THUNDER BAY, MIKE!

IT'S GOT A GYM, AN' A POOL AN' A PLAYGROUND AN' EVERYTHING!

YEAH?

DO YOU WANNA MOVE, LAWRENCE?

SURE! MOM SAYS IT'S GONNA BE NEAT!

MAYBE MOVING IS HARDEST FOR THE ONES WHO STAY BEHIND.

Lynn

YOU DID? CONNIE, THAT'S WONDERFUL!

SOLD IT, HUH. BOY, IT'S GONNA BE HARD TO IMAGINE SOMEONE ELSE IN YOUR HOUSE, LAWRENCE.

YEAH. I WONDER WHO'S GONNA GET MY BEDROOM.

...I HAD A LOT OF GOOD DREAMS IN HERE.

It was never my intention to have Connie and Lawrence move away. It just happened! Once Connie's relationship with Ted soured and Uncle Phil met Georgia, Connie's personal life was on hold. An opportunity for her to take a good job in another town seemed like a positive step, so the story took this turn. What the move did was give me another challenge to deal with and a new family to welcome. This helped to keep the story interesting.

SNOWSHOES, BOOKS, PUNCH BOWL, CAMPING TOASTER, HIBACHI ....
HIBACHI?!

CONNIE'S PACKING TO MOVE, AND SHE GAVE SOME THINGS TO ME.

BUT WHAT ARE WE GONNA DO WITH ALL THIS STUFF?!!
I DON'T KNOW.

GIVE IT TO SOMEONE ELSE WHEN WE MOVE!

I PACKED THOSE PICTURES IN WITH YOUR RECORDS, CONNIE.
THANKS!

BOY, THE PLACE IS STARTING TO LOOK BARE. NO PICTURES, NO ORNAMENTS...

IT USED TO BE OUR HOUSE.

NOW...IT'S JUST A HOUSE.

When we moved to the North Bay area, people confused it with Thunder Bay. These two Ontario towns are a long distance apart, and I wanted to make the distinction. I was hoping that readers would go to a map and see where Thunder Bay is — and they did! The next time you see a beautiful piece of amethyst, such as crystals in a large geode, it might have come from this area. Thunder Bay, among other things, is famous for its amethyst.

I wanted to explore the sense of loss we all share when a good friend moves away. I think this must be harder for children to deal with. In our case, we were the ones who left, and Aaron's friends were sad to see him go. It wasn't until we had settled in our new house and the excitement of moving was over that he began to feel the loss as well.

114

MY NEXT PATIENT CANCELED — LET'S GO FOR COFFEE!

WELL, JEAN, HOW DOES IT FEEL TO BE A BRAND-NEW MOM?!

FINE.

BUT THERE ARE SIDES TO THIS BUSINESS I NEVER EXPECTED.

SUCH AS?

HOW CAN SOMETHING THAT SLEEPS SO MUCH TAKE SO MUCH **TIME!**?

I NEVER REALIZED HOW A BABY COULD CHANGE YOUR LIFE, JOHN....

MY ENTIRE DAY REVOLVES AROUND HER SCHEDULE.

AND AT NIGHT I GET UP WITH HER EVERY 3 HOURS, WHILE MY HUSBAND JUST SNORES AWAY!

... ANOTHER EXCELLENT ARGUMENT FOR BREAST FEEDING.

JEAN CAME INTO THE CLINIC TODAY WITH HER NEW BABY.

SHE BROUGHT THE BABY? IS SHE CUTE? IS SHE LIKE HER MOM? WHAT DOES SHE LOOK LIKE?

SHE LOOKS LIKE .... A BABY! ALL BABIES LOOK ALIKE TO ME.

ASK ME TO DESCRIBE HER WHEN SHE'S SIXTEEN.

My folks used to take us to farms in the Fraser Delta for fresh strawberries. Both Alan and I were too young to enjoy picking, but we sure liked eating them. One day when our family was standing at the checkout with our baskets of strawberries, the man at the till looked at my brother with a curious smile. Alan was covered from his mouth to his navel in red juice. The man picked him up, put him on a big metal scale, and announced that he had to charge for the extra weight of the berries inside. He was kidding, but Dad paid him a little extra anyway.

Every summer we went as a family to get fresh fruit in season. In the Okanagan, we got peaches, plums, and apricots. It was a long drive but worth it. Mom canned everything, so we had the luxury of fruit preserves all winter long. Nothing tasted like the fresh stuff, though, and on one trip, Dad said we kids could eat whatever we wanted — so we did! As I said, it was a long drive home. With two kids full of fresh fruit, it's easy to imagine the results. We used the "roadside" washroom many times, with Mom hiding us behind her skirt as Dad looked madly around for paper!

HEY, WOW! LOOKIT THE NEAT BEACH!!

CAN WE TAKE OUR SHOES OFF? PLEASE, MOM?

WE DON'T HAVE YOUR BATHING SUITS WITH US, SO WE'RE JUST GOING TO WALK DOWN THE BEACH, UNDERSTAND?

AWW!

CAN WE JUST PADDLE UP TO OUR ANKLES, MOM?

LIZZIE—I SAID DON'T GO IN ABOVE YOUR KNEES!

I'LL ONLY GO IN UP TO MY THIGHS—HONEST!

MAAH! MICHAEL FELL IN!

HE'S IN THE WATER—WHY CAN'T I SWIM? MA? HUH? PLEASE?

I THOUGHT YOU WEREN'T GOING TO LET THEM GET WET!

WHAT'S THAT?

A POSTCARD FROM CONNIE.

(SIGH...) SHE WAS MY BEST FRIEND! I CAN'T BELIEVE SHE'S MOVED SO FAR AWAY.

I CAN.

HERE'S OUR PHONE BILL.

I DON'T THINK YOU UNDERSTAND HOW MUCH CONNIE MEANT TO ME, JOHN!

A WOMAN'S BEST FRIEND IS VERY IMPORTANT..... WE SHARED OUR MOST INTIMATE SECRETS!

....I TOLD HER EVERYTHING!

EVERYTHING?!!

MOM, THERE'S A BIG MOVING VAN IN FRONT OF LAWRENCE'S! WANNA SEE WHO'S MOVING IN?

OH... I DON'T KNOW, HONEY... COME WITH ME? PLEASE? MAYBE THEY'VE GOT A KID MY AGE!

THIS IS A CHANCE TO CHECK OUT THEIR FURNITURE WITHOUT GOING INSIDE!

THERE'S ALWAYS AN ANGLE.

THE MAN IN THE MOVING VAN SAID THE NEW PEOPLE WOULD BE ALL MOVED IN TODAY.

THAT'S NICE. I DIDN'T LIKE TO SEE CONNIE AND LAWRENCE'S HOUSE SIT EMPTY.

I DIDN'T MIND.

IT MADE ME HOPE THEY'D MOVE BACK.

LOOK OUT, KIDS—THIS IS PRETTY HEAVY!

LOOK, MOM—IT'S THE NEW KIDS, AN' THEY'RE—

SHH!

BUT MOM, THEY'RE—

MICHAEL, I SAID SHH!

BUT MOM! THEY'RE MY AGE!!

This strip received some nice mail. Folks expected to read a sarcastic punch line. Growing up in North Vancouver, we were always playing with and studying next to kids from China, Japan, and other Asian countries. In fact, it was hard to learn French as a second language when we were more familiar with Mandarin and Japanese. I wanted to draw an Asian family, and the Enjos stepped in.

HELLO, WE'RE CAROL AND KEITH ENJO. THIS IS BRIAN AND DAWN...

YOU MUST BE ELLY PATTERSON. YOUR FRIEND CONNIE TOLD ME SO MUCH ABOUT YOU!

I KNOW WHAT GOOD FRIENDS YOU WERE. IT'S GOING TO BE HARD FOR YOU—SEEING NEW PEOPLE IN HER HOUSE!

... MAYBE NOT AS HARD AS IT SEEMED!

The name "Enjo" was for my grade six home economics teacher. Miss Enjo was a sweet and lovely lady and must have been in her twenties at the time. My dad guessed that her last name had been longer and had been shortened when her family emigrated to Canada. The family I made up was based on the Masuda family, who had known my in-laws in Lynn Lake, Manitoba. They had also moved to North Bay, which was a nice coincidence: We had friends here to make us feel at home.

MOM, CAN DAWN AN' ME COME IN AN' PLAY?

I GUESS SO, ELIZABETH.

CRASH! CLATTER! SHUFFLE BAM! BAM! KLINK CLATTER!

SHE HASN'T SEEN ANY OF MY TOYS YET....

SO I'M SHOWIN' HER ALL OF THEM!

The Enjos provided both Elizabeth and Michael with friends to play with — I wanted the whole family to integrate with the Pattersons. This is always the hope when new folks move into the neighbourhood, and I could make it happen in the strip!

HELLOOOO.... I'VE BROUGHT YOU SOME COFFEE AND MUFFINS!

I THOUGHT YOU MIGHT LIKE A BREAK FROM UNPACKING.

YOU'RE WONDERFUL! HOW DID YOU KNOW WE WERE IN SUCH A MESS HERE?!

... WE MOVED ONCE.

YOU HAVE SOME VERY BEAUTIFUL THINGS, CAROL!

MY GRANDMOTHER BROUGHT THOSE OVER FROM JAPAN. THEY'RE HEIR-LOOMS.

DAWN...WHAT DOES "HEIRLOOM" MEAN?

IT MEANS IF YOU TOUCH ONE, SHE'LL KILL YA!

These ornate dolls were based on a collection in Louise Masuda's house. Children in Japan often receive these lovely figures as gifts. They form a large retinue of characters with different levels of importance, so after many years, you can have a sizeable number — arranged in order of their station. They are heirlooms not toys, and eventually a showcase is needed to display them in. I thought this was a wonderful idea and so I included them here.

IT'S NICE TO SEE OUR KIDS GETTING ALONG SO WELL TOGETHER, ELLY!

YES, MINE WERE BOTH LOOKING FORWARD TO HAVING SOMEONE NEW TO PLAY WITH!

MAAA! MICHAEL KEEPS BUGGING ME!

I THINK THE NOVELTY'S WORN OFF.

IS BRIAN JAPANESE, MOM?

HE'S JAPANESE-CANADIAN.

NOW, YOUR GRAND-PARENTS CAME FROM HOLLAND AND ENGLAND... SO, YOU'RE ANGLO-DUTCH-CANADIAN!

I AM?

WOW! AN' I THOUGHT I WAS JUST A REGULAR KID!!

After this strip ran, I had all kinds of letters from folks with similar backgrounds wondering where our family had originated and if there was any connection. I wished at the time we could have met some long-lost cousins, but sadly, that didn't happen.

HAVE THE ENJOS MOVED INTO CONNIE'S HOUSE OK?

I THINK SO.

IT'S FUNNY – I'VE BEEN IN THAT HOUSE SO MANY TIMES....

IT FELT STRANGE SITTING IN THAT FAMILIAR KITCHEN... DRINKING COFFEE WITH SOMEONE ELSE!!!

DON'T WORRY, EL. CONNIE WILL FORGIVE YOU.

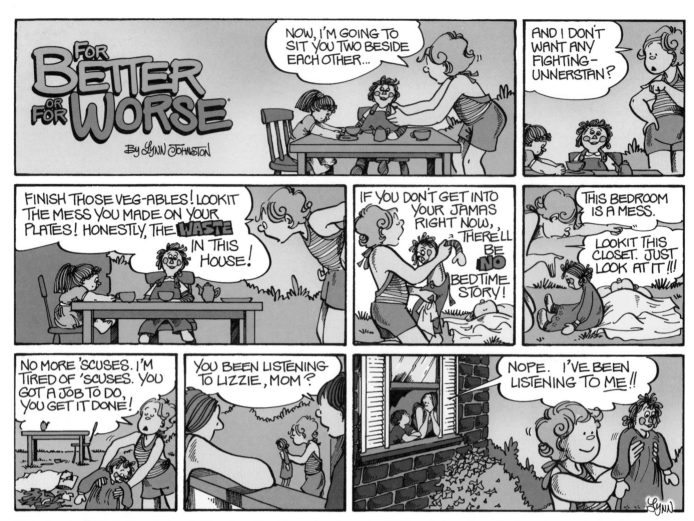

Listening to Katie talking to her dollies, I realized I was hearing myself. Her choice of words, her phrases, inflections, and body language, had all been learned from me. I'm sure I was parroting my mother when I directed my children, and now that I'm a grandmother, I'm waiting to hear if my granddaughter will talk the way HER mother does!

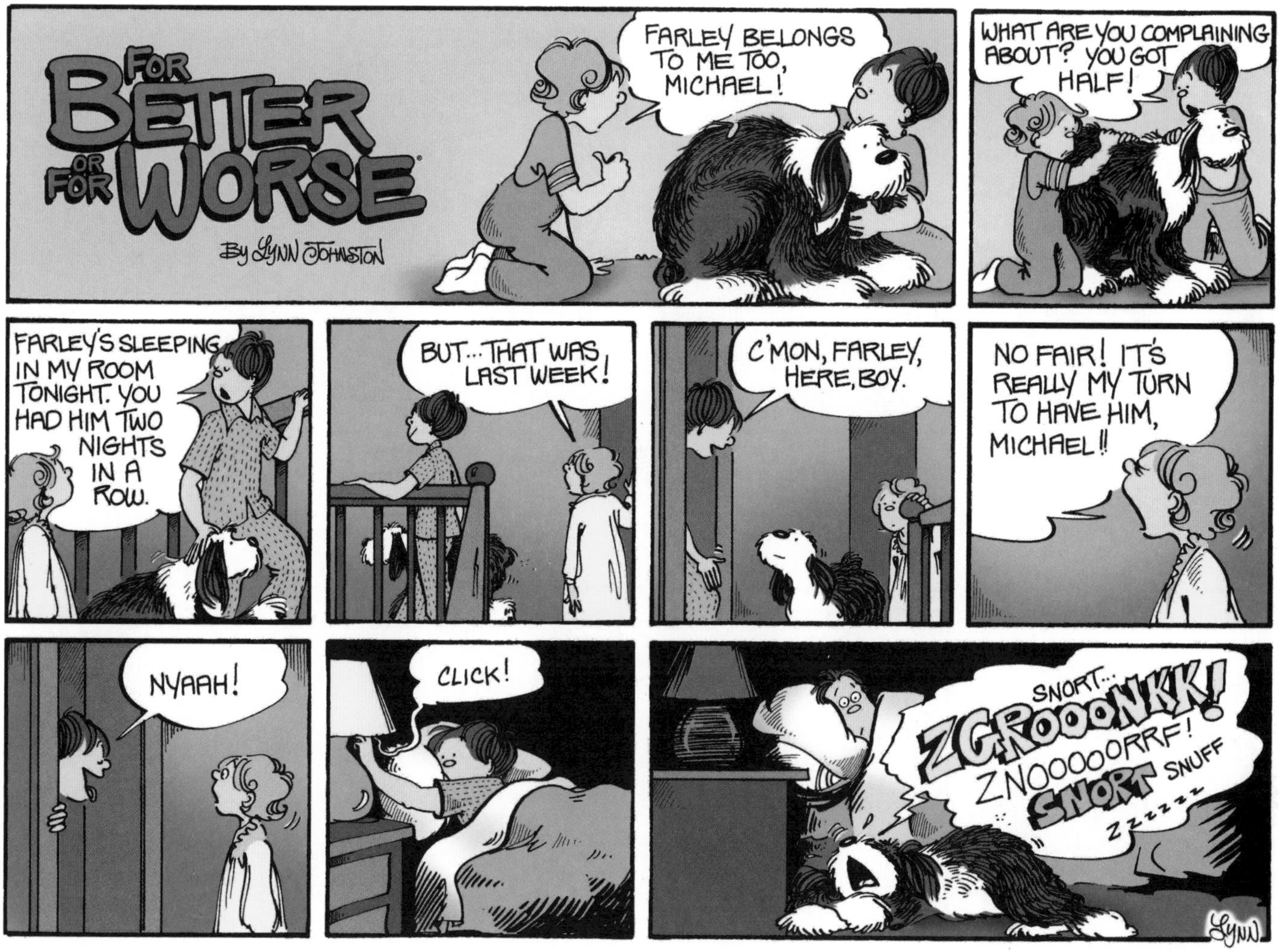
FOR BETTER OR FOR WORSE
BY LYNN JOHNSTON
FARLEY BELONGS TO ME TOO, MICHAEL!
WHAT ARE YOU COMPLAINING ABOUT? YOU GOT HALF!
FARLEY'S SLEEPING IN MY ROOM TONIGHT. YOU HAD HIM TWO NIGHTS IN A ROW.
BUT... THAT WAS LAST WEEK!
C'MON, FARLEY, HERE, BOY.
NO FAIR! IT'S REALLY MY TURN TO HAVE HIM, MICHAEL!!
NYAAH!
CLICK!
SNORT...
ZGROOOONKK!
ZNOOOOORRF!
SNORT SNUFF
ZZZZZZ
LYNN

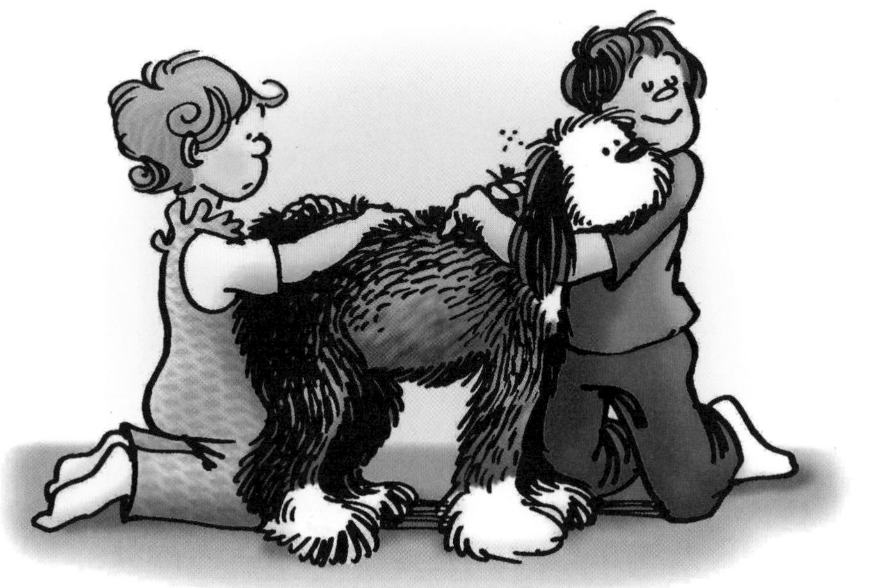

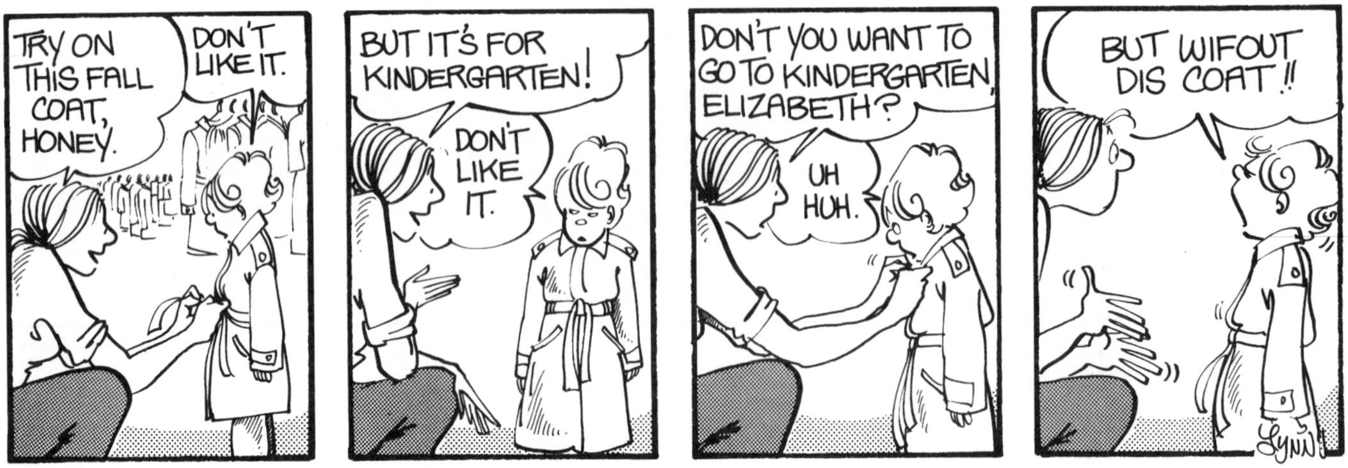
TRY ON THIS FALL COAT, HONEY.
DON'T LIKE IT.
BUT IT'S FOR KINDERGARTEN!
DON'T LIKE IT.
DON'T YOU WANT TO GO TO KINDERGARTEN, ELIZABETH?
UH HUH.
BUT WIFOUT DIS COAT!!
LYNN

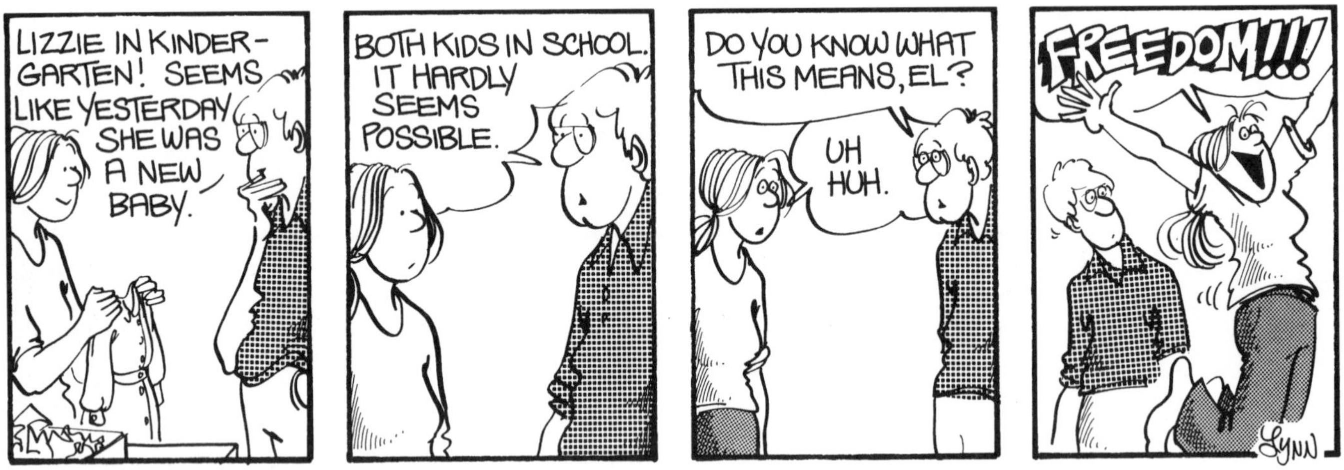
LIZZIE IN KINDER-GARTEN! SEEMS LIKE YESTERDAY SHE WAS A NEW BABY.
BOTH KIDS IN SCHOOL. IT HARDLY SEEMS POSSIBLE.
DO YOU KNOW WHAT THIS MEANS, EL?
UH HUH.
FREEDOM!!!
LYNN

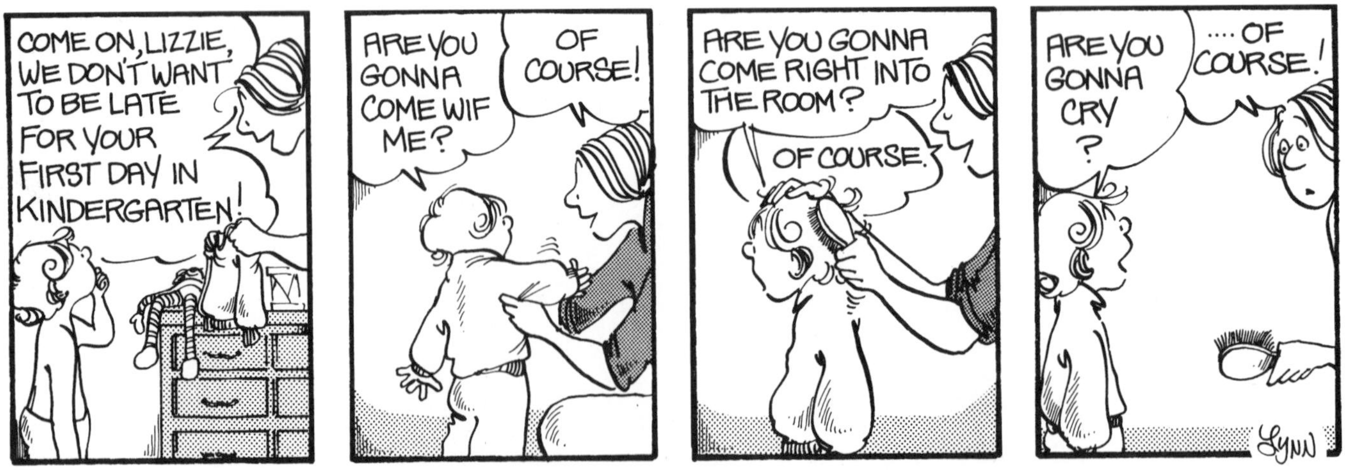
COME ON, LIZZIE, WE DON'T WANT TO BE LATE FOR YOUR FIRST DAY IN KINDERGARTEN!
ARE YOU GONNA COME WIF ME?
OF COURSE!
ARE YOU GONNA COME RIGHT INTO THE ROOM?
OF COURSE.
ARE YOU GONNA CRY?
....OF COURSE!
LYNN

Katie was starting grade two when we moved to North Bay. (The children in the strip were three years younger than Katie and Aaron.) The little school she attended was about a mile and a half down the road, next to a hobby farm. At lunchtime she and the other children could watch the animals through the fence: a donkey, chickens, and some rabbits. I said to her, "Katie isn't this a great place to have a school?!" and she replied, "But Mom, it stinks!"

Miss Lyon was indeed the name of Katie's Kindergarten teacher — she enjoyed being in the strip!

In Lynn Lake, we would walk the kids to school. After we moved, even though Kate's school was close by, the school bus would pick her up and drop her off at our mailbox every day. Aaron, too, caught the school bus, and because he went to a different school, he had to transfer to another bus in town. For both of them, it was another new experience in a new and very different place.

I never looked forward to phys ed, and as soon as I could, I dropped it in favour of … well, anything else! This series was done for the teachers who loved to watch us tail-draggers squirm! In their defence, they kept us in the best shape we'd ever been in.

In junior high, our teacher used to cut things so short we had no time to change before our next class. Her rule was, we HAD to shower. She'd watch us as we scrambled, slipped, and slid through the water and into our clothes — barking at those of us who tried to get away with not taking off our underwear. Some of us wondered if she was "unusual" or just plain mean!

I did get complaints about this one. People said I was stereotyping Asians as being intellectuals. Ironically, none of the complaints came from Asians.

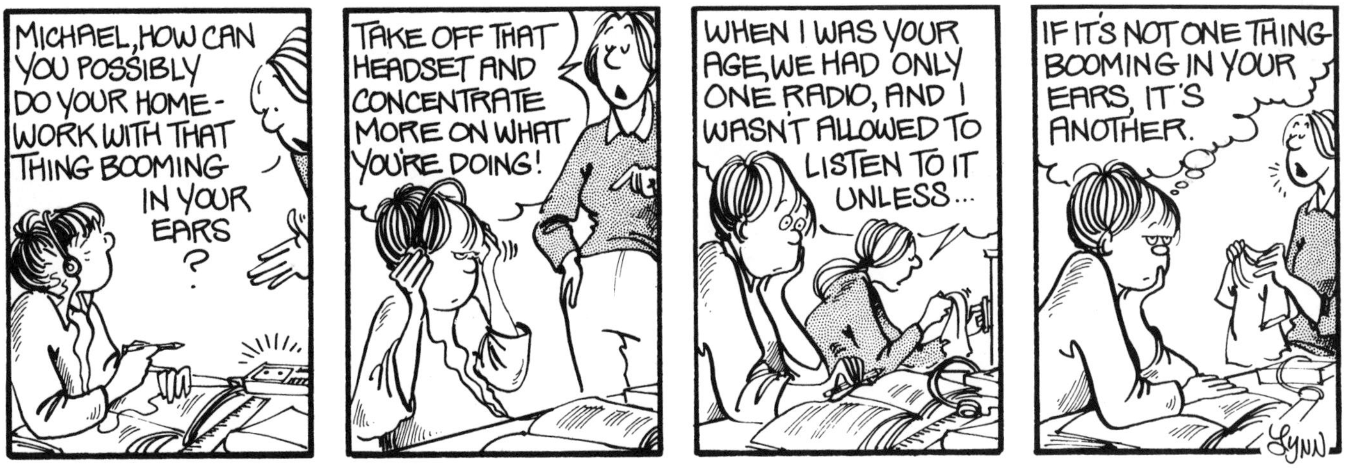
MICHAEL, HOW CAN YOU POSSIBLY DO YOUR HOME-WORK WITH THAT THING BOOMING IN YOUR EARS?
TAKE OFF THAT HEADSET AND CONCENTRATE MORE ON WHAT YOU'RE DOING!
WHEN I WAS YOUR AGE, WE HAD ONLY ONE RADIO, AND I WASN'T ALLOWED TO LISTEN TO IT UNLESS...
IF IT'S NOT ONE THING BOOMING IN YOUR EARS, IT'S ANOTHER.
LYNN

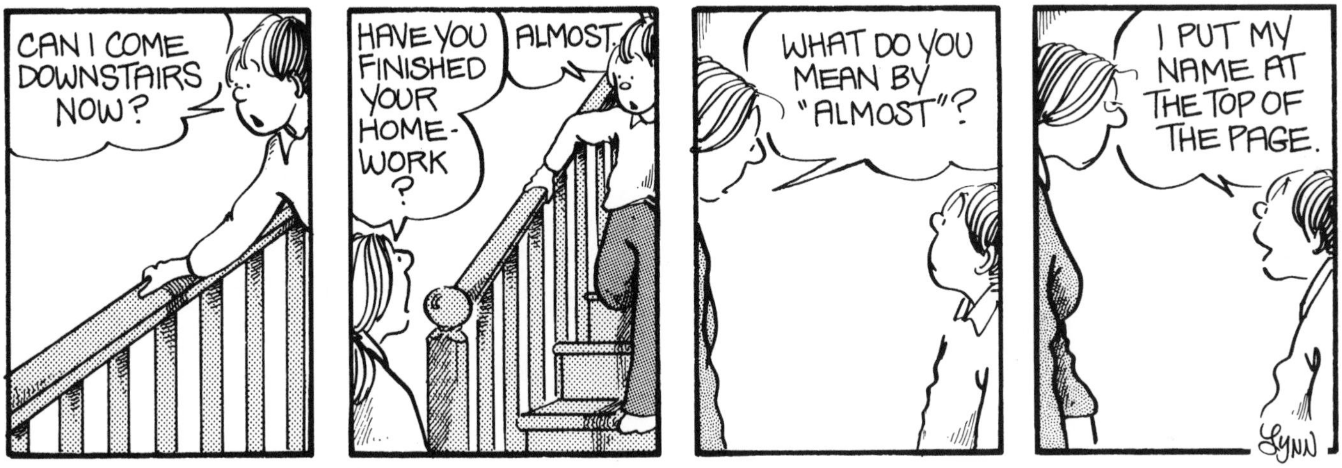
CAN I COME DOWNSTAIRS NOW?
HAVE YOU FINISHED YOUR HOME-WORK?
ALMOST.
WHAT DO YOU MEAN BY "ALMOST"?
I PUT MY NAME AT THE TOP OF THE PAGE.
LYNN

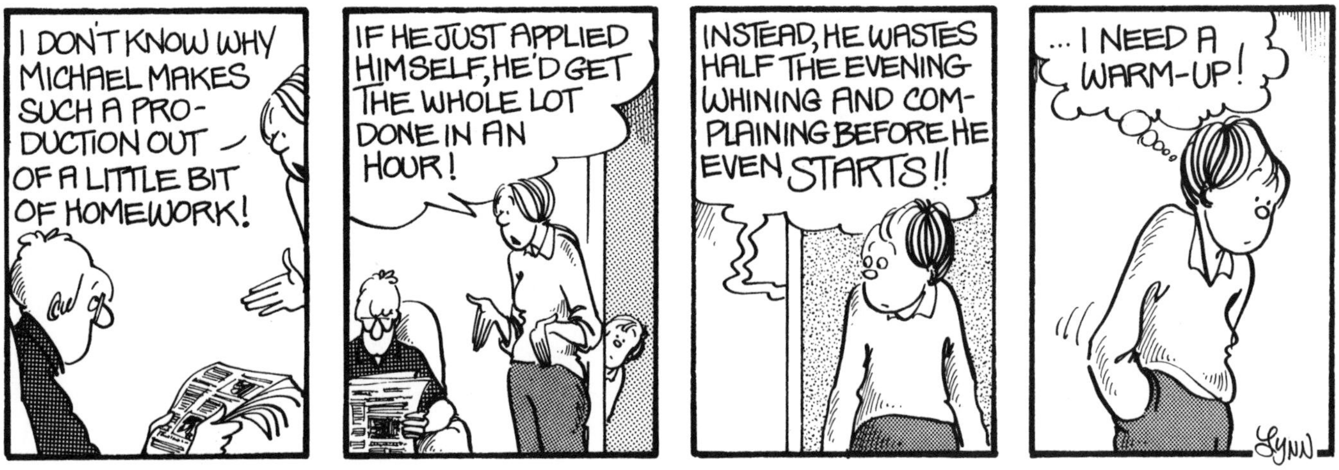
I DON'T KNOW WHY MICHAEL MAKES SUCH A PRO-DUCTION OUT OF A LITTLE BIT OF HOMEWORK!
IF HE JUST APPLIED HIMSELF, HE'D GET THE WHOLE LOT DONE IN AN HOUR!
INSTEAD, HE WASTES HALF THE EVENING WHINING AND COM-PLAINING BEFORE HE EVEN STARTS!!
... I NEED A WARM-UP!
LYNN

My kids liked most vegetables, so eating wasn't a problem. A cartoonist who draws on family stuff for gags, however, needs the gag reflex of unpalatable foods — and the thing about peas is, they're funny! Squash is funny because of the name, and of course the goofy shapes it can come in. A head of lettuce can be funny, I guess, but peas are made for comedy. They are hard to get on a fork, look like frog parts, and roll onto the floor easily. They are easy to spit, mash, or fling off a spoon. They can be bright or bilious green depending on how "left over" they are, and dogs, for the most part, hate them. Anything a dog won't eat is usually spurned by kids. I have done several gags about this maligned dicotyledon, and the surprising result is that I have had no complaints. I thought there was a reader out there for every complaint possible, but so far I have heard nothing from pea fanciers, associations, or "protect the pea" movements, and I'm curious: Now that I have mentioned this lack of interest, will I finally hear from these people?

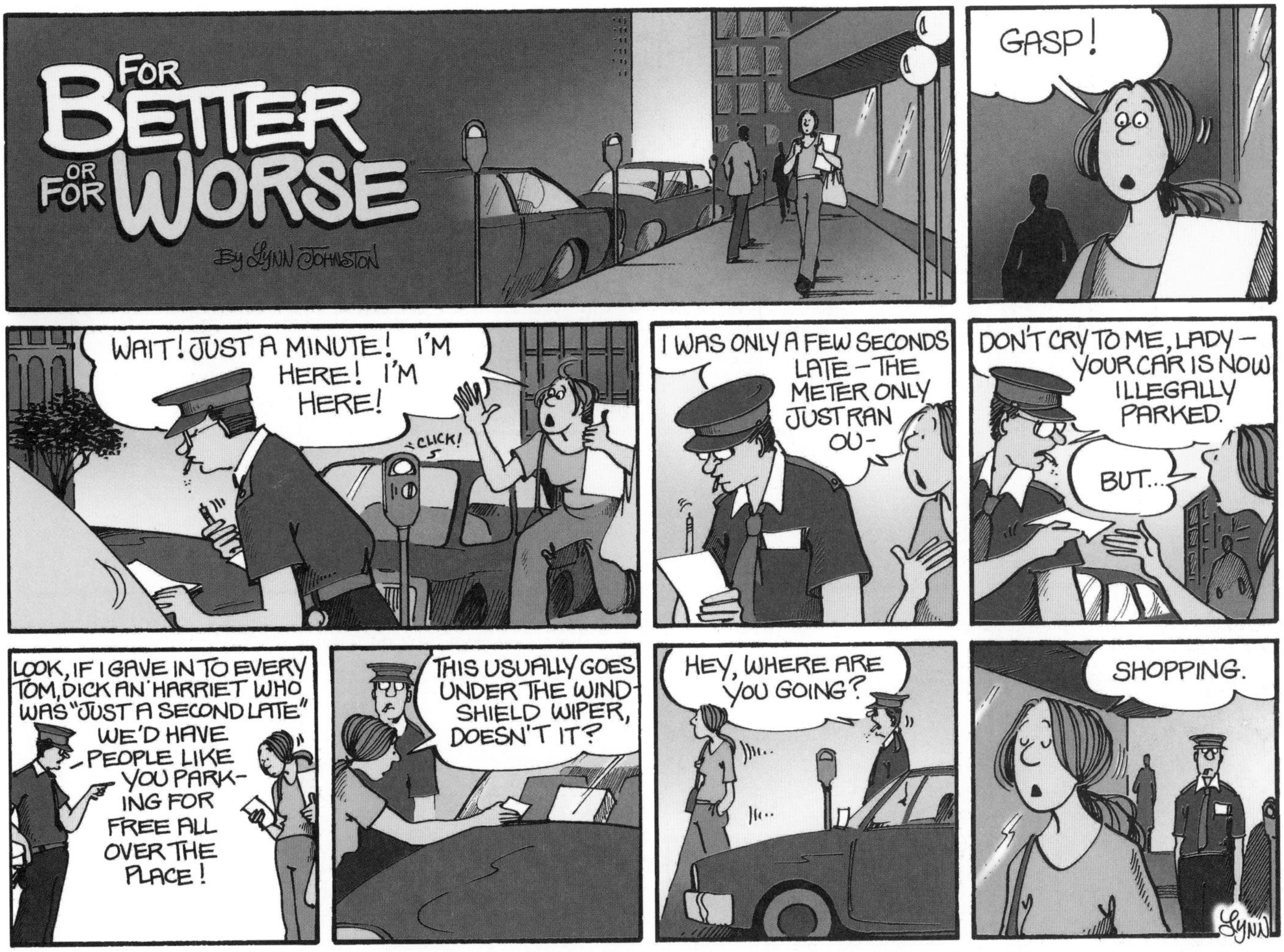
FOR BETTER OR FOR WORSE
By Lynn Johnston
GASP!
WAIT! JUST A MINUTE! I'M HERE! I'M HERE!
CLICK!
I WAS ONLY A FEW SECONDS LATE - THE METER ONLY JUST RAN OU-
DON'T CRY TO ME, LADY - YOUR CAR IS NOW ILLEGALLY PARKED.
BUT...
LOOK, IF I GAVE IN TO EVERY TOM, DICK AN' HARRIET WHO WAS "JUST A SECOND LATE" WE'D HAVE PEOPLE LIKE YOU PARKING FOR FREE ALL OVER THE PLACE!
THIS USUALLY GOES UNDER THE WINDSHIELD WIPER, DOESN'T IT?
HEY, WHERE ARE YOU GOING?
SHOPPING.
Lynn

We have a very dedicated parking authority here in North Bay. Leave your vehicle parked and unpaid for, and you will definitely receive a ticket. This reminds me of a story: It was my birthday, and friends had taken me to lunch at a favourite restaurant. I had so much fun that I forgot about the meter running outside. When I left the building, there was an attendant diligently writing a ticket as he leaned on my car. Naturally, I cried, "Wait! I'm here! I forgot!" He kept on writing. I stood and watched him, and when he looked up, he smiled. I was carrying a gift bag and huge bunch of helium-filled balloons. "Is it your birthday?" he asked. I said that it was. I reached out to take the ticket, but he tore it up in front of me and put it in his pocket. "Have a good one." he said, and he got on his bike and rode away. I thought it was time somebody said something GOOD about the guys who check the parking meters!

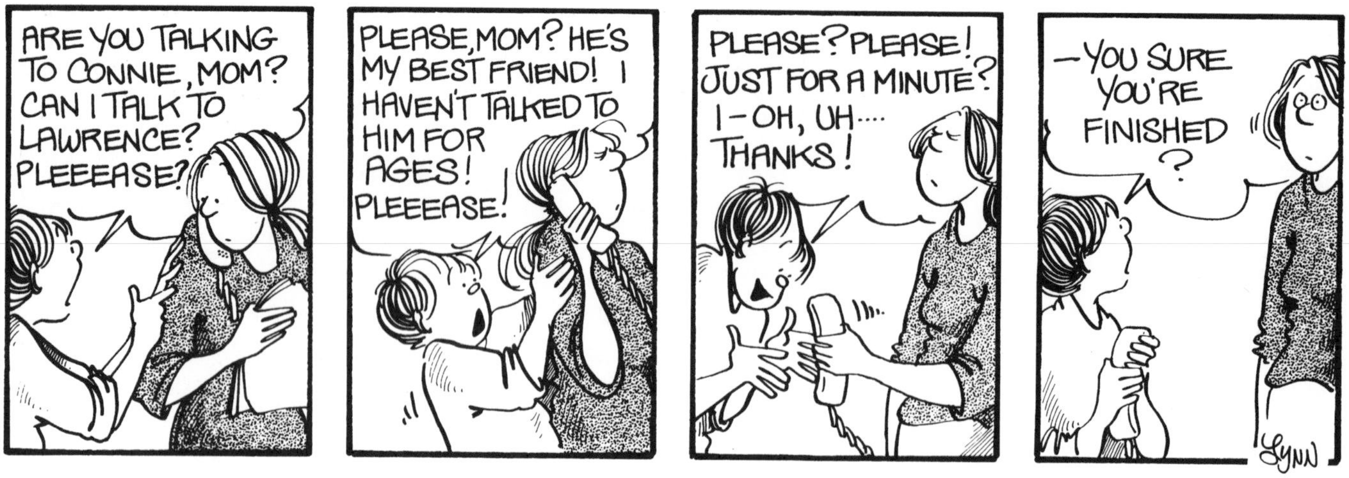
ARE YOU TALKING TO CONNIE, MOM? CAN I TALK TO LAWRENCE? PLEEEASE?
PLEASE, MOM? HE'S MY BEST FRIEND! I HAVEN'T TALKED TO HIM FOR AGES! PLEEEASE!
PLEASE? PLEASE! JUST FOR A MINUTE?
I-OH, UH.... THANKS!
–YOU SURE YOU'RE FINISHED?
LYNN

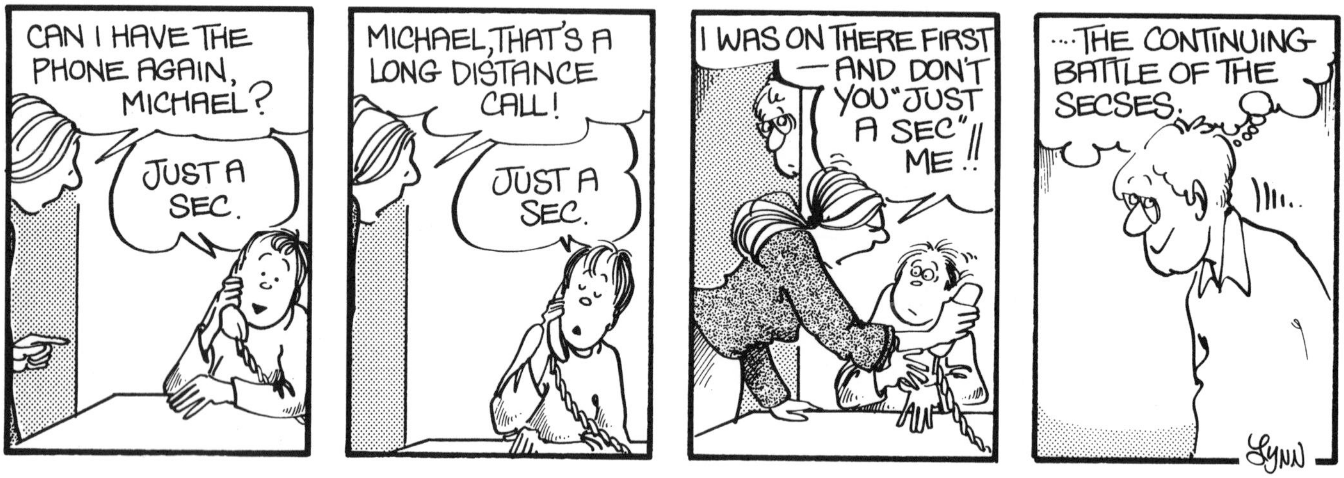
CAN I HAVE THE PHONE AGAIN, MICHAEL?
JUST A SEC.
MICHAEL, THAT'S A LONG DISTANCE CALL!
JUST A SEC.
I WAS ON THERE FIRST —AND DON'T YOU "JUST A SEC" ME!!
...THE CONTINUING BATTLE OF THE SECSES.
LYNN

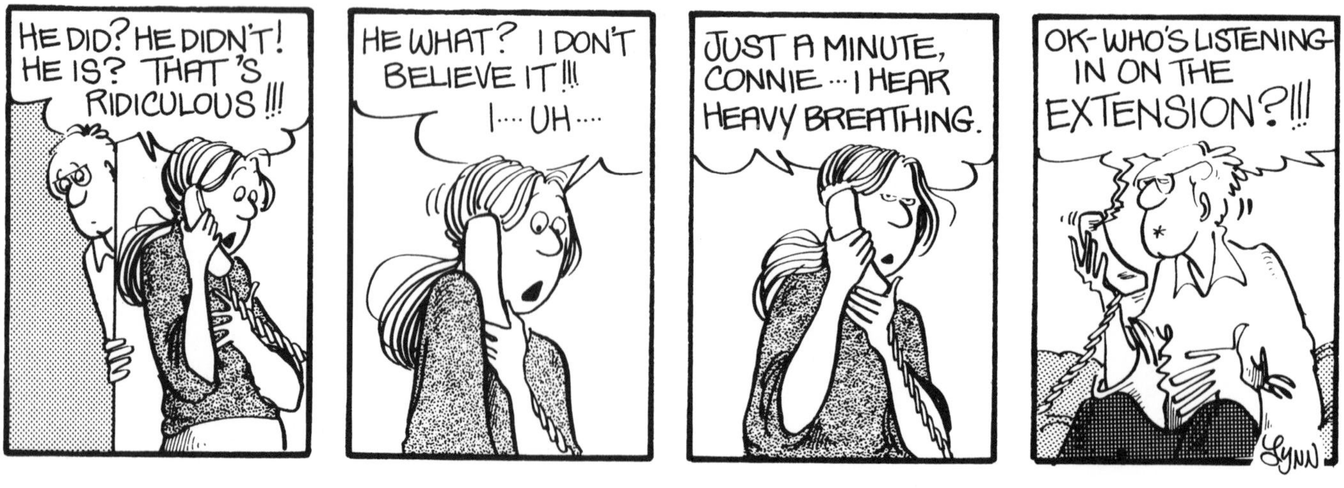
HE DID? HE DIDN'T! HE IS? THAT'S RIDICULOUS!!!
HE WHAT? I DON'T BELIEVE IT!!! I.... UH....
JUST A MINUTE, CONNIE... I HEAR HEAVY BREATHING.
OK-WHO'S LISTENING IN ON THE EXTENSION?!!!
LYNN

AMAZING! CONNIE MOVES ALL THE WAY TO THUNDER BAY TO GET AWAY FROM TED... AND GUESS WHO SHOWS UP ON HER DOORSTEP?!!

HE WANTS TO GET MARRIED, JOHN! HE DISCARDED HER LIKE AN EMPTY BOTTLE.... AND NOW HE WANTS HER TO COME BACK!

WHAT DID SHE SAY?

NO, OF COURSE!

NO DEPOSIT.... NO RETURN.

DO YOU THINK CONNIE AN' LAWRENCE WILL EVER MOVE BACK HERE, MOM?

IT'S HARD TO SAY.

YOU REALLY MISS LAWRENCE, DON'T YOU, HONEY?

YES.

YOU TALKED TO HIM ON THE PHONE YESTERDAY — WHY DIDN'T YOU TELL HIM HOW MUCH YOU MISS HIM?

....IT'S HARD TO SAY.

MESSAGE, DR.P. ... DR. MacCAULAY WOULD LIKE TO MEET YOU FOR LUNCH.

EVER SINCE CONNIE MOVED, I'VE BEEN IN AGONY, JOHN. WHY DID SHE HAVE TO GO — WHY?!!

YOU DUMPED HER, TED. YOU HURT AND HUMILIATED HER. YOU SAID SOME VICIOUS THINGS!

I WAS KIDDING! GOOD GRIEF, CAN'T SHE TAKE A LITTLE KIDDING?

Here's where the "soap opera" comes into *FBorFW*. There had to be some romantic conflict in the story, so when Connie moved away, I enjoyed exploring some of the "what-ifs." Would people like John and Ted meet and talk like this in real life? Maybe not. Still, it was a way to answer some of the questions a sympathetic fly on the wall might ask: What if Ted felt badly? What if he realized his mistake? Exploring questions like these gave me the incentive to produce and to stay on deadline.

The Barnstorf family lived across the street from us in Lynn Lake. Aaron and their youngest son, Roy, were great pals — always on the go, always getting into something. One would spur the other on, and although they could be troublesome, they never really got into trouble. The Barnstorfs' dog, Lady, was a wide, placid, and friendly English Springer Spaniel. She would put up with just about anything. One day, I went out to look for the boys and I heard the "Rmmmm-rummmm, neeeerooowwwww" sounds kids make when they're pretending to ride a motor bike. Around the side of the house, Aaron watched, waiting his turn — while Roy, standing astride Lady, loosely twisted her ears as if they were handles. Leaning forward like a racer, he drove Lady down an imaginary speedway, changing gears, changing lanes; you could almost see the wind whipping up their hair. Lady was expressionless, moving side to side, as if she were a hot machine and part of an improv comedy skit. I admonished both boys for teasing the dog, but inside, I laughed and looked forward to someday putting this scene into the strip.

IT'S POURING RAIN THIS MORNING, MIKE—YOU'D BETTER TAKE AN UMBRELLA.

NAH. I'M OK.

WHAT ABOUT YOUR BOOKS?

THEY'LL BE OK.

MATH

MICHAEL, I INSIST THAT YOU TAKE AN UMBRELLA!

NO!!

WHAT DOES SHE WANT ME TO DO.... LOOK STUPID?!!

Lynn

BOY, GORDON, I NEVER KNEW GRADE 5 WAS GONNA BE SO TOUGH!

ON TOP OF ALL THE EXTRA EXAMS AN' HOMEWORK.... WE GOTTA DO A SCIENCE PROJECT!

I HOPE NOTHING ELSE COMES ALONG TO COMPLICATE MY LIFE!

♡ HI, MICHAEL! ♡ ♡ ♡ ♡

Lynn

NOTICE ANYTHING DIFFERENT ABOUT ME THIS YEAR, MICHAEL?

NOPE.

GUESS!

YOU GOT YOUR FACE STRAIGHTENED?

I GOT MY EARS PIERCED, YOU DUMMY!!

I ADMIRE YOU, MIKE. YOU GOT A WAY WITH WORDS.

Lynn

Katie asked to have her ears pierced as soon as she saw other little girls with earrings. We said she could have pierced ears for her fifth birthday. We took her to the local jewellery store, and she was almost too excited to sit still; however, she didn't expect piercing to hurt so much and refused to get the second one done. It took a while to make a decision: Either take the one out or have the second earring put in. She decided to go ahead with the second one — as long as her brother couldn't watch!

KNOW WHAT? I JUST FOUND OUT WE'RE HAVIN' A BIG HALLOWEEN PARTY AT THE SCHOOL!

MR. WARREN'S ASKING ANY PARENTS WHO WANT TO CHAPERONE TO CALL HIM!

YOU GONNA ASK YOUR FOLKS TO CHAPERONE MIKE?

ARE YOU NUTS?

I WANNA HAVE FUN!!!

BOY! A REAL HALLOWEEN PARTY!

YEAH! MR. WARREN SAYS WE CAN EVEN DANCE IF WE WANT TO!

DANCE?... YOU MEAN WITH **GIRLS??**

I DON'T MIND... LONG AS I DON'T HAVE TO TOUCH ONE!!

MRS. ENJO TELLS ME THAT YOUR SCHOOL NEEDS CHAPERONES FOR A HALLOWEEN PARTY!

MICHAEL, WHY DON'T YOU EVER BRING HOME THESE NOTICES FROM SCHOOL?

I DO BRING THEM HOME!

FUMBLE FUMBLE

YOU JUST NEVER READ THEM!

In this strip, Mike hands his mother a shredded note. I usually found them in the washing machine, small papier-mâché lumps, too mangled to read.

WHAT'S THAT YOU'RE MAKING, ELIZABETH?

EV'RYBODY GOTS TO MAKE A HARVEST PICTURE FOR KINDERGARTEN ....AN' I'M DOIN' A PUNKIN!

BUT HONEY, YOU'VE COLORED THE ENTIRE PAGE ORANGE!

I KNOW.

IT'S A CLOSE-UP!

EVERY YEAR SINCE I CAN REMEMBER, I'VE SPENT HALLOWE'EN WITH LAWRENCE ...I WISH HE HADN'T MOVED AWAY.

IF I WAS MAGIC, I COULD FLY AN' VISIT HIM! LIKE ON A BROOMSTICK MAYBE!

WITCHES DON'T REALLY EXIST, THOUGH - DO THEY, DAD?

SAY IT.... AND THE CAULDRON LANDS IN YOUR LAP.

WHAT'RE YOU GONNA BE FOR HALLOWEEN? ·· I DUNNO, WHAT'RE YOU GONNA BE? I DUNNO...

HEY, GUYS- NEAT IDEA: WHY DON'T WE ALL GO OUT AS EXACTLY THE SAME THING!!

AWWRIGHT!

WICKED, MAN!

FAR OUT! LET'S GO FOR IT!

WHAT'RE WE GONNA BE?···I DUNNO, WHAT DO YOU WANNA BE? I DUNNO,WHAT DO YOU···

137

Yes, this happened — and with all the theatrical sarcasm seen here. This was what made our marriage so much fun. We were both able to laugh and make jokes out of just about anything.

Our house in Corbeil was hidden in quite a dense forest, so leaves and clippings could easily be tossed into the woods or piled somewhere for compost. Our house in Dundas, though (on which the Pattersons' house was based), was in a busy, upscale neighbourhood, where leaves had to be piled, pushed into bags, and left for city workers to remove. After a discussion about the waste we made with plastic bags, I decided to take a load of leaves to the dump myself, but in the back of the car, bagless. I only did this once. It was a nuisance, a mess, and created a lot of work!

LOOKIT, MOM! LOOKIT THE BEAUTIFUL LEAVES I FOUND!

MISS LYON WANTS US TO FIND 4 DIFFERENT FALL LEAVES, AN' TO SAY WHAT KINDA TREE THEY CAME FROM!

AND DO YOU KNOW WHICH TREE EACH OF THESE CAME FROM?

UH HUH!

THAT ONE, THAT ONE, THAT ONE, AN' THAT ONE.

OF ALL THE SEASONS OF THE YEAR, I THINK FALL IS MY FAVORITE!

EVERYTHING BURSTS INTO ONE BRILLIANT FRENZY OF COLOR! ONE LAST CELEBRATION OF LIFE BEFORE THE LONG DAYS OF WINTER SET IN!

MOTHER NATURE'S MID-LIFE CRISIS.

HERE, MICHAEL, I WANT YOU TO GIVE THIS NOTE TO MR. WARREN.

I'VE VOLUNTEERED TO HELP CHAPERONE YOUR SCHOOL HALLOWEEN PARTY.

YOU DID? BUT WHY?!!

YOUR TEACHERS PUT UP WITH YOU EVERY DAY OF THE WEEK, DON'T THEY?

SO?

I OWE THEM ONE.

When I was a kid, my friends would come to my house to talk to my mother. She and I didn't always see eye to eye, so it surprised me when my friends considered her advice worth seeking. I accepted her relationship with them with admiration and jealousy: admiration for her, jealousy because I couldn't confide in her the way they did.

My friend Carolyn Sadowska (a professional comedienne who's known for her comic impressions of Her Majesty the Queen) and coincidentally Aaron's Grade 1 Teacher once told me that our monarch ate bacon with her fingers, which would render this approved mealtime etiquette. I wondered, then, how she would tackle a cob of corn. Food for thought.

Carolyn as "The Queen."
www.queencomedy.com

My mom could make a casserole out of anything. In turn, I too have no fear of this classic leftover surprise. My friend Kelly once told me that her husband refused to eat leftovers. I asked if she had offered them to him in a casserole. She said, "No, because he'd find out." "What do you think quiche and stir fry and pizza and soup are made of?" I argued. "Bits of stuff from the refrigerator, cut up and fashioned into something ELSE!" She said she hadn't thought of that, and we set about making a great pot of soup out of what was left in her fridge. It was a delicious brew, and her husband ate it with relish (and buns). When he was done, he asked her how she'd made it, and she replied, "soup mix," referring to a mix of stuff from the refrigerator. "Good," he said, "as long as it's not made from leftovers."

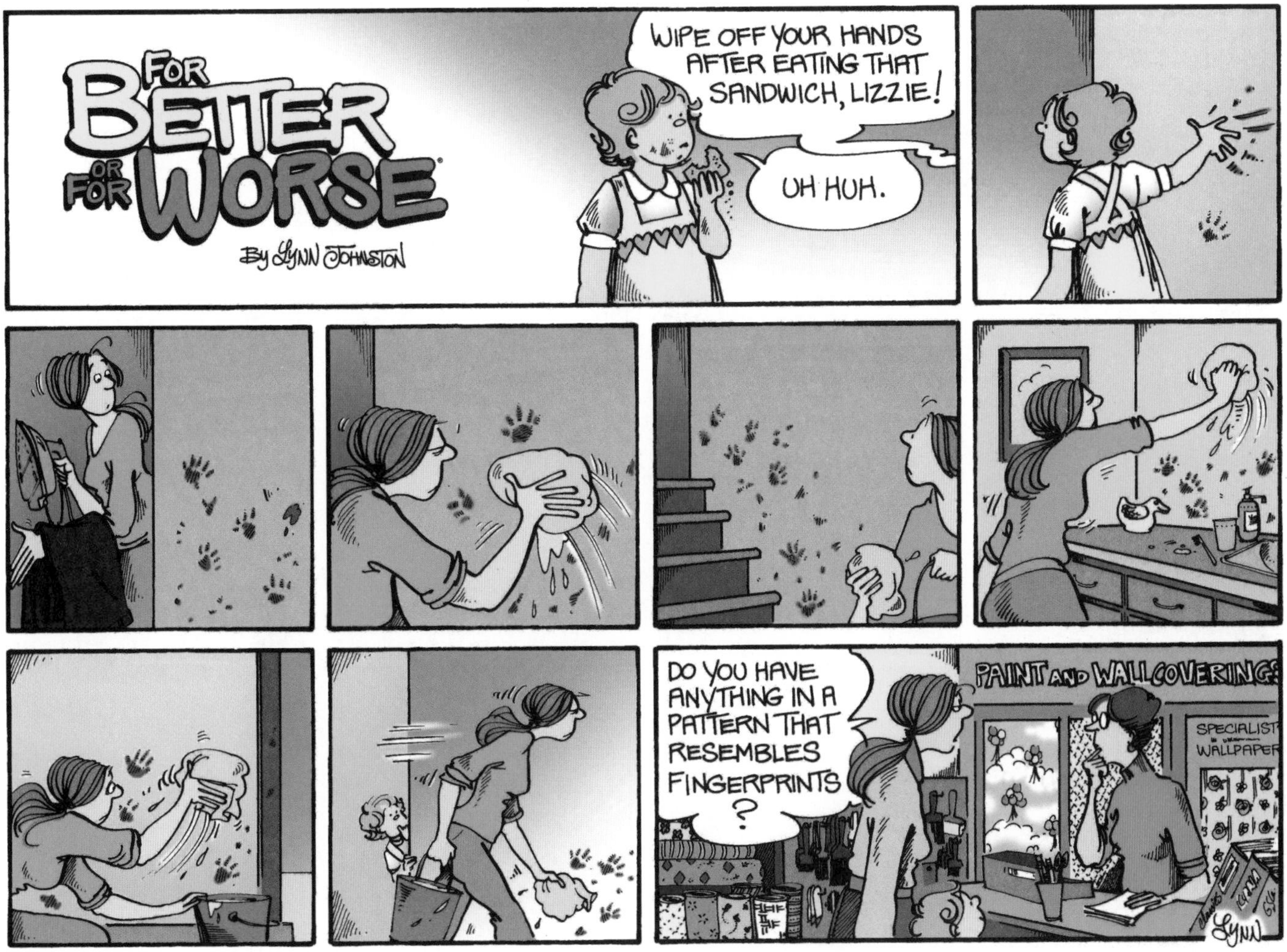
FOR BETTER OR FOR WORSE
BY LYNN JOHNSTON
WIPE OFF YOUR HANDS AFTER EATING THAT SANDWICH, LIZZIE!
UH HUH.
DO YOU HAVE ANYTHING IN A PATTERN THAT RESEMBLES FINGERPRINTS?
PAINT AND WALLCOVERINGS

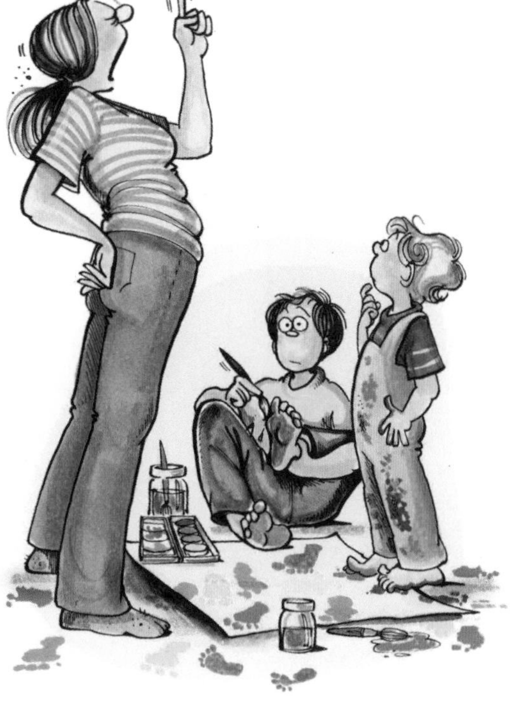

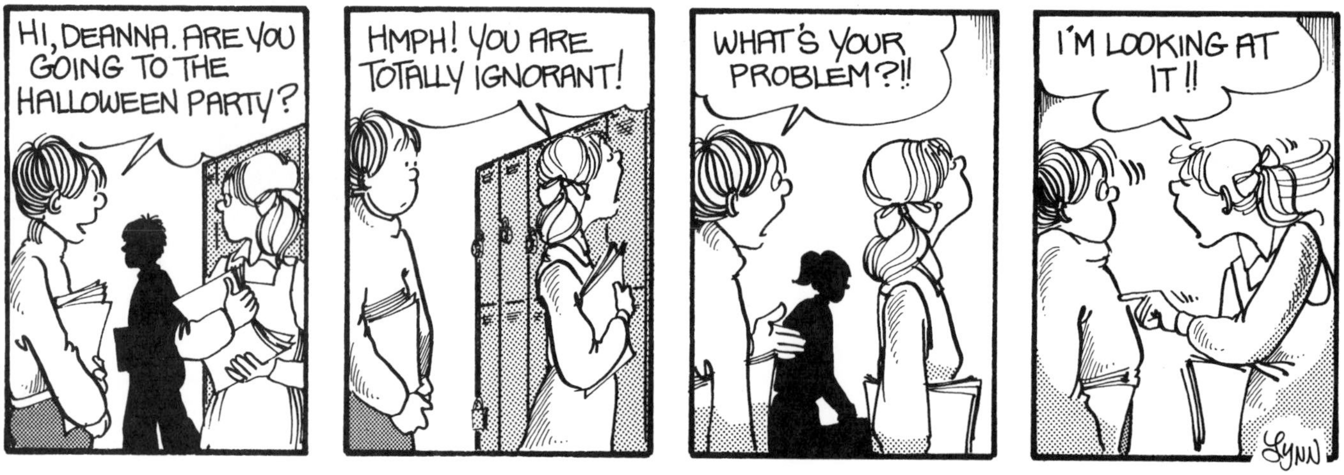
HI, DEANNA. ARE YOU GOING TO THE HALLOWEEN PARTY?
HMPH! YOU ARE TOTALLY IGNORANT!
WHAT'S YOUR PROBLEM?!!
I'M LOOKING AT IT!!
LYNN

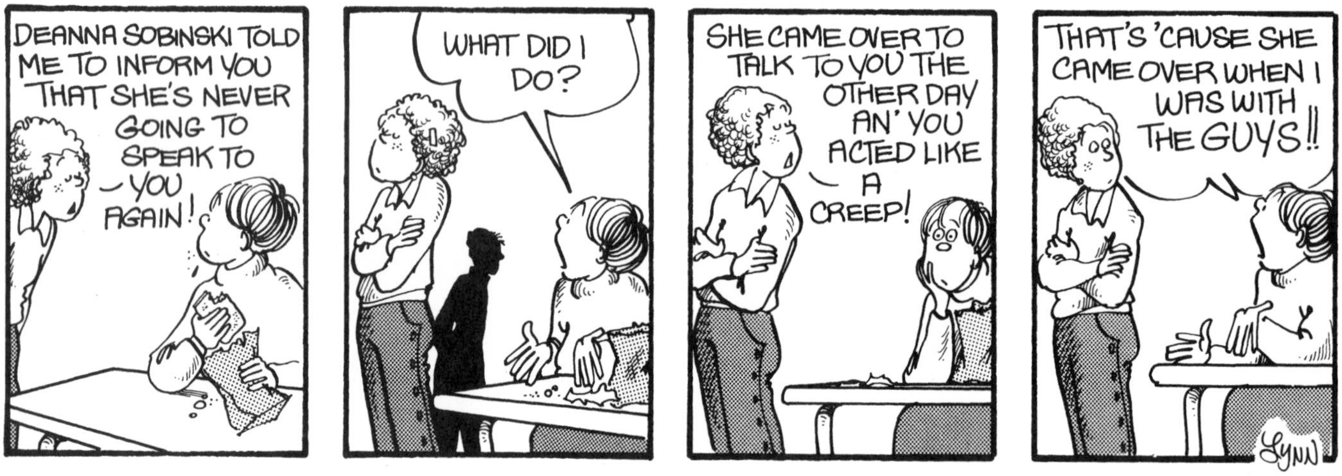
DEANNA SOBINSKI TOLD ME TO INFORM YOU THAT SHE'S NEVER GOING TO SPEAK TO YOU AGAIN!
WHAT DID I DO?
SHE CAME OVER TO TALK TO YOU THE OTHER DAY AN' YOU ACTED LIKE A CREEP!
THAT'S 'CAUSE SHE CAME OVER WHEN I WAS WITH THE GUYS!!
LYNN

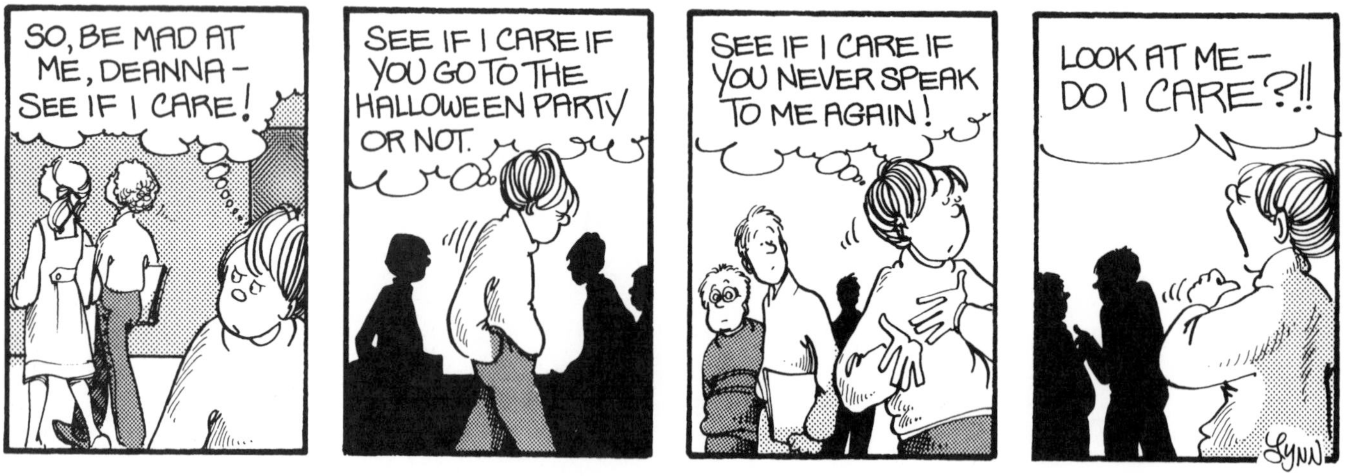
SO, BE MAD AT ME, DEANNA - SEE IF I CARE!
SEE IF I CARE IF YOU GO TO THE HALLOWEEN PARTY OR NOT.
SEE IF I CARE IF YOU NEVER SPEAK TO ME AGAIN!
LOOK AT ME - DO I CARE?!!
LYNN

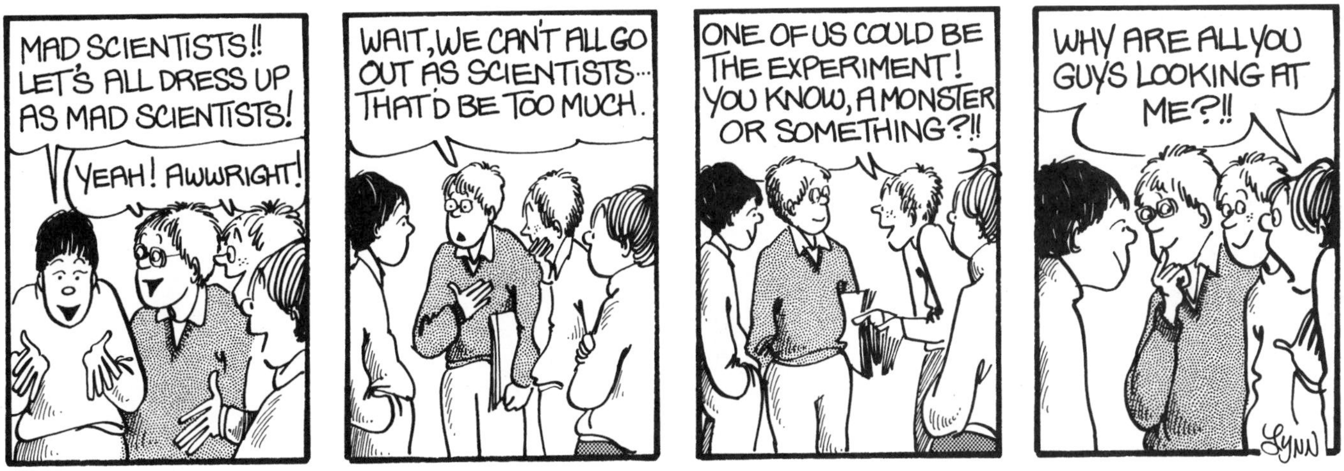
MAD SCIENTISTS!! LET'S ALL DRESS UP AS MAD SCIENTISTS!
YEAH! AWWRIGHT!
WAIT, WE CAN'T ALL GO OUT AS SCIENTISTS... THAT'D BE TOO MUCH.
ONE OF US COULD BE THE EXPERIMENT! YOU KNOW, A MONSTER OR SOMETHING?!!
WHY ARE ALL YOU GUYS LOOKING AT ME?!!
LYNN

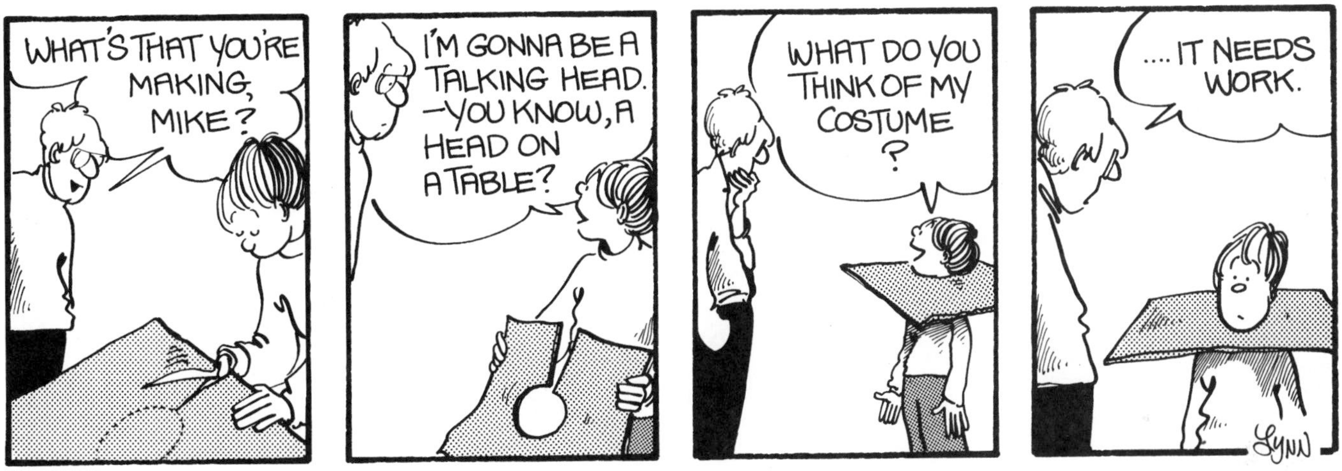
WHAT'S THAT YOU'RE MAKING, MIKE?
I'M GONNA BE A TALKING HEAD. —YOU KNOW, A HEAD ON A TABLE?
WHAT DO YOU THINK OF MY COSTUME?
....IT NEEDS WORK.
LYNN

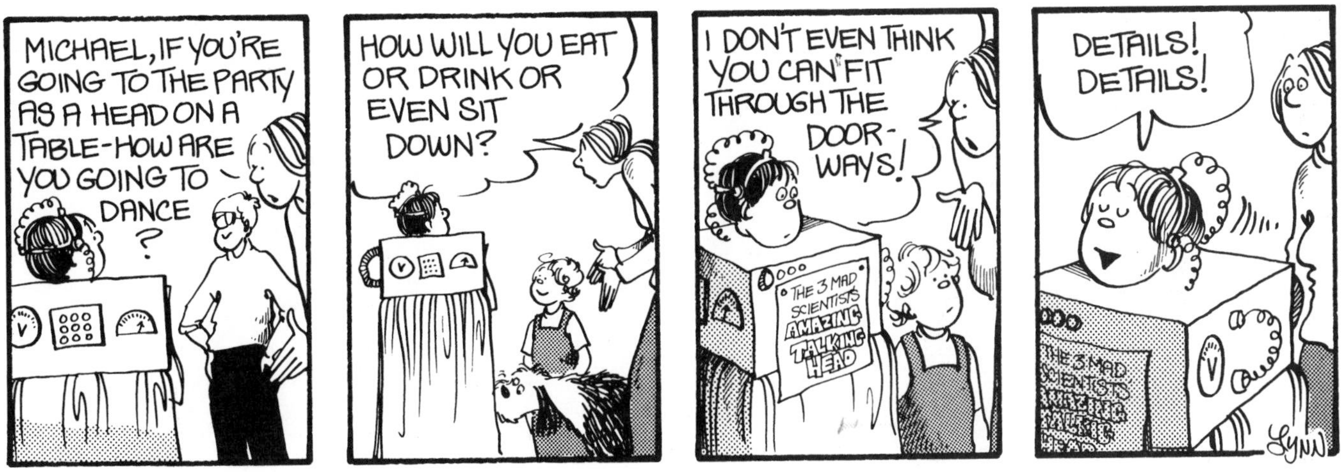
MICHAEL, IF YOU'RE GOING TO THE PARTY AS A HEAD ON A TABLE-HOW ARE YOU GOING TO DANCE?
HOW WILL YOU EAT OR DRINK OR EVEN SIT DOWN?
I DON'T EVEN THINK YOU CAN FIT THROUGH THE DOOR-WAYS!
THE 3 MAD SCIENTISTS AMAZING TALKING HEAD
DETAILS! DETAILS!
LYNN

Nope. Nobody in our family ever made a talking head on a table as a Halloween costume. This was another descent into the "writer's mind" where silly ideas lie. The prospect of sustaining such a monstrosity made me think about how a small group of boys would treat their experimental pal; whatever they did, it would be messy!

FIRST PRIZE WAS A TOUGH ONE, KIDS—SO THE JUDGES HAVE TIED IT BETWEEN MIKE PATTERSON AND DEANNA SOBINSKI!

CONGRATULATIONS! HOW 'BOUT YOU TWO STARTING THE NEXT DANCE?

DANCE?!! BUT, SIR... WE'RE NOT EVEN SPEAKING TO EACH OTHER!

BOOM

BOOM CHA-BOOM BOOM

WHAT DOES THAT MATTER—WITH THIS MUSIC, YOU CAN'T HEAR ANYTHING ANYWAYS!

CHA-BOOM BOOM CHA-CHA-BOOOMP BOOM BOOM BOOM!

HOW WAS THE PARTY, MIKE?

OK.

WERE THERE LOTS OF COSTUMES? DID YOU PLAY GAMES? WAS IT FUN?!

I GUESS.

YOU MEAN THERE'S NOTHING TO TELL?

NAH.

SHE DANCED WITH ME! DEANNA SOBINSKI DANCED WITH ME!!

BOY, I'M EXHAUSTED! CHAPERONING THAT HALLOWEEN PARTY WORE ME RIGHT OUT!

I WIPED SPILLS, STOPPED ARGUMENTS, FIXED COSTUMES, POLICED THE HALLS, KEPT THE PEACE....

IT'S HARD DISCIPLINING A LARGE GROUP OF KIDS THESE DAYS, JOHN....

THEY NEVER SEEMED TO TAKE ME SERIOUSLY!

When my brother was moved to his new bedroom in the basement, I thought I'd love having a room to myself. My mother replaced the kiddie curtains with flowered drapes and made a bedspread to match. I had a new dressing table and a white headboard for my bed. It was a room to be proud of. Still, when the trees outside whistled in the wind and their branches made stark, skeletal patterns on the walls, I'd lie there, terrified. Now that I was alone, spooks, goblins, and other imaginary evils were coming nightly to "get me." During one very bad storm, my mother got out of bed to see if I was all right. As she opened the door to my room, lightning shook the house, and the flash turned my mother into a silhouette shrouded in a glowing, transparent gown. I screamed as hard as I could! She never did understand why I was so frightened by her — I couldn't explain what I'd seen. It was something I couldn't describe. This is the way I remember that evening.

After Halloween, Katie would save up her goodies until Aaron went dry. Unlike her older sibling, she could restrain herself from eating all of her stash at once — which surprised me. Of the two children, she had the sweetest tooth. We even called her "Cake" instead of "Kate" because she liked desserts so much. At the end of October, however, willpower set in. She could hoard her gains in full view, then savour each morsel after Aaron's was long gone. I remember watching him as he pretended not to be fazed by the sounds of crinkling wrappers followed by lip smacking and the sound of "mmmmmm." I was surprised that he didn't pounce on her or ask me for a treat to make up for the discrepancy. He just put up with the injustice, and I wondered when and how he'd get even, because this would come about, guaranteed. Like my brother and me, my kids were creative teases!

OOF!

LOOK OUT, FARLEY! MOVE! OUT OF THE WAY!

DARNED DOG! WHY IS IT EVERY TIME YOU TURN AROUND, THAT DOG IS IN THE WAY?!!

MAYBE HE JUST WANTS TO BE NOTICED!

LOOKIT THAT, LIZZIE— WHEN WE DRIVE ALONG, THE SUN FOLLOWS US!

THE SUN DOESN'T FOLLOW US!

DOES SO!

NO IT DOESN'T, MISS LYON TOLD US IN KINDERGARTEN!

IT'S JUST A OBSTACLE ILLUSION.

The malapropisms kids use while learning the language are so much fun. Words like "awfuls" for "waffles" and "Anointed Stakes of America" made me laugh out loud. My mother told me she once wrote an essay on the copulation of Canada and how it grew bigger after the first world war. Oh, how I'd have loved to use that one!

YAAAAY!! GO BOYS GO! SKATE! SKATE

YAY! SKATE!

GO BOYS ...GO

IT'S A LONG PRACTICE .... ISN'T IT, MOM.

When they moved to a new building, the folks at Universal Press asked all of the artists for a portrait to put on their walls. A proud "northern Canadian," this is the one I sent — and I think it's still hanging there!

NOW, YOU'RE LEANING TOO FAR FORWARD, MIKE, YOU'VE GOT TO BEND YOUR KNEES, DIG IN, KEEP UP TO THE PUCK!

AND LOOK BEHIND YOU, MAKE SURE YOU KNOW WHAT'S GOING ON AT ALL TIMES....

PUSH YOUR BLADES INTO THOSE TURNS! HEAD UP!

LOCKER ROOM B

I KNOW HOW YOU FEEL, MIKE....MY MOTHER DOESN'T SKATE EITHER.

DID YOU SEE THE NEW ARENA SCHEDULE, MOM?

I HAVE HOCKEY MONDAYS, WEDNESDAYS AN'SATURDAYS...

AN'LIZZIE'S IN BEGINNER FIGURE-SKATING TUESDAYS AN' FRIDAYS!

THE EASTGATE ARENA ....MY HOME AWAY FROM HOME.

In North Bay, we had access to some great sports facilities, so the kids were soon skating, swimming, and playing hockey. My car was on the road constantly — ferrying them to the rink or the "Y," or wherever the game was to be, and I had a rule: four trips only. I would only drive into town four times in a day. This was met with some confusion, as I had counted each way, there and back, as separate trips! The rule was then changed to eight trips. AAAUGH!

MICHAEL HAS HOCKEY, COMPUTER CLUB, SWIMMING AND MUSIC LESSONS...

ELIZABETH HAS SKATING, ART CLASS AND SATURDAY SWIM!

THERE ISN'T ONE NIGHT THAT ONE OR BOTH OF US WON'T BE CHAUFFEURING KIDS SOME-WHERE!

TAXI!!

LINEUPS OF WOMEN AND CHILDREN WAIT FOR THEIR ONE CUP OF MILK...MANY TOO WEAK TO STAND.

UNABLE TO FIND ENOUGH FOOD, PEOPLE ARE DIGGING INTO ANT HILLS HOPING TO FIND RICE THAT MAY HAVE BEEN CARRIED IN BY....

WHAT'S FOR SUPPER, MOM? WE'RE STARVING!!

Having gone on several Medical Missions to Honduras and Peru, I am well aware of how little some people have and how much we in North America take for granted. When my kids said they were "starving," I was grateful that they had no idea what "starving" meant.

I HAVE TO GO TO WORK, NOW, FARLEY. YOU STAY HERE.

DOESN'T HE JUMP UP ON THE FURNITURE WHILE YOU'RE GONE, ELLY?

OH, NO-HE NEVER DOES THAT, I'VE GOT HIM TRAINED!

I'M SO GLAD YOU COULD DROP US OFF DOWNTOWN, ELLY.

IT MAKES MORE SENSE THAN TAKING TWO CARS WHEN WE'RE BOTH GOING IN THE SAME DIRECTION!

MOM, BABY RICHARD JUST DUMPED HIS BOTTLE ALL OVER THE BACK SEAT!

HENCE THE NAME "CAR POOL", EH, ELLY? HEH, HEH......UH.... -ELLY?

MORNING, EL—YOU LOOK FRAZZLED!

I JUST DROVE MY NEIGHBOR INTO TOWN, AND HER KIDS DESTROYED MY CAR!

YOU MEAN ANNIE JUST SAT THERE? DOESN'T SHE DISCIPLINE THEM?

ANNIE CONFUSES DEMOLITION WITH CREATIVITY.

WHAT DO YOU THINK OF OUR IDEA FOR A DISPLAY WINDOW THIS YEAR, ELLY?

IT'S DICKENS' "A CHRISTMAS CAROL"! ...YOU COULD BUILD A WHOLE SCENE— STRAIGHT OUT OF THE BOOK!

OF COURSE, WE DON'T HAVE MUCH OF A BUDGET. THE BOARD WANTS IT DONE AS CHEAPLY AS POSSIBLE!

SCROOGE LIVES.

SPEAKERS, READINGS, FILMS, PLAYS, CONTESTS...

THIS IS A PRETTY AMBITIOUS CHRISTMAS PROGRAM YOU HAVE HERE, SUE.

I KNOW—BUT HOW ELSE CAN WE ATTRACT A LOT OF PEOPLE TO THE LIBRARY?

...WE COULD APPLY FOR A BINGO LICENSE!

I was a member of the Art Centre board in North Bay for a few years. In an effort to make the theatre more profitable, a friend and I drove to a neighbouring town's theatre to find out how they managed to stay in the black. Thinking they had a magical formula, I begged them to tell us the secret to their financial success. The answer, sadly, was Bingo. Bingo became one of our main resources, too. You'd think the wonderful art of live theatre would have brought in enough to pay the bills!

One of the reasons I don't volunteer to be a board member now is that I always have suggestions. My philosophy is — if you make a suggestion, you should be willing to act on it! With this in mind, I graciously decline opportunities to be a board member. Even at the age of 65, I still can't keep my mouth shut!

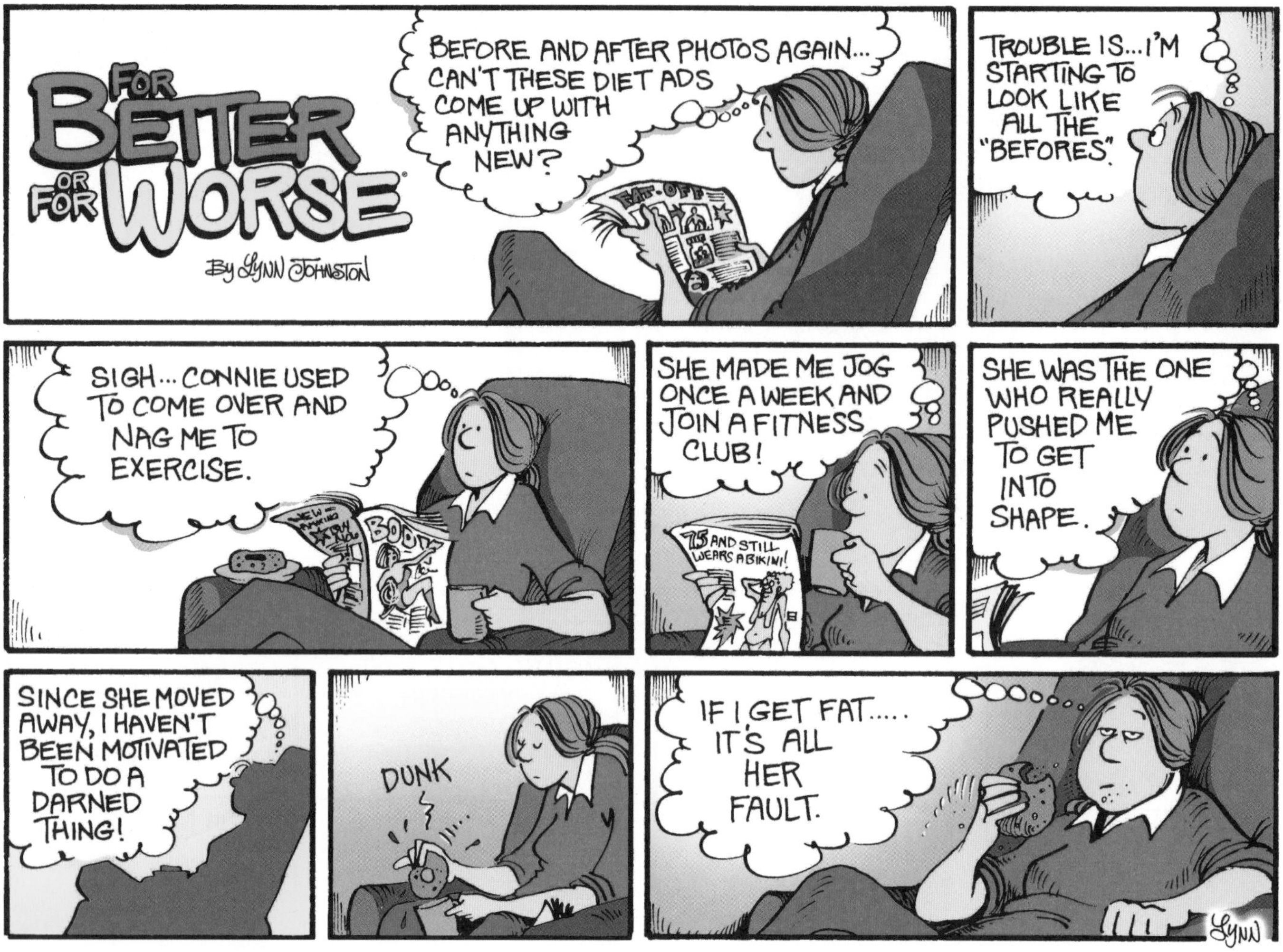
FOR BETTER OR FOR WORSE
BY LYNN JOHNSTON
BEFORE AND AFTER PHOTOS AGAIN... CAN'T THESE DIET ADS COME UP WITH ANYTHING NEW?
TROUBLE IS...I'M STARTING TO LOOK LIKE ALL THE "BEFORES."
SIGH... CONNIE USED TO COME OVER AND NAG ME TO EXERCISE.
SHE MADE ME JOG ONCE A WEEK AND JOIN A FITNESS CLUB!
75 AND STILL WEARS A BIKINI!
SHE WAS THE ONE WHO REALLY PUSHED ME TO GET INTO SHAPE.
SINCE SHE MOVED AWAY, I HAVEN'T BEEN MOTIVATED TO DO A DARNED THING!
DUNK
IF I GET FAT..... IT'S ALL HER FAULT.
LYNN

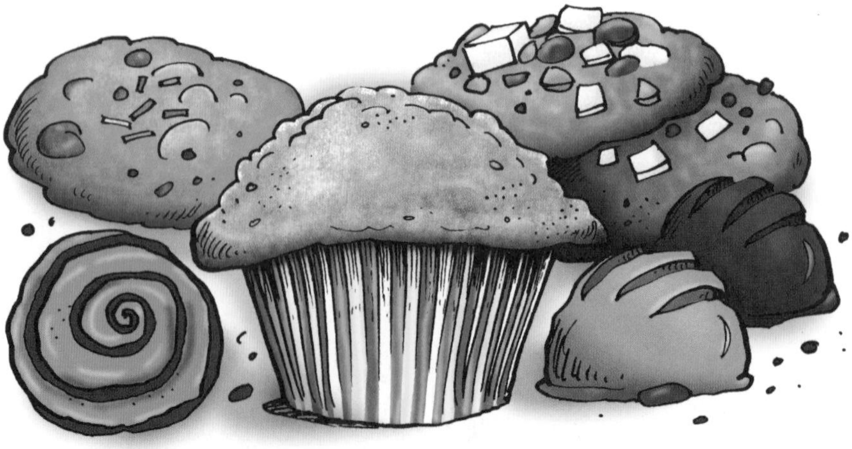

This was one of my father's "tricks of the trade." He had many ways to make tears disappear. He had stories and sayings and jokes and songs. He made faces, he danced and clowned — we had our own private vaudeville show complete with costumes, music, mime, and verse. He could be silly. He could delve into fantasy as easily as we could, and he saw things through our eyes, something few grown-ups have the imagination to do. Dad was like another kid who sometimes sided with us — against Mom. I remember her telling us and Dad to, "Please … GROW UP!!!"

My father and me, circa 1950. The back of this photo says, "Daddy & daughter setting out for the corner store where he will purchase a loaf of bread & get talked into buying a chocolate bar."

THE REASON YOUR JAW ACHES, TED, IS BECAUSE YOU'RE GRINDING YOUR TEETH AT NIGHT!

I CAN'T HELP IT, JOHN. I KEEP THINKING ABOUT CONNIE.

I CAN'T EAT, I CAN'T SLEEP..... I..... I'VE LOST 10 LBS. SINCE SHE MOVED AWAY!

BEATS DIETING!

FACE IT, TED. CONNIE IS GONE. YOU HAD YOUR CHANCE, AND IT'S OVER.

TROUBLE WITH YOU IS— YOU'RE SO AFRAID OF GETTING TRAPPED THE ONLY WOMEN YOU WANT ARE THE ONES YOU CAN'T HAVE!

YOU'RE A DENTIST! WHEN I WANT A PSYCHIATRIST—I'LL SEE ONE!!

GETTING YOU TO A PSYCHIATRIST WOULD BE LIKE PULLING TEETH!

YOU WON'T BELIEVE THIS, CONNIE! TED WANTS US TO TALK TO YOU ON HIS BEHALF!

HE SAYS HE WANTS YOU TO GIVE HIM ANOTHER CHANCE. HE SAYS HE CARES, AND HE NEEDS YOU....

ARE YOU SOFTENING? .... NO, HUH.

JOHN — COULD YOU PUT ON SOME VIOLINS?!

Farley was couch height; his face was perfectly aligned with yours if you were in repose. Should you then feel the smog of dog breath, hear the sound of heavy breathing, and smell kibble, it was not advisable to stir. Once you let Farley know you were conscious, he'd smother you with affection ... and drool!

ELLY, WAIT! CAN WE CATCH ANOTHER RIDE WITH YOU?

THIS IS SO CONVENIENT, YOU GOING DOWN-TOWN EVERY MORNING LIKE THIS!

SIT DOWN, BOYS, FEET OFF THE SEATS! NO SPITTING!

DON'T WORRY ABOUT THE GAS, ANNIE... YOU CAN PAY ME IN ASPIRIN!

ANOTHER DOCTOR'S APPOINTMENT? ARE YOU OK?

I GUESS I CAN'T KEEP IT A SECRET ANY LONGER, EL—I'M EXPECTING AGAIN!

SINCE WE'RE SUCH CLOSE NEIGHBORS... WE WANTED YOU TO BE THE FIRST TO KNOW.

YOU MIGHT WANT TO BUILD A HIGHER FENCE.

ANOTHER BABY! ANNE, THAT'S PRETTY EXCITING NEWS!

WE'RE HAPPY ABOUT IT—I LOVE BEING PREGNANT!

MY PREGNANCY WITH RICHARD WAS SO EASY!!

...IT'S THE ONLY TIME THE KID WAS EVER UNDER CONTROL!

ANNIE AND STEVE ARE GOING TO HAVE ANOTHER BABY?

YEAH. ANNIE SAYS IT'S AMAZING - SHE SEEMS TO GET PREGNANT AT THE DROP OF A HAT!

HOW DOES STEVE FEEL ABOUT ALL THIS?

HE SAYS HE'S GOING TO STOP WEARING HATS.

FAR OUT, MOM! HERE'S A LETTER FROM LAWRENCE!!

THEY'RE COMING HERE FOR CHRISTMAS!! HE AN' HIS MOM ARE COMING HOME!!!

CUT IT OUT, MICHAEL'! WHAT'S THE MATTER WIF YOU?

I'M HAVING A HAPPY ATTACK!!

CONNIE AND LAWRENCE WILL BE HERE, PHIL AND GEORGIA ARE COMING, MY FOLKS WILL BE HERE....

THIS IS GOING TO BE A BUSY HOLIDAY.

I'LL BE CLEANING AND COOKING AND ORGANIZING FOR A SOLID MONTH!

I HOPE THE NUMBER OF CALORIES I BURN OFF OVER CHRISTMAS ARE EQUAL TO THE NUMBER I TAKE IN!

Once again ... a true-to-life bit of stupidity became a Sunday strip. It was one of those things that made me say to myself, "What was I thinking? I KNEW that would happen!" Because these events made such good material, I was almost HAPPY to have done something silly! When I could use a situation, make fun of it, exaggerate it, draw all of the expressions, delve into the body language ... I was grateful! Knowing this, my kids would try to diminish a situation by saying, "Hey, you can use that in the strip!" Using the strip as an outlet was convenient. I didn't need a therapist; I just poured my thoughts into the ether and waited for the results to come back. Always, there was someone out there who felt the same way I did, someone had had the same experience exactly and could identify. Their letters were wonderful. There's nothing more comforting than knowing you're not alone!

I am someone who procrastinates until stuff HAS to be done. In order to force myself to do ironing, say, I give myself a deadline — I have learned from the strip that deadlines provide the pressure I need to produce. I'll invite friends for dinner at 6:00 on Saturday, for example, so I'll definitely have the kitchen clean by the time they get here. I'll promise someone an article of clothing, and then I HAVE to go through my closet. I'll have a garden party to force myself to weed my garden, and on it goes. This strip was done when I was in a panic. I had procrastinated for so long that I was late; my editor expected to get this strip several days beforehand, and if I didn't get it done ASAP, I'd be fined for missing my deadline. I wondered what in the world I would do for this Sunday page … and it hit me! Why not write about procrastination!

IT'LL BE SO NICE HAVING MY FOLKS HERE, JOHN. WE HAVEN'T SEEN THEM FOR ALMOST A YEAR!

IT SCARES ME. EVERY TIME I SEE THEM, THEY LOOK OLDER.

I DON'T MIND **ME** GETTING OLDER....

—BUT I WANT THEM TO STAY THE SAME!

At this time, my parents lived in Hope, British Columbia. To get to North Bay was quite a haul: a two-hour drive to Vancouver, a flight to Toronto, and another to North Bay. With two kids, it was even more hassle for us to go to them. The few times we did get together for Christmas were much-celebrated events.

I THINK WE'LL GIVE MY FOLKS OUR ROOM, JOHN —AND WE'LL TAKE THE FAMILY ROOM.
OK.

THEY'D LIKE THEIR PRIVACY, AND BESIDES, IT'LL BE FUN CAMPING OUT ON THE OLD COUCH.
SURE. FINE.

I LOVE YOU, JOHN— YOU'RE SO FLEXIBLE!!

IT HELPS...WHEN YOU HAVE TO "BEND OVER BACKWARD" ...

We were fortunate to have enough space that we didn't have to reorganize our sleeping arrangements. The game of musical beds was, however, good fodder for the strip.

WE'RE GONNA DO A PLAY, DADDY— AN' GUESS WHAT! I GET TO BE THE STAR!!

SHERRILEE GETS TO BE THE VERGING MARY, GERARD GETS TO BE JOSEPH, THE TWINS AN' KELLEY ARE THE 3 KINGS, JAIME IS A SHEPHERD, BECKY AN' MATT ARE COWS....

WAIT A MINUTE! YOU SAID YOU WERE A STAR!

I AM! I GET TO HOLD A FLASHLIGHT ON A STICK!!

Some of the names used here were Katie's friends. Other were kids that had bullied her at school because of the strip, so this was a way to include the local children and show that we wanted to include everyone we could, whenever possible.

164

WE'RE DOIN' THE CHRISTMAS STORY, CHRISTOPHER—AN' I GET TO BE THE STAR OF BETHLEHEM!

MISS LYON SAYS THAT ALL THE KIDS WHO ARE KINGS AN' SHEPHERDS HAFTA WEAR THEIR 'JAMAS AN' BATH ROBES!

HOW COME?

TSK! DON'T YOU KNOW ANYTHING?!!

...IT HAPPENED AT NIGHT, DIDN'T IT?!!

I think I was in grade three when I was cast in a school Christmas pageant as a wise person. I was told to wear my bathrobe as a costume, but my mom was so upset by its frayed condition that she hurriedly made me a new one out of striped material — much like the robes worn in Christian-Hollywood flicks. Though my behaviour wasn't particularly saintly, I wore my pageant bathrobe for years, pretending I was right out of the Bible!

MOM, CAN CHRIS STAY FOR SUPPER?

I DON'T KNOW, HONEY... I...

WHAT ARE WE HAVING?

UM...THERE'S A BIT OF STEW, A BIT OF CORN, SOME LEFT-OVER RICE CASSEROLE AND....

MOM? CAN I GO TO CHRISTOPHER'S HOUSE FOR SUPPER?

LOOK, THE PLANE ISN'T GOING TO COME ANY FASTER BY YOU TWO ACTING WILD AND SILLY — SO SETTLE DOWN!!

BUT WE WANNA SEE GRANDMA AN' GRAMPA! HOW COME THEY'RE TAKING SO LONG GETTING HERE?

GATE 76

I DON'T KNOW. MAYBE THE WEATHER'S BAD...MAYBE THEIR FLIGHT WAS DELAYED...

—MAYBE THEY KNOW WHAT THEY'RE IN FOR!

I used this family photograph when I did this series. It was taken in Ruth and Tom's living room when my folks came all the way to Lynn Lake for Christmas, early 1980s. Because everyone was in the picture, I used this as a reference for years until we had all grown older and our faces had changed.

Standing in the back (L to R): Rod and Katie; Rod's father, Tom, and cousin Chrissy; Uncle Don and cousin Lauren.
Seated: my father, Merv; me; Rod's mother, Ruth; my mom, Ursula; Rod's sister Beth; my brother Al; and Aaron on the floor.

166

YOUR ROOM? BUT, ELLY!

—WE'D BE PERFECTLY FINE IN THE FAMILY ROOM ON THE SOFA!

OH, MOM! I COULDN'T HAVE YOU SLEEP THERE!

WHY NOT?

'CAUSE THIS IS THE ROOM SHE CLEANED!

I USED TO SIT AND READ TO YOUR MOM LIKE THIS FOR HOURS, ELIZABETH.

THEN, ONE DAY, JUST LIKE MAGIC.... EVERYTHING CHANGED.

SHE GREW UP?!!

NO.

WE BOUGHT A TELEVISION.

LOOK, I SAID — UPSTAIRS! IN BED! NOW!!

NO FAIR! I GET TO STAY UP LONGER THAN LIZZIE, AN' YOU'RE MAKING US GO TO BED AT THE SAME TIME!!

REMEMBER WHEN WE WERE YOUNG PARENTS WITH SMALL CHILDREN, DEAR?

UH-HUH.

...AND I WOULDN'T GO BACK FOR THE WORLD!

167

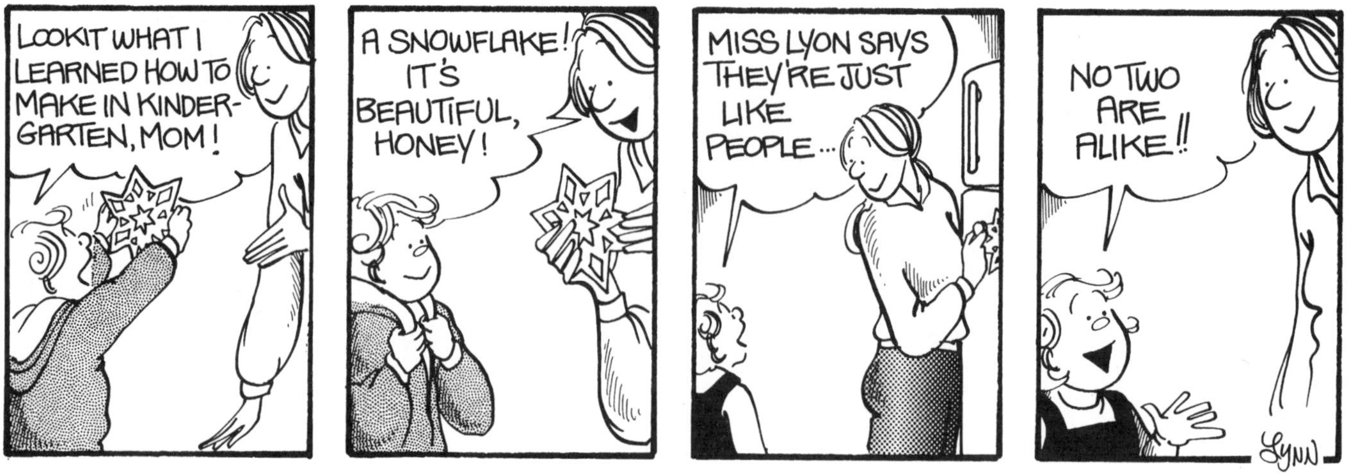
LOOKIT WHAT I LEARNED HOW TO MAKE IN KINDER-GARTEN, MOM!
A SNOWFLAKE! IT'S BEAUTIFUL, HONEY!
MISS LYON SAYS THEY'RE JUST LIKE PEOPLE...
NO TWO ARE ALIKE!!
LYNN

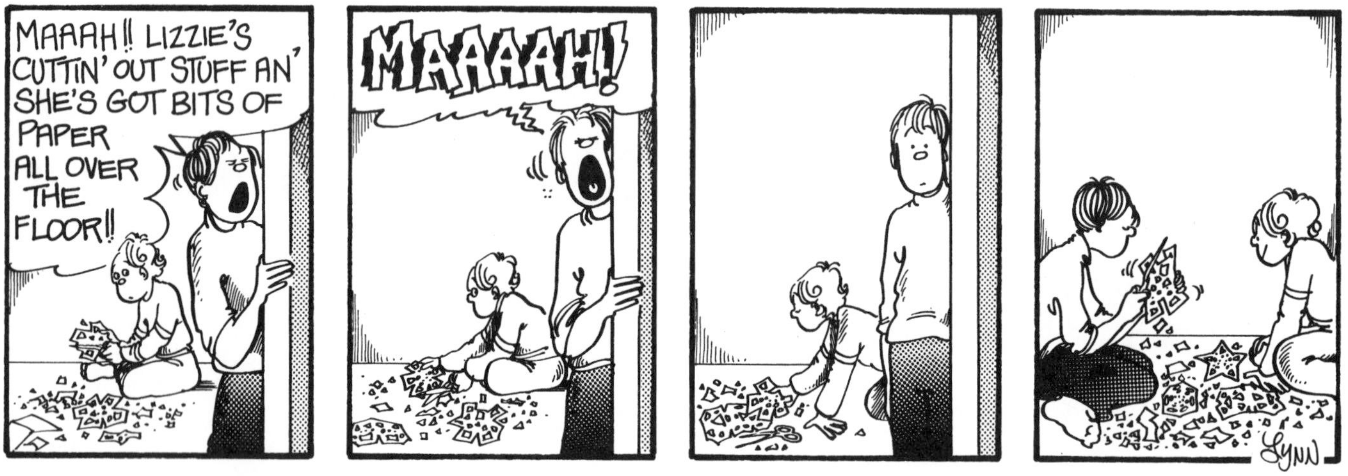
MAAAH!! LIZZIE'S CUTTIN' OUT STUFF AN' SHE'S GOT BITS OF PAPER ALL OVER THE FLOOR!!
MAAAAH!
LYNN

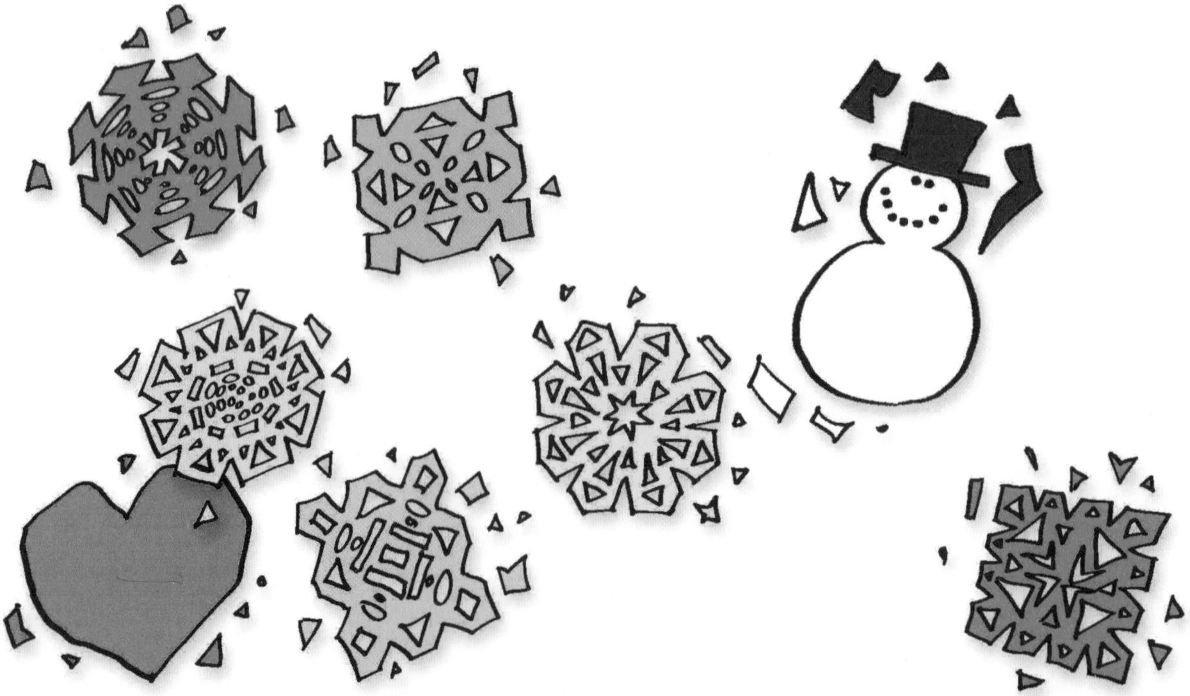

Dear Everyone! ......

AAGH! NO! IT'S NOT... NOT one of those horrible, Xeroxed CHRISTMAS NEWSLETTERS?!!!

After a year (& A BIT) of living in Corbeil, I think we are finally beginning to feel at home (we're clued in to the more colorful gossip & have met most of the neighbors... Rod regularly takes coffee to the dump lady, but has been overshadowed by Gary Barham from the marina who took her a beer) recently.

Rod is now supervising the dental hygiene & assisting program at Canadore College .... & has become accustomed to wearing the odd tie...

30 young, lovely girls....
30 young, lovely girls....
30 young, lovely girls.....

Aaron & Kate have taken to swimming and are working their way up the YMCA LADDER

← ODD TIE. (he has another one for good).

Aaron is still immersed in computer logic. We hope that at some time he will immerse himself in bathwater. (annually is not enough.)

The Yule "special" was completed with much hoopla & advertising & ran on Dec. 9TH. We're all relieved to have it over & done with ... but it was a wonderful year! With some time on my hands, I enrolled in flying lessons. "If the bozos we met up north can do it, then so can I!"... I've since taken my hat off to the bozos.

Katie is a Brownie ... & struggling thru piano lessons. She has some good chums & loves school.

Both have decisions made about their futures. Aaron wants to go into broadcasting ... Kate wants to be a dentist. This week.

look out Red Baron!

Willie the dog discovered an affinity for skunks. Twice. For some reason he still lives here.

That was 1985... Everyone here is well and happy and...

Wishing you all a happy holiday and all the best in the new year!!

Lynn, Rod, Aaron AND Katie J.

Our family newsletter, 1985.

A recall card for Sharper Cards.

This strip was missing for some reason. All we had in our archives was the newspaper clipping below, and it had been edited down to fit into smaller format. Eventually, we did get our hands on a print with the top panels included. I redrew the whole thing (so Kevin could do the colouring and send it to the syndicate) and took the liberty of changing the punch line. What I wanted to do was connect "rat race" and "running through a maze" (like a mouse) with CHEESE! The original punch was weak. I mean, other than a rodent, who makes a meal out of just cheese? I think the new ending works better, but it's still a stretch! This is an example of when I had a workable idea but couldn't quite figure out how to word it!

171

I DON'T BELIEVE HOW MUCH I'VE SPENT ON CHRISTMAS ALREADY!

I'VE TRIED TO STAY WITHIN A BUDGET, BUT THINGS ARE SO EXPENSIVE!

WHY DON'T YOU ASK SANTA TO BRING ALL THE CHRISTMAS PRESENTS?!

THEN IT WOULDN'T COST YOU ANYTHING!

TELL GRAMPA HE'S WRONG! THERE'S STILL SOOT IN THE FIREPLACE!

One of our traditions at Christmas was to clean out the fireplace. This was a good thing. We'd have forgotten otherwise. This is a pretty accurate illustration of our living room in Lynn Lake ... complete with the crud on the rug.

DADDY, DO WE HAFTA WAIT 'TILL GRANDMA AND GRAMPA GET UP BEFORE WE CAN OPEN UP OUR PRESENTS TOMORROW?

OF COURSE YOU DO! YOU KNOW THE OLD SAYING....

AGE BEFORE BOOTY!!

BESIDES YOUR FOLKS, WHO ELSE WILL BE HERE ON THE 25TH, ELLY?

UM... PHIL, GEORGIA, CONNIE, LAWRENCE — MAYBE CONNIE'S FOLKS, ANNIE, STEVE AND THE KIDS, MRS. BAIRD....

LET'S JUST SAY IT'S GOING TO BE A GOOD OLD-FASHIONED CHRISTMAS!

ABSOLUTE CHAOS!

... AND LET THE SPIRIT OF GIVING AND GOOD WILL BE WITH US, NOT FOR JUST THIS DAY, BUT...

AWK! BUCK-BUCK-BUCK! AWK! BUCK-BUCK-BUCK

This is something that didn't happen but should have. Brought up in the Anglican Church, I endured countless hours sitting through painfully dull sermons and kneeling as the litany droned on. I would have given anything to see a kid launch a toy down the aisle ... and I'm sure the adults would have appreciated it, too!

SORRY, I...UH...CAN'T QUITE FIGURE OUT HOW TO WORK THIS CASH REGISTER

SIGH...THIS CLERK IS INCREDIBLE!

HMM—FROSTY PRUNE LIP-LUSHER! GEE, I DUNNO IF I'VE GOT THIS IN STOCK!

YES, YOU DO—IN THAT CABINET OVER THERE!

SHE'S ONLY WORKED HERE TWO MONTHS...HOW SHOULD SHE KNOW?

HAH. CAN'T EVEN FILL OUT A SALES RECEIPT!

MAYBE YOU NEED A LOBOTOMY TO WORK IN THIS PLACE!

MA'AM? EXCUSE ME, MA'AM?

YOU FORGOT YOUR PEN, YOUR GLOVES, AND YOUR CHECKBOOK!

I have always had fun with sound effects and radio broadcasts, labels and names. Jim Borecki is the name of a good friend, with whom I have lost touch. I tried to contact him by putting his name in this strip, but so far I have not been able to find him.

It was fun to give Connie a new look. A big change in your life affects you mentally and physically, and it seemed to me that after ridding herself of the annoying Ted, Connie was renewed, refreshed, and recharged.

It seemed right to have Ted arrive, to see his lost love feeling great and looking spectacular.

That wonderful Joni Mitchell song, which goes, "Don't it always seem to go that you don't know what you've got 'til it's gone," went through my head as I drew this strip.

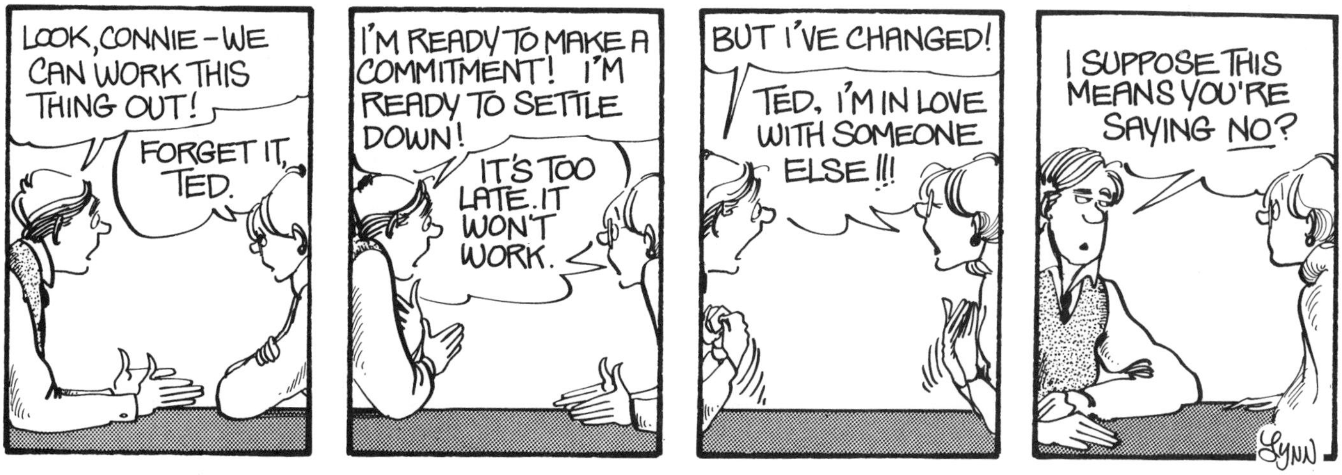
LOOK, CONNIE - WE CAN WORK THIS THING OUT!
FORGET IT, TED.
I'M READY TO MAKE A COMMITMENT! I'M READY TO SETTLE DOWN!
IT'S TOO LATE. IT WON'T WORK.
BUT I'VE CHANGED!
TED, I'M IN LOVE WITH SOMEONE ELSE!!!
I SUPPOSE THIS MEANS YOU'RE SAYING NO?
LYNN

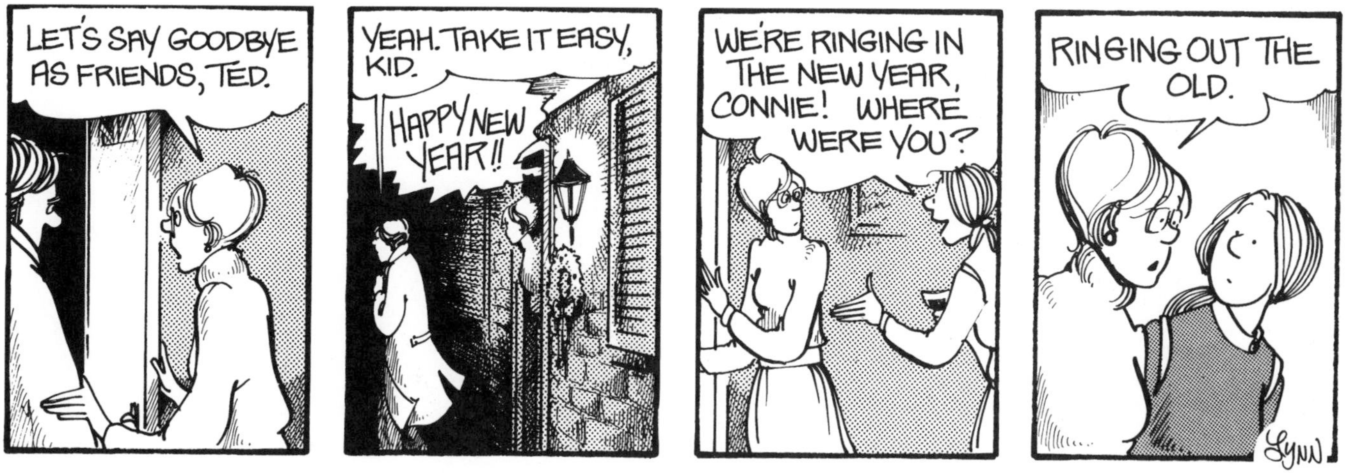
LET'S SAY GOODBYE AS FRIENDS, TED.
YEAH. TAKE IT EASY, KID.
HAPPY NEW YEAR!!
WE'RE RINGING IN THE NEW YEAR, CONNIE! WHERE WERE YOU?
RINGING OUT THE OLD.
LYNN

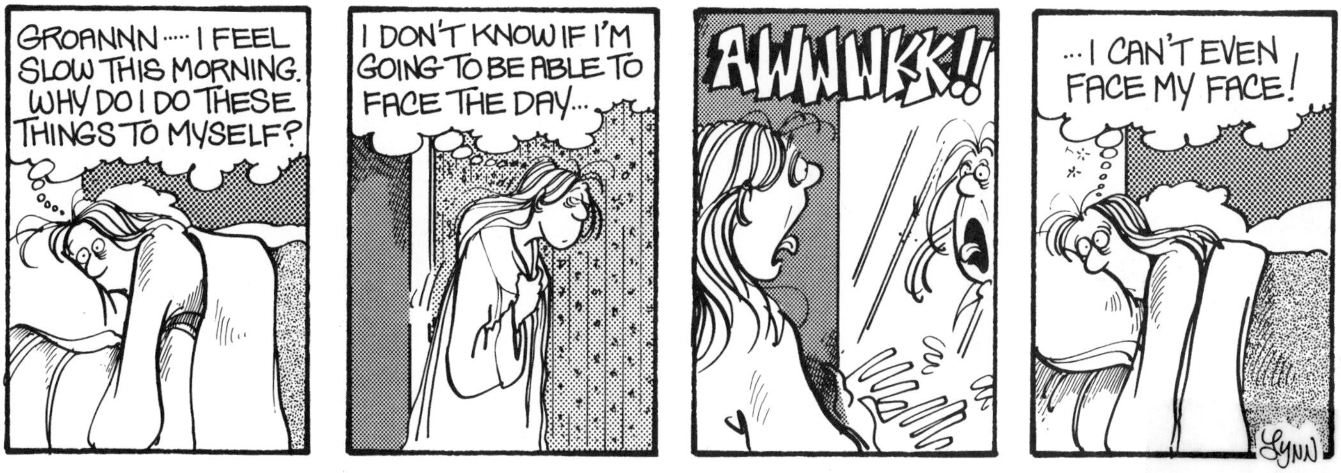
GROANNN..... I FEEL SLOW THIS MORNING. WHY DO I DO THESE THINGS TO MYSELF?
I DON'T KNOW IF I'M GOING TO BE ABLE TO FACE THE DAY...
AWWWKK!!
...I CAN'T EVEN FACE MY FACE!
LYNN

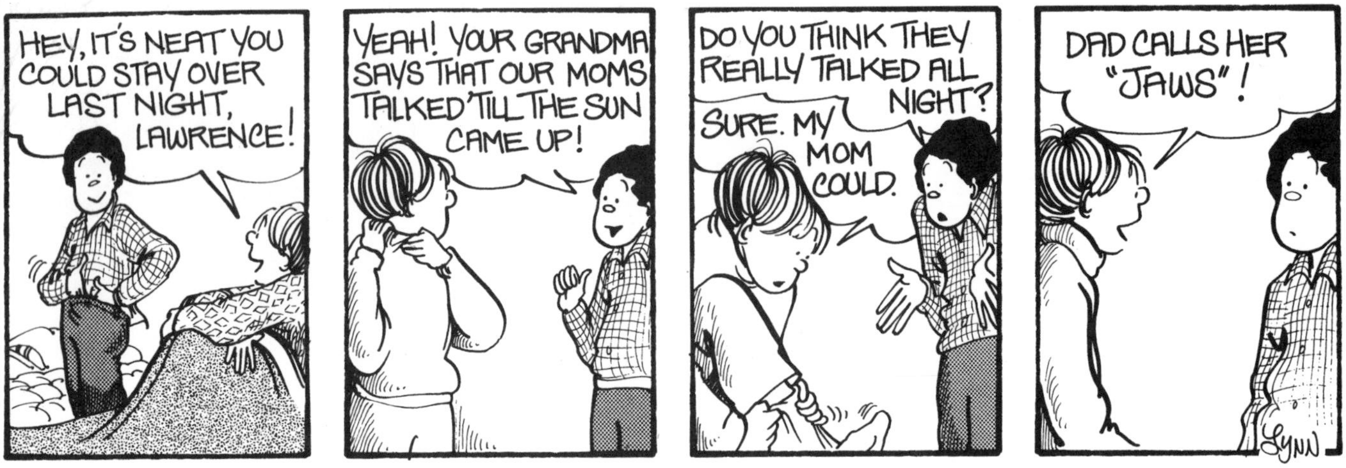
HEY, IT'S NEAT YOU COULD STAY OVER LAST NIGHT, LAWRENCE!
YEAH! YOUR GRANDMA SAYS THAT OUR MOMS TALKED 'TILL THE SUN CAME UP!
DO YOU THINK THEY REALLY TALKED ALL NIGHT?
SURE. MY MOM COULD.
DAD CALLS HER "JAWS"!
LYNN

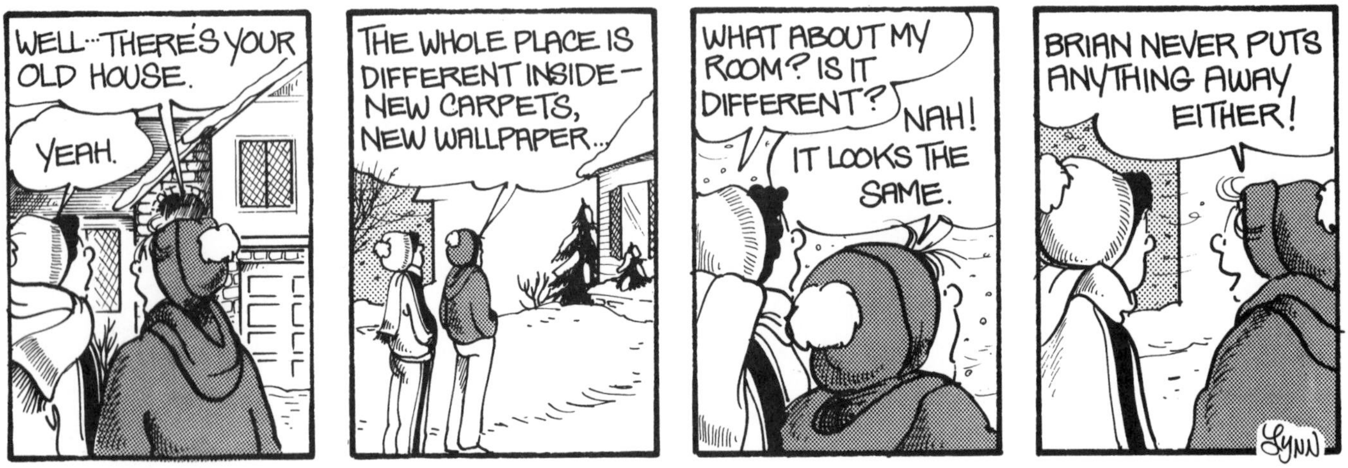
WELL... THERE'S YOUR OLD HOUSE.
YEAH.
THE WHOLE PLACE IS DIFFERENT INSIDE — NEW CARPETS, NEW WALLPAPER...
WHAT ABOUT MY ROOM? IS IT DIFFERENT?
NAH! IT LOOKS THE SAME.
BRIAN NEVER PUTS ANYTHING AWAY EITHER!
LYNN

I tried to imagine what it would be like for Lawrence to stand outside his old house in a neighbourhood that he loved. He must have felt a sense of loss and confusion. Children have no choice when it comes to enormous decisions like moving, so I assumed he would stand there, wondering why he was now living somewhere else!

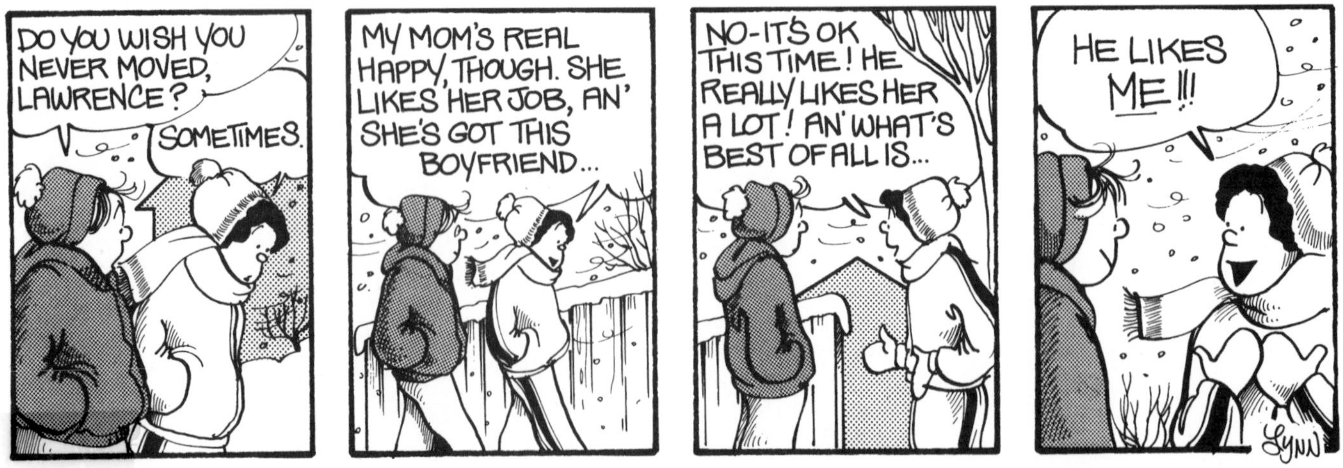
DO YOU WISH YOU NEVER MOVED, LAWRENCE?
SOMETIMES.
MY MOM'S REAL HAPPY, THOUGH. SHE LIKES HER JOB, AN' SHE'S GOT THIS BOYFRIEND...
NO-IT'S OK THIS TIME! HE REALLY LIKES HER A LOT! AN' WHAT'S BEST OF ALL IS...
HE LIKES ME!!!
LYNN

Having someone new come into a family is an enormous adjustment. Aaron and I had been a team before I married Rod — and even though Rod adopted Aaron and gave him his last name, their personalities were never really compatible. I wanted Lawrence and Connie's story to be a happy one — one in which everyone adapted and the relationships worked. Having this kind of control over their lives was like playing God!

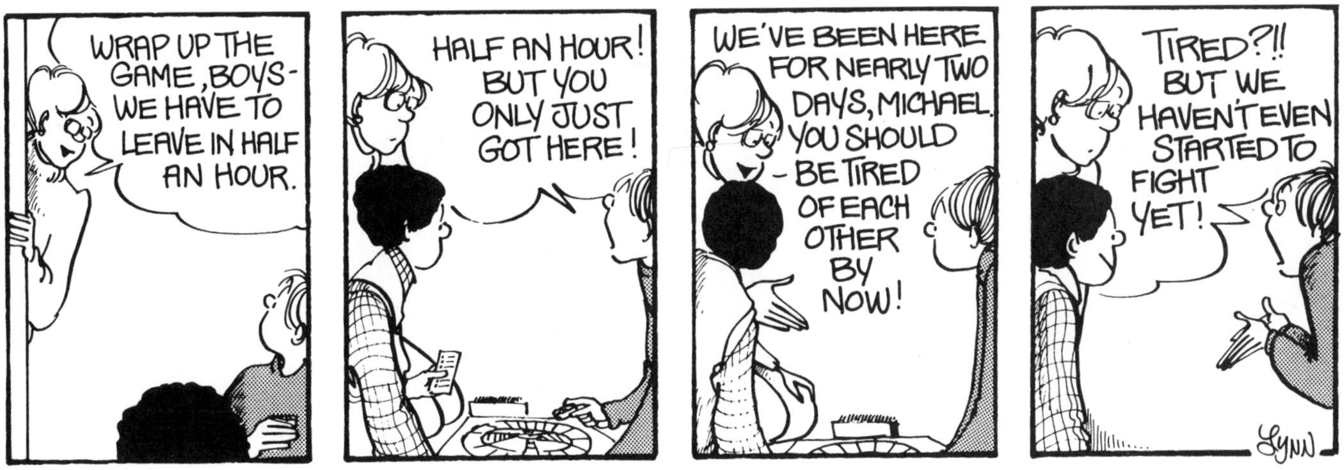
WRAP UP THE GAME, BOYS - WE HAVE TO LEAVE IN HALF AN HOUR.
HALF AN HOUR! BUT YOU ONLY JUST GOT HERE!
WE'VE BEEN HERE FOR NEARLY TWO DAYS, MICHAEL. YOU SHOULD BE TIRED OF EACH OTHER BY NOW!
TIRED?!! BUT WE HAVEN'T EVEN STARTED TO FIGHT YET!
LYNN

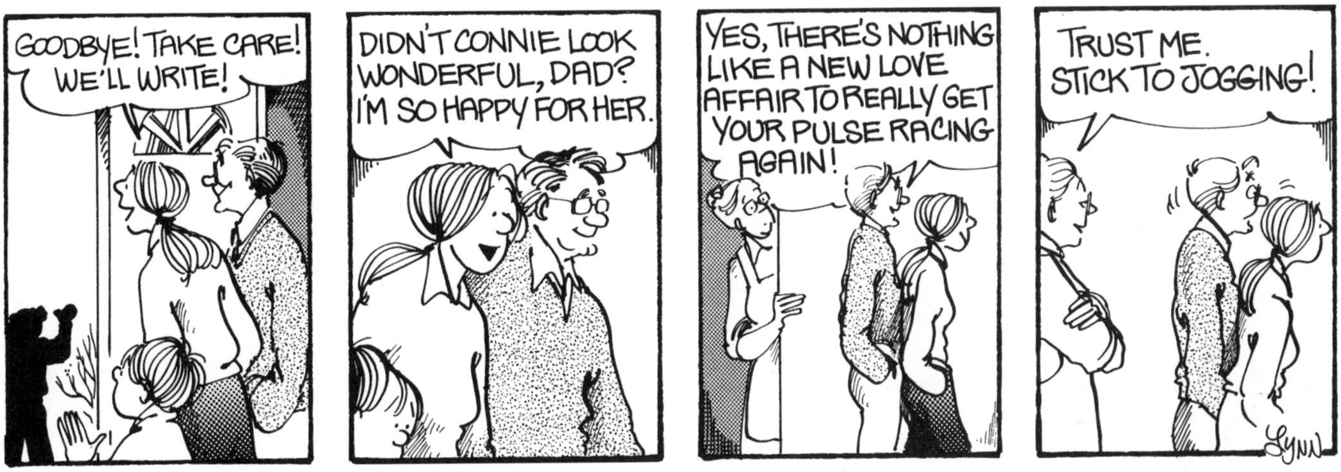
GOODBYE! TAKE CARE! WE'LL WRITE!
DIDN'T CONNIE LOOK WONDERFUL, DAD? I'M SO HAPPY FOR HER.
YES, THERE'S NOTHING LIKE A NEW LOVE AFFAIR TO REALLY GET YOUR PULSE RACING AGAIN!
TRUST ME. STICK TO JOGGING!
LYNN

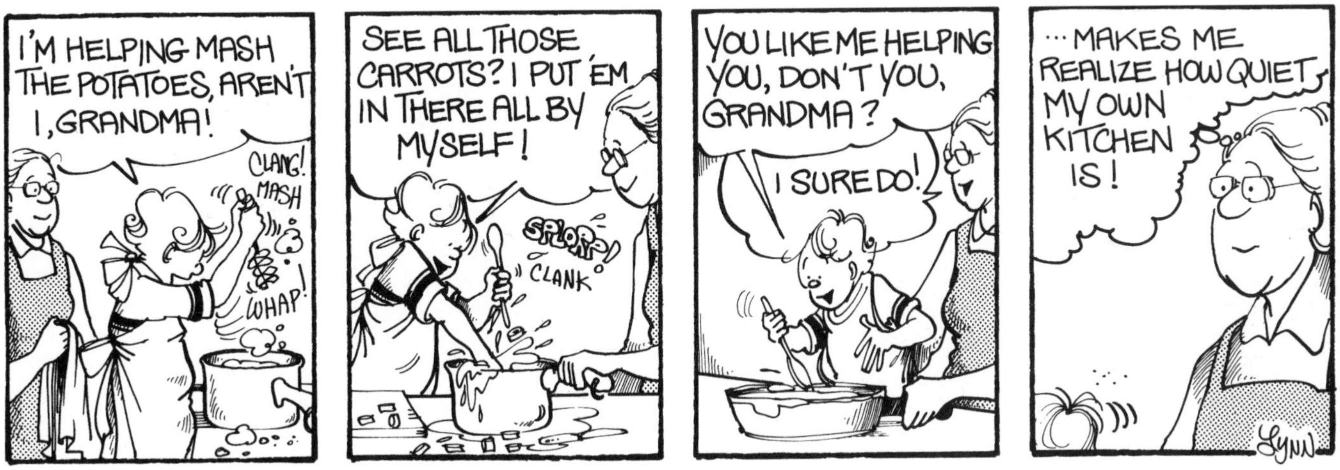
I'M HELPING MASH THE POTATOES, AREN'T I, GRANDMA!
CLANG! MASH
WHAP!
SEE ALL THOSE CARROTS? I PUT 'EM IN THERE ALL BY MYSELF!
SPLOP!
CLANK
YOU LIKE ME HELPING YOU, DON'T YOU, GRANDMA?
I SURE DO!
... MAKES ME REALIZE HOW QUIET MY OWN KITCHEN IS!
LYNN

WOW! ANOTHER SUPER MEAL? MOM, THIS LOOKS FANTASTIC!!

COME NOW, DEAR. OUR ELLY MAKES WONDERFUL DINNERS!

ARE YOU KIDDING?!! WE HAVEN'T EATEN LIKE THIS SINCE THE FREEZER BROKE DOWN!!

This is a true story. The freezer didn't break down, but it did have to be moved and therefore defrosted. I pulled out an archive of forgotten leftovers, summer fruit and fishing acquisitions, dry pie crusts, soup stock, and more. Some of this was still recognizable, so a mess of reconstituted fodder graced our plates for a week or two. People actually ate what I served — and the freezer was then refilled with the leftovers from the leftovers. We recycle.

MOM, YOU HAVE TO STOP DOING ALL THIS BAKING — I'M REALLY GAINING WEIGHT!

NONSENSE, DEAR. YOU'RE NOT OVER-WEIGHT!

AN ENVELOPE JUST CAME IN THE MAIL, MOM — MUST BE FOR YOU.

IT SAYS "BULK".

TELL ME A STORY ABOUT THE WAR, GRAMPA!

WELL...ONE NIGHT, AFTER A FEW BREWS AT THE LOCAL PUB, SOME OF THE BOYS AND I DECIDED TO STAGE A PANTY RAID ON...

NO, I WANNA HEAR ABOUT THE BOMBS AN' GUNS AN' FIGHTING!!

DON'T YOU REMEMBER ANY OF THE GOOD STUFF?!!

My dad talked a lot about the war, and any time the subject came up in the strip, I received letters from veterans happy to see it mentioned.

Aaron and my dad had a hard time playing board games. Aaron wanted to learn and Dad wanted to teach him, but they both wanted to win!

181

I have always loved making up names on things like cereal boxes. In art school, one of the things we had to do for commercial design was to come up with an entire cereal box — from the size to the ingredients to the illustration on the cover. This meant we had to figure out how much space we needed for type (in two official languages): brand name, logos, contents, weight, nutritional value, and directions. Packaging is a whole industry of its own, so this was a really good exercise. The cereal I came up with was "Sugar Soggs." The art showed a kid eating some gruesome candy-coated gruel. It was okay, but the best design was done by one of the guys in the class; he called his cereal "Uncle Brian's Grumpies." On the cover was a grimacing caricature of the instructor, whose name was Brian, and the ingredients he made up were hilarious. In terms of funny, he had me beat by a mile. Neither of us got a good mark because we hadn't taken the project seriously. It seemed to us that despite the prof's objections, cartoons do sell!

Later, when I worked for Standard Engravers, a packaging firm in Hamilton, Ontario, I was given the opportunity to design a giveaway on a cereal box. I thought this would be neat, until I was given a space about 2 inches square on the bottom right corner. This was a real challenge — and that's good. If you give a cartoonist or graphic artist a blank page and say "draw something," they have to think for a while. Give them a tiny, awkward space, and suddenly the ideas come out of the blue. A great example of this is Sergio Aragones' "marginals" — the tiny cartoons that tumble around the page borders in *Mad* magazine. When he suggested he be hired to do these, he was told that he'd run out of ideas. Some 45 years later, he's still producing them, and each one is wonderfully different.

For the small corner space on the cereal box, I designed finger puppets, pencil toppers, decals, and "spinners" (a top made from paper). It was fun. I thought this could be a surprisingly satisfying career, but things went in other directions. I still get to work on cereal boxes but in a different way!

I never went shopping with my husband; having a man wait patiently, or impatiently, while I peruse a dress shop would be horrible! I would have to rush, which would take away from the true shopping experience. Whenever I see some sad chap sitting uncomfortably outside the change room in some frou-frou boutique, my heart goes out to him. I want to say, "Get off your duff, go do something YOU want to do, and meet her somewhere else!" This strip was done in solidarity with those who shop and those who wait.

BOY, IT'S HARD TO HAVE OTHER PEOPLE LIVING WITH YOU! (CLAMP.)

I WANT MY OWN BED! I WANT TO BE ABLE TO WALK TO THE BATHROOM IN MY SHORTS!! (EXPLORER)

I LOVE MY IN-LAWS, BUT THE TENSION IS DRIVING ME CRAZY. BZZZZ ZZZZ ZZ

...IT'S A GOOD THING I CAN TAKE OUT MY FRUSTRATIONS ON MY WORK!

WHAT IS IT, JOHN? IT'S TED. HE NEVER SHOWED UP FOR WORK AT THE MED CENTER TODAY.

I KNEW HE'D BEEN ACTING STRANGELY LATELY, BUT....

BREAKING UP WITH CONNIE WAS AWFULLY HARD ON HIM— HOW'S HE TAKING IT?

HE'S JUST MARRIED HIS SECRETARY !!!

AFTER THEIR DIVORCE, CONNIE'S FIRST HUSBAND WENT BACK TO SOUTH AMERICA, AND CONNIE STARTED TO DATE PHIL....

SHE BROKE UP WITH PHIL TO DATE TED, BUT TED BROKE UP WITH HER WHEN SHE WANTED TO GET MARRIED...

AFTER SHE MOVED NORTH TED WANTED HER BACK, BUT SHE SAID NO— SO, HE MARRIED HIS SECRETARY!

ELLY DOESN'T GOSSIP. SHE GIVES CASE HISTORIES.

Here's a strip that was written with the express purpose of letting the readers know what was going on behind the scenes.

MOM, I CAN'T FIND MY CASSEROLES.

I PUT THEM DOWN HERE, DEAR.

WHERE ARE MY POT HOLDERS AND OVEN MITTS?

IN THIS DRAWER!

MOM—YOU HAVE RE-ARRANGED MY ENTIRE KITCHEN!

I KNOW.

IT MAKES IT SO MUCH EASIER TO FIND EVERY-THING!

SIT DOWN, DEAR — HAVE A CUP OF TEA.

I DON'T WANT A CUP OF TEA — I WANT TO DO SOMETHING!!

YOU'RE NOT SUPPOSED TO DO ANYTHING, DAD — YOU'RE ON HOLIDAY!

I'M RETIRED, ELLY!— MY WHOLE LIFE IS A HOLIDAY!!

LET'S SEE.. GRANDPA'S FIXED THE SINK, THE TOWEL RACK, THE GARAGE DOOR, THE HALL CLOCK...

HE LOOKS BORED. I WISH I HAD SOME-THING ELSE FOR HIM TO FIX.... BUT I DON'T.

HEY, MOM— WANT ME TO BREAK SOMETHING?!!

WHERE'S GRANDPA?

UP IN THE ATTIC. HE SAID WE DIDN'T HAVE ENOUGH INSULATION.

THAT'S CRAZY. DAD? DAD!!!

AAAAAH CHOOOH!

DON'T YOU EVER DUST UP HERE?

MOM, WHY IN THE WORLD WOULD DAD WANT TO INSPECT OUR INSULATION?

HE'S TRACKING DUST ALL OVER THE PLACE, THERE'S FIBERGLASS IN THE CARPETS...

WELL, YOU KNOW YOUR FATHER, DEAR....

HE LIKES TO BE USEFUL!

CRAACK!

CRUMBLE!

MOMMY! MOM! COME QUICK! GRAMPA'S IN THE ATTIC!!

I KNOW, DEAR.

BUT HIS FOOT IS IN MY ROOM!!

This story was told to me by our good friend Larry Boland. We were sitting in his living room. His wife, Marilyn, was bringing in the tea, when I looked up and admired their lovely ceiling. Marilyn smiled and said that thanks to Larry, it had just been redone. Larry described putting his foot through the plaster with such detail that I had to put the story in the strip. Things people WANTED me to include rarely made the grade. I preferred the embarrassing stuff!

186

OH, MY GOSH-- DAD! ARE YOU ALL RIGHT?

*G☆!¢

GO GET THE OTHER FLASHLIGHT, MICHAEL! I'M GOING INTO THE ATTIC.

I CAN'T REACH YOU. I'LL HAVE TO BRING UP SOME PLYWOOD.

TSK, TSK... AND IN HIS GOOD PANTS, TOO!

GET YOUR OTHER KNEE ONTO THE PLYWOOD, DAD...

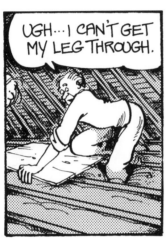

UGH... I CAN'T GET MY LEG THROUGH.

MAYBE IF I TOOK YOUR SHOE OFF, DEAR!

BOY, THAT'S THE UGLIEST CHANDELIER I EVER SAW!

OOOH!

WHAT HAPPENED?

DAD WENT INTO THE ATTIC AND... UH... PUT HIS FOOT THROUGH THE CEILING.

ELLY, HOW ON EARTH AM I GOING TO FIX A HOLE LIKE THAT?

WE COULD HANG A PICTURE OVER IT!

WHAT WAS YOUR DAD DOING IN THE ATTIC ANYWAY?

CHECKING THE INSULATION.

DON'T GET SO UPSET, JOHN – THERE'S A GOOD SIDE TO EVERYTHING.

YOUR FATHER PUTS HIS FOOT THROUGH THE CEILING? WHAT COULD POSSIBLY BE GOOD ABOUT THAT?!

THE INSULATION IS FINE!

THERE. WE'VE PUT A PLASTIC COVER OVER THE HOLE, ELIZABETH.

A CONTRACTOR WILL BE HERE TO FIX IT TOMORROW.

IT'S RIGHT OVER YOUR BED, LIZZIE. ALL THE BOOGIE MEN IN THE ATTIC WILL BE ABLE TO CRAWL INTO YOUR ROOM TONIGHT!

MIKE, YOU HAVE JUST VOLUNTEERED TO SWITCH ROOMS!

DUMB HOLE IN THE CEILING CAN'T BOTHER ME ... THERE'S NO SUCH THING AS BOOGIE MEN.

WHISTLLLEEEE FWEEEEO°°OOO°°° WSHHHHHH

WELL ·· I WONDER HOW MICHAEL'S MANAGING TO SLEEP IN THAT ROOM TONIGHT!

YOU DIDN'T MEAN TO CAUSE ANY DAMAGE, DEAR — YOU WERE JUST TRYING TO HELP.

ELLY AND JOHN AREN'T ANGRY. ANYBODY COULD HAVE PUT THEIR FOOT THROUGH THE CEILING!

WHY ARE YOU SO ANGRY WITH YOURSELF?

SOMEBODY'S GOT TO BE ANGRY WITH ME !!!

WHATCHA DOING, GRAM?

WAKING UP GRANDPA.

PERK PERK SIZZLE

FLAP FLAP!

SNIFF? SNEEEFFFFF!!

AWESOME!

I once saw my mother-in-law flapping her apron at the top of the basement stairs. I asked her what in the world she was doing, and she explained that the menfolk were in the middle of a project down there and she wanted them to come up for dinner. She was wafting the smell of roast beef, mash, and gravy down into the basement. It worked!

ELIZABETH— COME OUT OF THAT SUITCASE !!

OH, DEAR—WE'RE LEAVING TONIGHT AND NOW YOU'VE MESSED EVERYTHING ALL UP!

WHY DID YOU GO AND DO A THING LIKE THAT?

I WANTED TO COME WIF YOU!

WHY COULDN'T WE GO WITH GRANDMA AN' GRAMPA TO THE AIRPORT?

MOM SAID THERE JUST WASN'T ENOUGH ROOM IN THE CAR.

BESIDES, IT'S EASIER THIS WAY. OUR FAMILY DOESN'T GO FOR LONG, DRAWN-OUT, TEARFUL FAREWELLS.

FINAL CALL FOR FLIGHT 183 TO VANCOUVER... GATE 76

THE PLASTERER IS HERE TO FINISH YOUR CEILING, ELIZABETH!

SEE? HE'S GOING TO MAKE A PATTERN WITH A LITTLE BROOM!

COULD YOU MAKE THE CIRCLES LARGER? HOW ABOUT SOME STIPPLING? I'D LIKE A BORDER AND...

LADY! YOU THINK DIS IS MAYBE THE SISTINE CHAPEL?!!

HOLY SMOKES!! ALL THAT TO FIX A CEILING?!!

BILL

WELL, WHILE THE CONTRACTOR WAS HERE, I GOT HIM TO DO SOME PAINTING, FIX THE CLOSET, WALLPAPER THE STAIR-WELL...

JOHN- IT WAS A GREAT OPPORTUNITY!!

EVERY TIME OPPORTUNITY KNOCKS ... I HAVE TO OPEN MY CHECKBOOK TO LET IT IN.

190

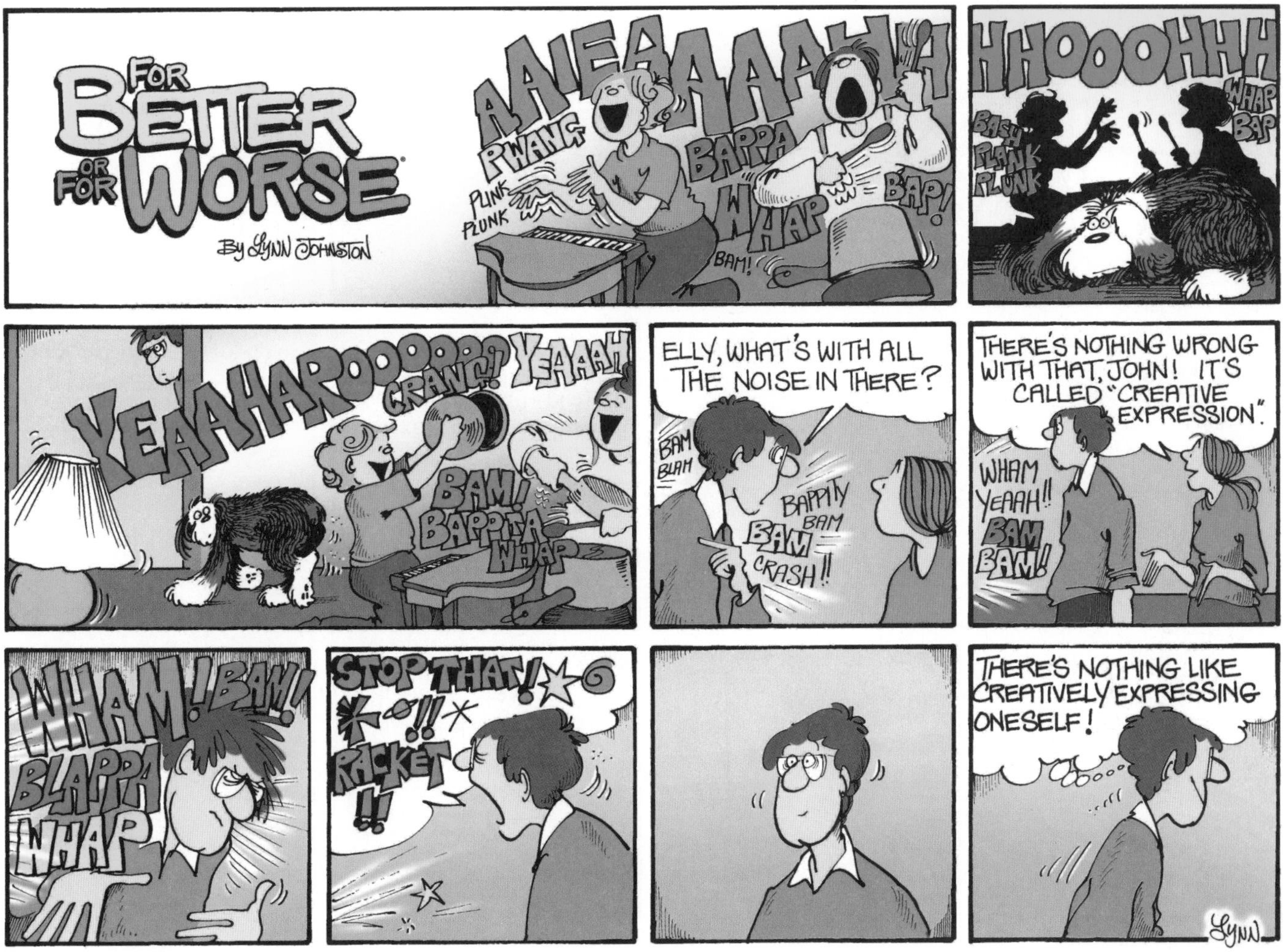
FOR BETTER OR FOR WORSE
BY LYNN JOHNSTON
AAIEEAAAAAHHH
PWANG
PLINK PLUNK
BAPPA
WHAP
BAP!
BAM!
HHOOOHHH
BASH PLANK PLUNK
WHAP BAP
YEAAHAROOOOO
CRANG!
YEAAAH
BAM! BAPPITA WHAP
ELLY, WHAT'S WITH ALL THE NOISE IN THERE?
BAM BLAM
BAPPITY BAM
BAM CRASH!!
THERE'S NOTHING WRONG WITH THAT, JOHN! IT'S CALLED "CREATIVE EXPRESSION".
WHAM YEAAH!!
BAM BAM!
WHAM! BAM!
BLAPPA WHAP
STOP THAT!
RACKET!!
THERE'S NOTHING LIKE CREATIVELY EXPRESSING ONESELF!
LYNN

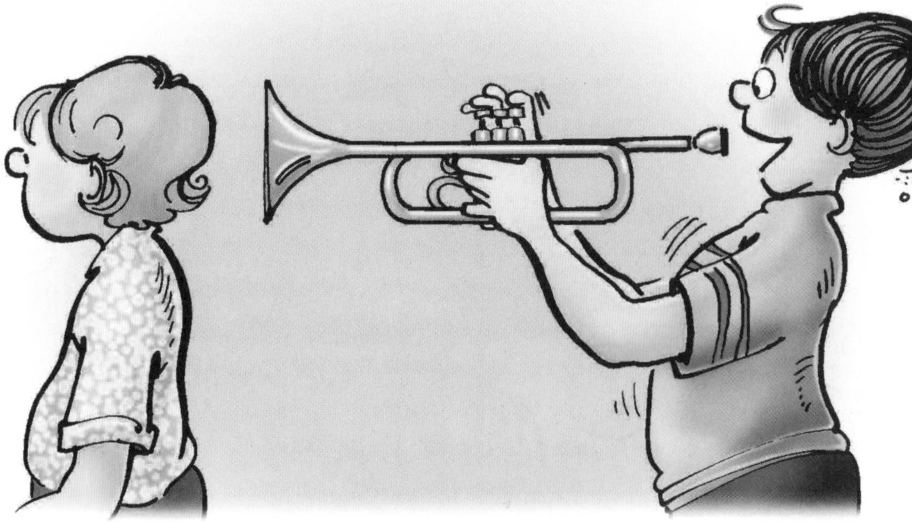

One day, I got tired of seeing the pile of single socks and mittens that had accumulated next to the dryer, and I threw them all out. A while later, I was cleaning out the storage room, going through camping gear, old toys, and outdoor clothing, and I found a collection of single socks and mittens — mates to the ones I had thrown out. I wished I had looked through the camping gear first … but I might have tossed out all the single things only to discover their mates in the laundry.

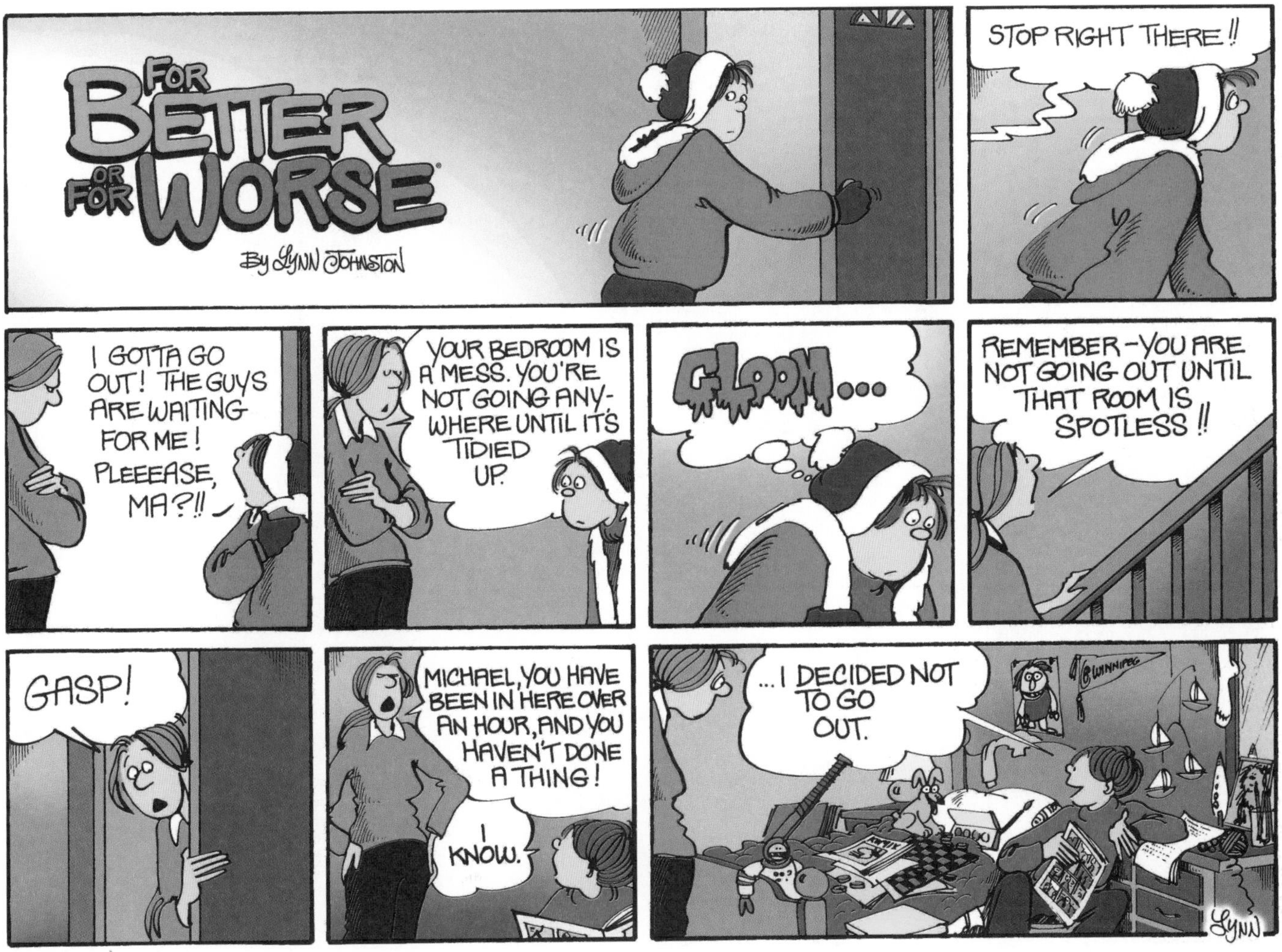
FOR BETTER OR FOR WORSE
BY LYNN JOHNSTON
STOP RIGHT THERE!!
I GOTTA GO OUT! THE GUYS ARE WAITING FOR ME! PLEEEASE, MA?!!
YOUR BEDROOM IS A MESS. YOU'RE NOT GOING ANYWHERE UNTIL IT'S TIDIED UP.
GLOOM...
REMEMBER—YOU ARE NOT GOING OUT UNTIL THAT ROOM IS SPOTLESS!!
GASP!
MICHAEL, YOU HAVE BEEN IN HERE OVER AN HOUR, AND YOU HAVEN'T DONE A THING!
I KNOW.
...I DECIDED NOT TO GO OUT.
LYNN

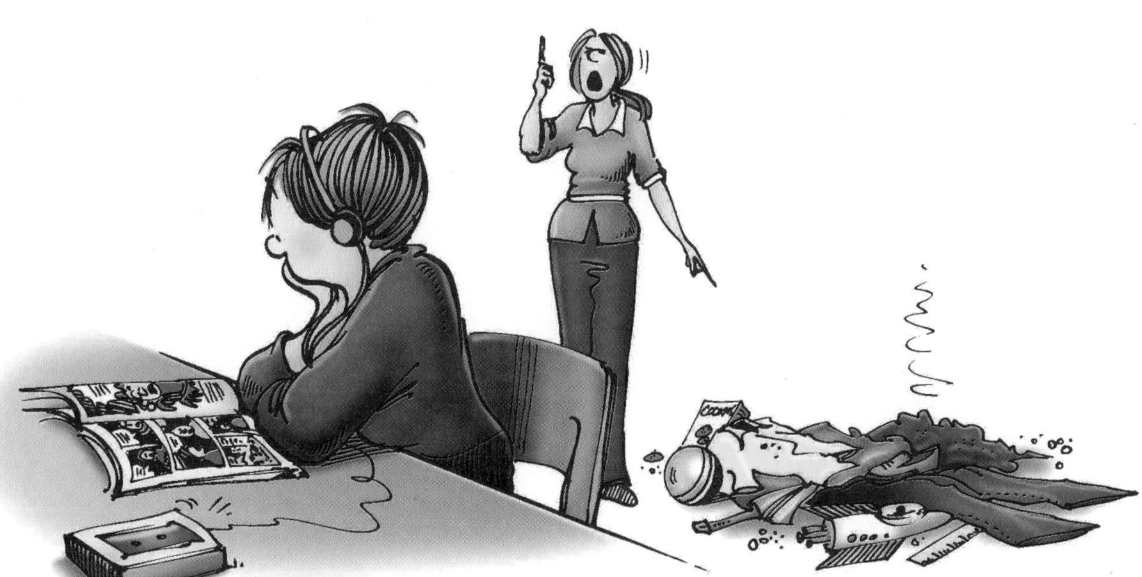

IT'S BEEN ONE OF THOSE DAYS, EL. MY ASSISTANT GAVE NOTICE. SHE'S LEAVING IN 2 WEEKS.

WOMEN!! YOU TRAIN THEM TO DO THINGS EXACTLY THE WAY YOU WANT THEM—AND THEY GO AND QUIT ON YOU!

WHAP!

PERHAPS I SHOULD REPHRASE THAT!

JEAN'S BABY IS NEARLY A YEAR OLD, JOHN, WHY DON'T YOU ASK HER IF SHE'D LIKE HER OLD JOB BACK?

BUT SHE SAID SHE WANTED TO STAY HOME AND RAISE HER FAMILY. SHE PLANNED TO SPEND EVERY MOMENT WITH HER CHILD!

YOU'RE SUGGESTING THAT I ASK A WOMAN WHO'S DEVOTING HER LIFE TO MOTHERHOOD TO COME BACK TO WORK?

TRUST ME.

SHE'LL DO IT! JEAN SAYS SHE'LL COME BACK TO WORK!

BUT SHE'LL ONLY BE ABLE TO COME IN PART TIME UNTIL SHE GETS BRITTANY INTO DAY-CARE.

IF I COULD ONLY GET SOMEONE TO ASSIST ME FOR HALF DAYS. IF I COULD JUST GET SOMEONE IN FOR A COUPLE OF WEEKS....

WHY ARE YOU LOOKING AT ME LIKE THAT?

JOHN, I HAVEN'T ASSISTED AT THE CLINIC FOR YEARS! BESIDES, WHAT ABOUT THE LIBRARY?

YOU COULD GO THERE IN THE MORNING AND COME TO THE CLINIC AT NOON! ANNIE WILL LOOK AFTER OUR KIDS! PLEASE?

NO, JOHN. NO, NO, NO, NO, NO!!!

FINE. I'LL GIVE YOU A WHILE TO THINK ABOUT IT.

When we first arrived in Lynn Lake, we had no front desk person for the clinic and no chairside assistant. With Aaron in kindergarten and my mom-in-law willing to look after Katie, I thought I might be able to work with Rod part-time while he trained someone else.

SO, I TOLD HIM I'D WORK IN THE CLINIC UNTIL JEAN CAN COME IN FULL TIME.

I DON'T KNOW WHY I LET HIM TALK ME INTO IT, ANNIE. YOU'LL BE FINE.

I KNOW WHAT YOU'RE THINKING: "WILL I REMEMBER EVERYTHING? WILL I MANAGE WITH THE PATIENTS? WILL I FUMBLE THE INSTRUMENTS?

... WILL I FIT INTO MY OLD UNIFORMS?!!

I had assisted Rod when he was in dental school. There was a free clinic in the evenings, and students got extra experience if they volunteered to work on patients after class for free. Spouses often accompanied the students — just so they could spend some time together. University took a toll on relationships. With this bit of training under my belt, I believed I could fill in for a while in our new clinic.

WHAT IS IT, ANNIE? I FELT THE BABY KICK.

LET ME FEEL! ME TOO!

WELL?.... DO SOMETHING!!

How wild your imagination becomes if someone you love is late coming home. You're sure they're safe, but … what if? What if your family is one of those about whom the headlines are written? After all, it's the luck of the draw. Nobody is absolutely secure. Bad things can happen to any of us. In your mind, you go from imagining fatal accidents to acts of violence to kidnapping — all the stuff you see in the movies. Perhaps what we do is prepare ourselves for the worst. Maybe this is a good exercise, but it's often far too stressful and far too frightening.

When folks ask how writers come up with so many weird ideas, I use the "missing at night" scenario to explain: Give yourself a situation in which you have no control, something that could go in any direction — this is when your writer's hat goes on. You want to resolve the situation now; you want to be able to handle whatever happens, and so you let your imagination loose. The next thing you know, you are in the mind of a writer. One small idea bubbles into another. Could there have been an accident? You visualize this awful possibility: the car, the people inside. Are they on a roadside? In the water? Soon, you're bringing in sirens — an ambulance and police to the scene. You go from imagining the accident to living through the aftermath: the hospital, the anguish, the lives on the line. You argue with nurses, you fight for the right to know. You call relatives and tell them the news. You wait for the recovery, or you plan for the wake. This is how a writer works; even though you're telling a story, you feel as though it's real.

For a writer, imagination is a gift. For someone who is waiting and wondering, it's a nuisance. The good thing is, by the time you reach the most agonizing chapter in your imaginary scenario, your missing person shows up and you have nothing to show for your night of woe but relief. And … isn't that a great way for this all to end?

I enjoy cutting hair. My hairdresser thinks I should leave this art to the professionals. In his lovely Italian accent, Gino will say, "Lynn … you can-a do-a lots of a-things! You good at-a lots-a of things! But PLEASE! Do not-a cut-a your hair!!!!"

When my kids were small, they'd run from me when I appeared with my cape, scissors, and slim, black comb. I'd wet their hair, then follow them around the house. Every time their attention would waver, I'd reach out and snip off a bit more hair. If I was lucky, they'd allow me to use the comb: lifting tufts like they do in salons, cutting along the leading edge of my fingers. This gave the best results. Waiting until they fell asleep was another workable tactic … but, messy.

Aaron eventually made cutting his hair an impossibility, so I took him to the hairdressing school on the advice of a friend whose kids enjoyed going there. Aaron was immediately taken with the students, who were eager to make him feel at home. The supervisor suggested I leave him in their care, and I did so, relieved that it was their turn to do some chasing! When I came to get him, he was happily waiting for me — neatly shorn, with a toy in his hand that was given to him for good behaviour. On the way home, I asked him why he sat still and was so good for the girls in the hairdressing school but wouldn't sit still for me. He replied, "They promised me a good boy toy, and … they're pretty." *Sigh* Kids grow up so fast!!!

I was so happy while drawing this. A good gag gave me great expressions to work with as I built up to the punch line. Not only did I enjoy the process here, but I was getting back at my mother and all the teachers who told me to "get down to business and hit the books." This strip was a cleansing experience.

Tough exams gave me stomachaches, sleepless nights, and bouts of depression ... but I always managed to pass!

OK, MIKE.... IF 5 OUT OF 10 IS 50%, WHAT IS 10 OUT OF 10?

THINK ABOUT IT - 100% IS THE WHOLE WORKS, SO 10 OUT OF 10 WOULD BE....?

LOOK, THIS IS EASY! IT'S JUST PLAIN AND SIMPLE LOGIC!

I KNOW!

....BUT IT DOESN'T MAKE SENSE.

FINALLY! MIKE UNDERSTANDS PERCENTAGES AND DECIMAL POINTS.

I WENT OVER IT AGAIN AND AGAIN AND AGAIN!

HONEY, UH... COULD YOU NOT HANG YOUR SHIRT ON THE MIRROR? IT DRIVES ME CRAZY!

FUNNY HOW YOU CAN TELL SOMEONE SOMETHING A MILLION TIMES... AND IT JUST DOESN'T SINK IN!

OH, NO! NOT AGAIN! YOU MEAN WE HAFTA GO TO ANNIE'S HOUSE AFTER SCHOOL?

JUST FOR A WHILE, MICHAEL. I HAVE TO WORK AT THE CLINIC.

ANNIE LIVES RIGHT NEXT DOOR... WHY CAN'T I JUST DROP LIZZIE OFF, AN' SPEND THE REST OF THE DAY AT HOME!

YEAH! THAT'S WHAT HE ALWAYS DOES ANYHOW!

Fortunately for Alan, he was never a patient. My mother, however, allowed me to practice on her. I remember her under the gas, which was a lot of fun. I had never seen her so relaxed and funny.

THIS IS A BIG DAY FOR ME, SIS. NO TRUMPET PLAYER WANTS ANYTHING DONE TO HIS FRONT TEETH.

IF JOHN CHANGES THEIR SHAPE EVEN A TINY BIT, IT COULD CHANGE MY WHOLE CAREER.

I CAN'T AFFORD A MISTAKE!

THAT'S OK, PHIL— JOHN DOES RELATIVES FOR FREE.

YOU KNOW THE CLINIC ROUTINE, ELLY....

A GOOD ASSISTANT MUST LEARN TO ANTICIPATE EVERYTHING THE DOCTOR IS ABOUT TO DO.

CLAMP...EXPLORER, TOPICAL ANESTHETIC, COTTON ROLL, SYRINGE AND SUCTION...

GET ME A RESTORATIVE KIT, THE RESIN KIT AND...

WAIT A MINUTE!

WHAT? WHAT'S WRONG?— SOMETHING'S WRONG?

YOU HAVEN'T ONCE SAID PLEASE.

This very situation brought my assisting career to an end. Dentistry is a fiddly business with many frustrating procedures. When my husband sharply asked for an instrument or for suction, I expected a polite "thanks" for my efforts, but he just carried on. His brusque manner wasn't personal — I just took it the wrong way!

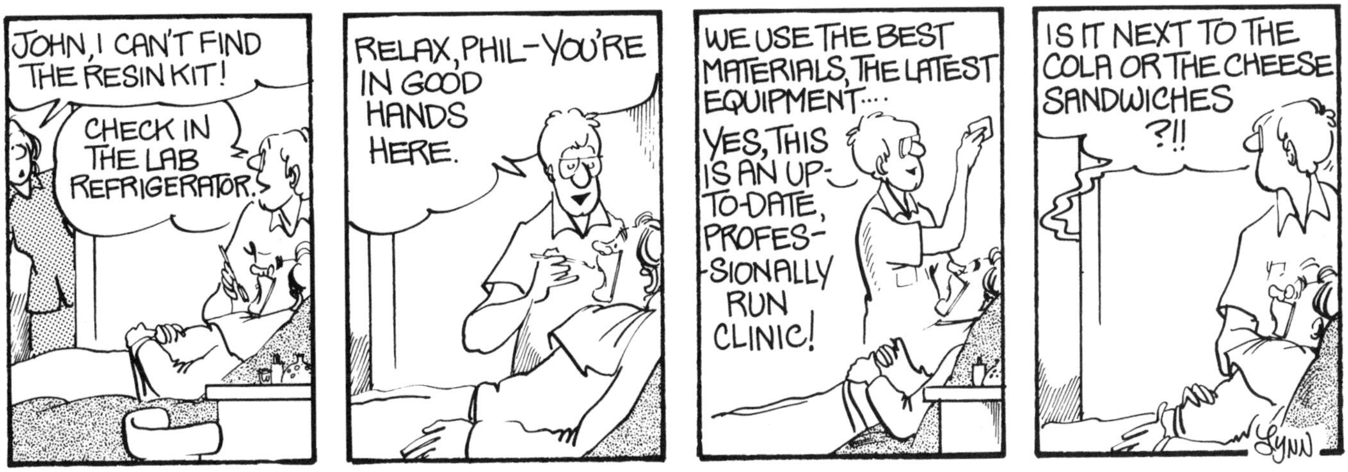
JOHN, I CAN'T FIND THE RESIN KIT!
CHECK IN THE LAB REFRIGERATOR.
RELAX, PHIL–YOU'RE IN GOOD HANDS HERE.
WE USE THE BEST MATERIALS, THE LATEST EQUIPMENT....
YES, THIS IS AN UP-TO-DATE, PROFES-SIONALLY RUN CLINIC!
IS IT NEXT TO THE COLA OR THE CHEESE SANDWICHES ?!!
LYNN

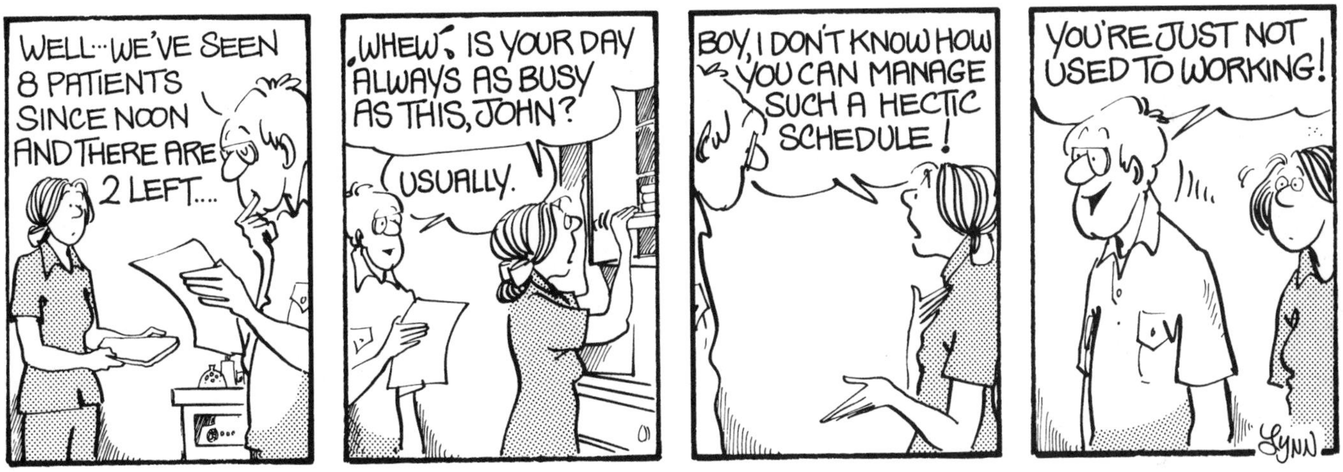
WELL... WE'VE SEEN 8 PATIENTS SINCE NOON AND THERE ARE 2 LEFT....
WHEW! IS YOUR DAY ALWAYS AS BUSY AS THIS, JOHN?
USUALLY.
BOY, I DON'T KNOW HOW YOU CAN MANAGE SUCH A HECTIC SCHEDULE!
YOU'RE JUST NOT USED TO WORKING!
LYNN

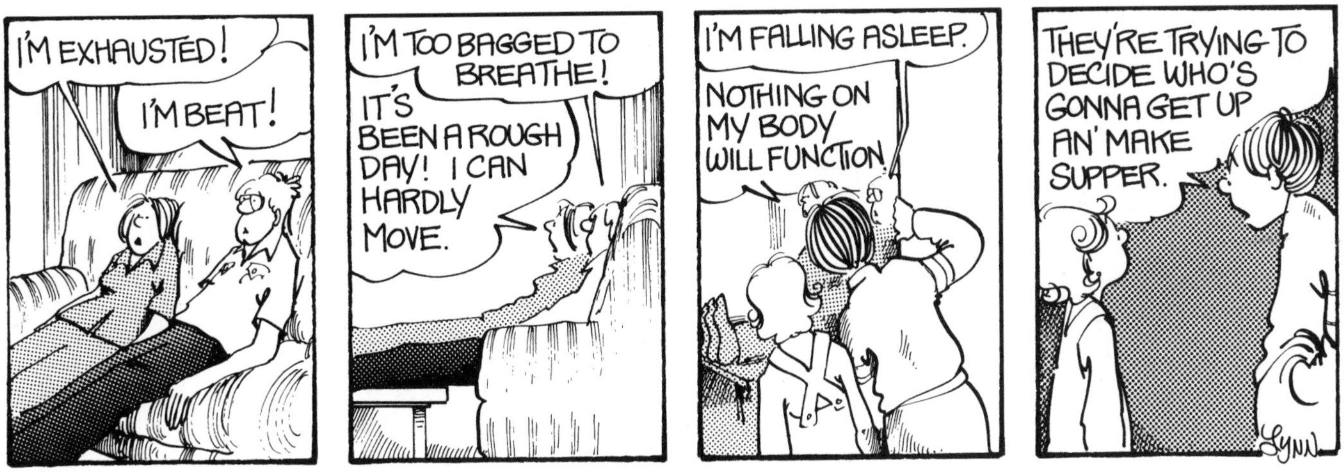
I'M EXHAUSTED!
I'M BEAT!
I'M TOO BAGGED TO BREATHE!
IT'S BEEN A ROUGH DAY! I CAN HARDLY MOVE.
I'M FALLING ASLEEP.
NOTHING ON MY BODY WILL FUNCTION.
THEY'RE TRYING TO DECIDE WHO'S GONNA GET UP AN' MAKE SUPPER.
LYNN

DADDY'S FIXING MY PORTABLE RADIO, LIZ...

YOU SURE YOU KNOW WHAT YOU'RE DOING?

FIZZZ

STUPID RADIO! THEY MAKE THESE THINGS ALMOST IMPOSSIBLE TO REPAIR!

FIZZZZZZZ

ACME HASSLE FREE SOLDERING KIT

CLICK!

OOOHHH AWWRIGHT BAY-BEEE GONNA GIT DOWNNN

HERE IT IS, MICHAEL! YOUR RADIO IS FIXED!

NEAT. THANKS.

I'VE SPENT ALL AFTERNOON SWEATING OVER A HOT SOLDERING IRON —AND THAT'S ALL YOU CAN SAY ?!!!

HI, HONEY! I'VE JUST WASHED, PRESSED AND REPAIRED ALL YOUR SHIRTS AND PANTS!

NEAT. THANKS.

Lynn

I am a militant shopper sometimes. I sneer at able-bodied folks who park in the handicap zone, grumble when they squeeze all the tomatoes, and will audibly sigh if there's a long checkout line and some bozo decides to redeem a wad of coupons. On a busy weekend outside my favourite grocery store, someone had parked across the ramp. Shoppers couldn't get to the parking lot without heaving their carts over the curb. The situation I drew in this strip was based on this incident, but it has a different ending.

I waited a minute, wondering how long this inconsiderate person would be. He certainly had to know that he'd blocked everyone's path. I had a couple of choice comments to make like, "Couldn't get any closer, hum?" or "The parking lot's THAT way!" Soon the doors opened and an elderly man appeared. He was helping a woman who was pushing a small, half-filled shopping cart. He smiled at me as he held her steady and eased her forward. "My wife had a stroke," he said, "this is her first time outdoors since she managed to walk again and she wanted to shop for groceries." I opened the passenger door and kept the cart from rolling forward as he lovingly helped her into the car. I then handed him their grocery bags as he loaded them into the trunk. He explained that he'd moved the car closer to the door for her and was sorry for the inconvenience. He thanked me sincerely as he worked himself into the driver's seat. As they drove away I thought to myself, "Thank heavens I didn't say anything!" It was another lesson; a good story — and I guess I didn't have the courage to tell it the way it was!

LOOK OUT THERE! IT'S TED AND IRIS!!

IRENE.

THEY'VE JUST COME BACK FROM THEIR HONEYMOON IN JAMAICA!

BARBADOS.

I CAN'T BELIEVE THEY'RE MARRIED — SHE WAS HIS SECRETARY FOR 15 YEARS!

12 YEARS.

IF YOU'RE GOING TO GOSSIP.... GET IT RIGHT!

TED, YOU DEVIL — I NEVER EXPECTED YOU AND IRENE TO PULL A STUNT LIKE THIS!

AFTER 12 YEARS OF WORKING IN THE SAME OFFICE — YOU SUDDENLY DECIDE TO RUN OFF AND GET MARRIED?!!

SO — HOW DOES IT FEEL TO BE MARRIED TO THE BOSS?!

I GUESS IT BEATS BEING "THE OTHER WOMAN"!

Like other twists in the story line, this revelation came as a surprise to me. I had no idea that Ted had been interested in his receptionist/secretary! The neat thing about Irene was that she took Ted away from Connie. Connie could move on. Irene had a "throw-away" part; her character didn't need to be rounded out. I invented a character I could play with for a while and then ignore — the kind of role in which an actor would hate to be cast!

ELLY, HOW COULD YOU SAY THAT?!! HOW COULD YOU EMBARRASS TED AND IRENE?

BUT IT'S TRUE! IF TED'S BEEN IN LOVE WITH HIS SECRETARY ALL THESE YEARS — WHY DID HE PROPOSE TO CONNIE?!!

IF SHE'D MARRIED HIM, THEY'D PROBABLY HAVE ENDED UP HAVING AN AFFAIR BEHIND HER BACK!

IT'S STILL NO AFFAIR OF YOURS!!

WHY DID I SAY THAT AWFUL THING TO TED AND IRENE? WHY?!!

BECAUSE YOU'RE AN INSENSITIVE CLOD!

WHY DON'T I EVER THINK BEFORE I SPEAK?

YOU NEVER LEARN FROM EXPERIENCE, DO YOU, DIMWIT?

I HATE AGONIZING OVER THINGS AFTER MIDNIGHT....

THE ONLY ONE WHO ANSWERS MY QUESTIONS IS ME!!

SHOULD I APOLOGIZE TO TED AND IRENE?

IT'S UP TO YOU.

SHOULD I MAKE AN APPOINTMENT TO SEE THEM ALONE IN THEIR OFFICE?

IT'S A START.

I FEEL AWFUL. I DON'T KNOW WHAT TO SAY. HOW AM I GOING TO FACE THEM?

TRY TURNING LIKE THIS.

UH...TED? IRENE?...I WANT TO APOLOGIZE FOR THAT WISECRACK I MADE THE OTHER DAY.

IT WAS CRUDE AND INAPPROPRIATE AND I WANT YOU TO KNOW THAT I FEEL TERRIBLE.

I'VE DIED A THOUSAND DEATHS! I'VE LAIN AWAKE AT NIGHT!! I'VE WISHED A MILLION TIMES I'D NEVER SAID IT!

WHAT WISECRACK?

I'm the kind of person who lies awake, going over and over something I said or did, turning the deed into an Everest of woe. I can't see past the infraction until I've confronted the offended party and apologized.

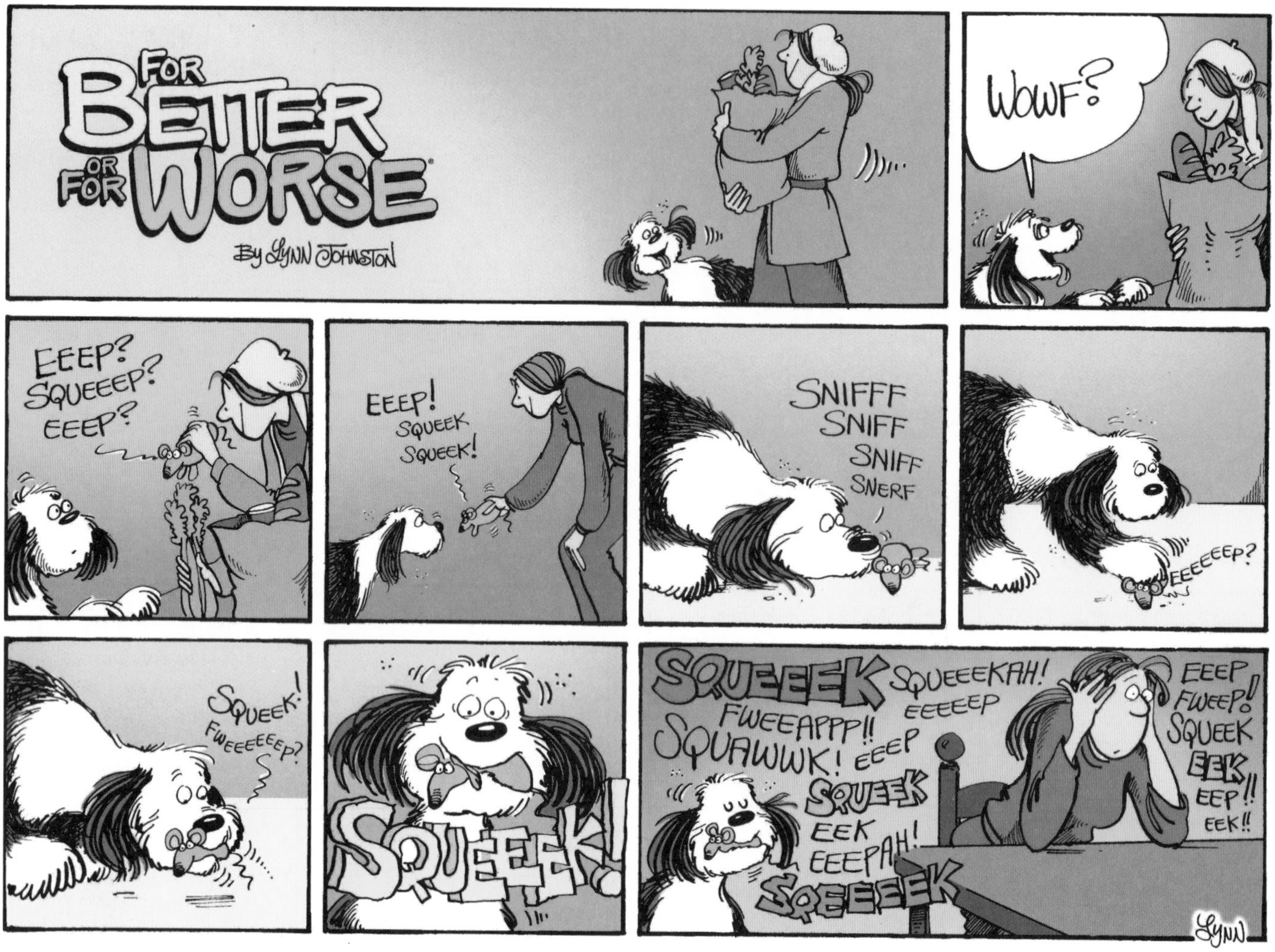
FOR BETTER OR FOR WORSE
By Lynn Johnston
WOWF?
EEEP? SQUEEEP? EEEP?
EEEP! SQUEEK SQUEEK!
SNIFFF SNIFF SNIFF SNERF
EEEEEEEP?
SQUEEK! FWEEEEEEP?
SQUEEK!
SQUEEEK SQUEEEKAH! EEEEEP FWEEAPPP!! SQUAWWK! EEEP SQUEEK EEK EEEPAH! SQEEEEK
EEEP FWEEP! SQUEEK EEK EEP!! EEK!!
Lynn

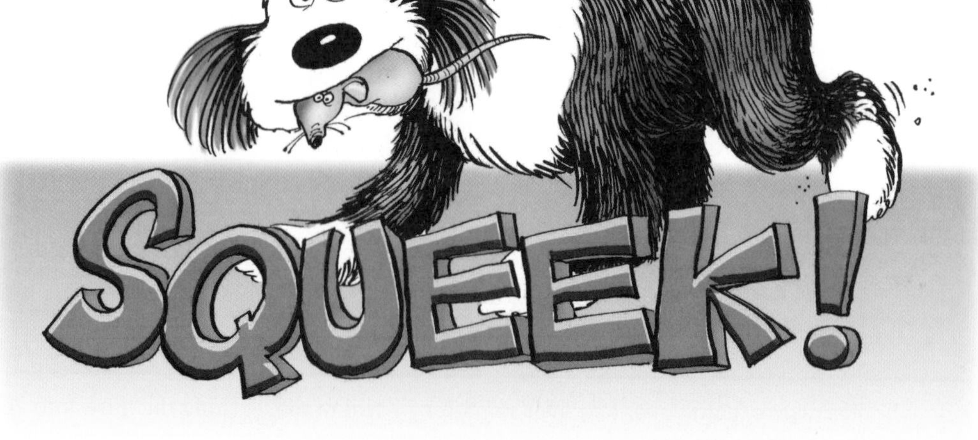
SQUEEK!

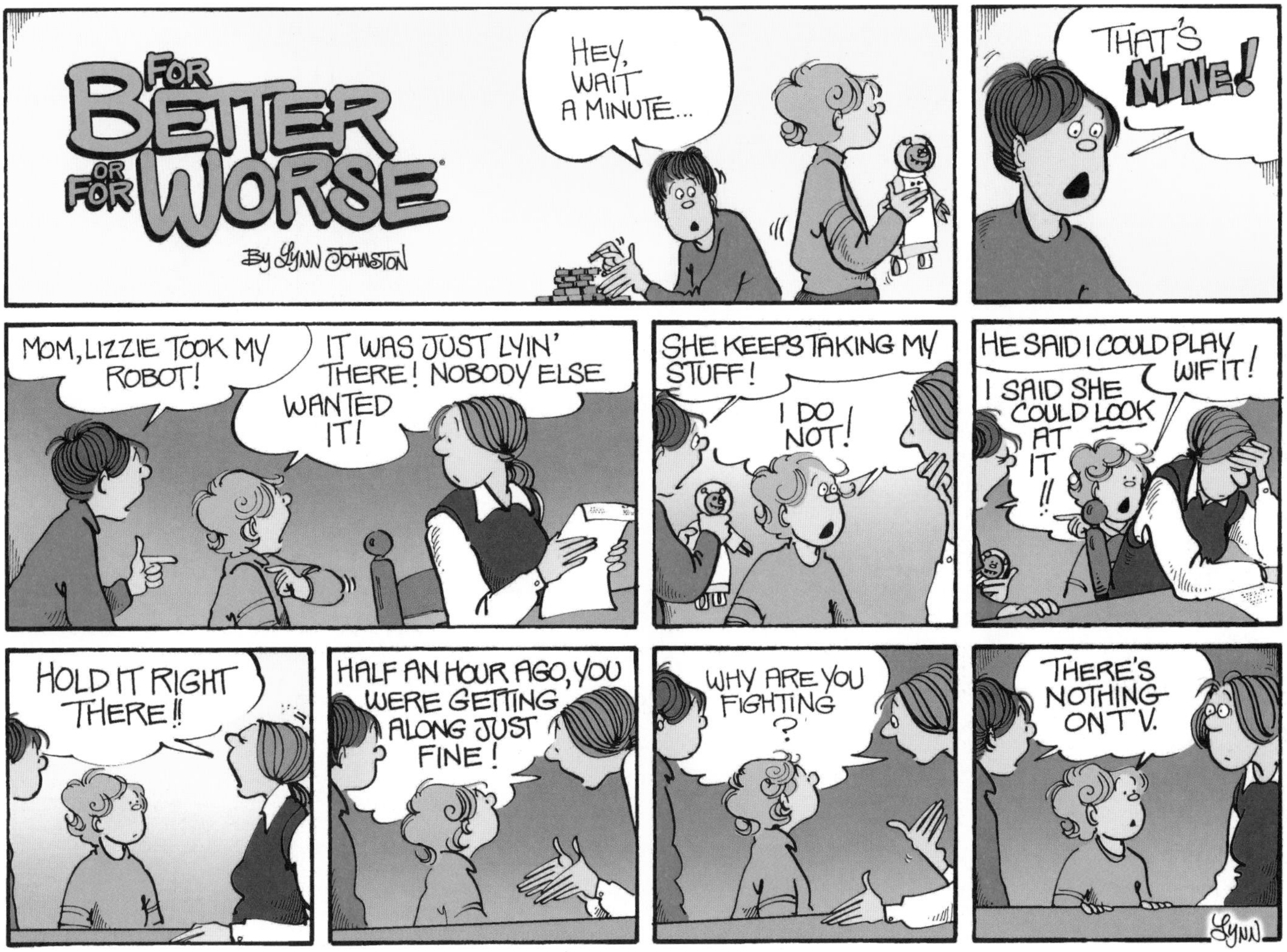
FOR BETTER OR FOR WORSE®
BY LYNN JOHNSTON
HEY, WAIT A MINUTE...
THAT'S MINE!
MOM, LIZZIE TOOK MY ROBOT!
IT WAS JUST LYIN' THERE! NOBODY ELSE WANTED IT!
SHE KEEPS TAKING MY STUFF!
I DO NOT!
HE SAID I COULD PLAY WIF IT!
I SAID SHE COULD LOOK AT IT!!
HOLD IT RIGHT THERE!!
HALF AN HOUR AGO, YOU WERE GETTING ALONG JUST FINE!
WHY ARE YOU FIGHTING?
THERE'S NOTHING ON TV.
LYNN

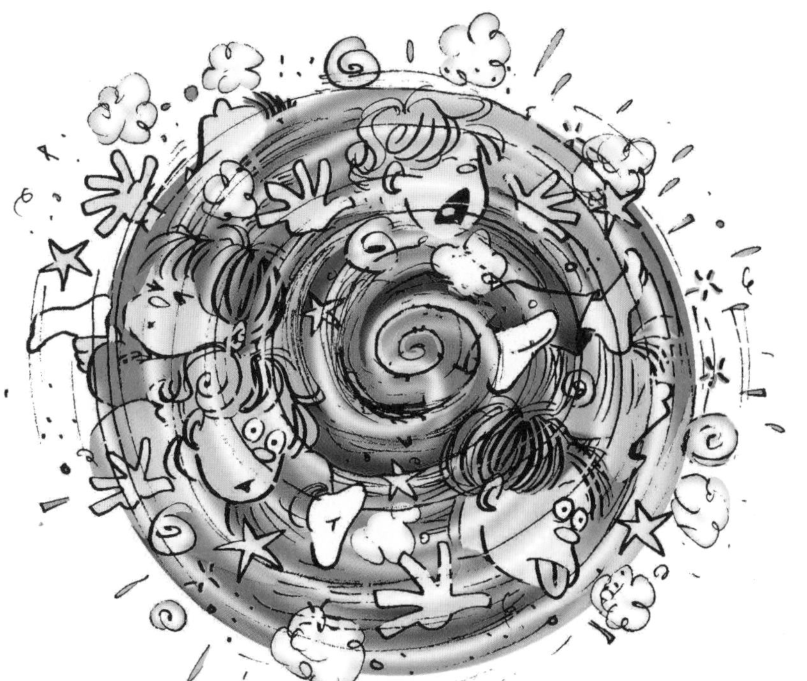

Michael, being five years older than Elizabeth, was allowed to stay at home alone for a couple of hours after school — before his mother came home from work. The sitter (and good friend) lived next door and kept an eye on him, but still, I got complaints about this "unhealthy situation."

When Mom went to work at the jewellery store, my brother and I stayed in the house after school by ourselves. We had strict rules of conduct and some serious responsibilities! We took pride in our roles, which made us surprisingly compatible. We fought less when we were unsupervised. Who would have guessed!

The strip was starting to realistically show a family's weaknesses as well as its strengths, which I think made it more believable. I was trying to show real life: What happened to me and to the character Michael happens all the time. In an ideal world, I guess someone should be there to chaperone a child at all times, but like me, Mike was a responsible kid who was capable of helping out. Sometimes we could all use an extra hand to help make ends meet!